Reputation Management

Building and Protecting Your
Company's Profile in a Digital World

Reputation Management

Building and Protecting Your Company's Profile in a Digital World

Edited by
Andrew Hiles

qatar
FINANCIAL CENTRE
AUTHORITY

BLOOMSBURY

Copyright © Bloomsbury Information Ltd, 2011
Chapters copyright © their respective authors

First published in 2011 by

Bloomsbury Information Ltd
50 Bedford Square
London
WC1B 3DB
United Kingdom

Bloomsbury Publishing, London, Berlin, New York, and Sydney
www.bloomsbury.com

The information contained in this book is for general information purposes only. It does not constitute investment, financial, legal, or other advice, and should not be relied upon as such. No representation or warranty, express or implied, is made as to the accuracy or completeness of the contents. The publisher and the authors disclaim any warranty or liability for actions taken (or not taken) on the basis of information contained herein.

The views and opinions of the publisher may not necessarily coincide with some of the views and opinions expressed in this book, which are entirely those of the authors. No endorsement of them by the publisher should be inferred.

Every reasonable effort has been made to trace copyright holders of material reproduced in this book, but if any have been inadvertently overlooked then the publisher would be glad to hear from them.

A CIP record for this book is available from the British Library.

Standard edition
ISBN-10: 1-84930-042-9
ISBN-13: 978-1-84930-042-1

Middle East edition
ISBN-10: 1-84930-049-6
ISBN-13: 978-1-84930-049-0

Project Director: Conrad Gardner
Project Manager: Ben Hickling
Assistant Project Manager: Sarah Latham

Typeset by Marsh Typesetting, West Sussex, UK
Printed and bound by CPI Group (UK) Ltd, Croydon, CR0 4YY

Contents

Introduction

Up to 90% of an organization's assets are not tangible: the most important are reputation, brand value, relationships, and know-how. The first three of these are interlinked, but arguably the most important of them is reputation, since both brand value and relationships may be destroyed by loss of reputation.

This important book brings together provocative and thoughtful insights on reputation management by thought leaders from around the world. The book is studded with true-life examples, real case studies, and lessons learned the hard way. It will prove an invaluable companion and guide to all those involved in, or interested in, the concepts of reputation creation and management.

Because of the breadth, diversity, and richness of these experts' input, you may be stimulated by opposing ideas; or occasionally see similar references in different contexts; and, because great minds think alike, you may find some minor overlap, which we have retained to preserve the individual integrity of each contribution. To provide further food for thought, we have deliberately juxtaposed chapters that have similar or contrasting themes.

Chapter 1 sets the scene with an outline of how rumors begin and spread, and how to deal with them. This is followed by Chapters 2 to 7, which put reputation management within the corporate context, and cover key themes such as reputation governance and stakeholder engagement. Chapters 8 to 11 deal with aspects of media management—crucial to any reputation management program. Reputation from the financial perspective is discussed in Chapters 12 to 15, and includes emerging topics such as long-term reputation management, and the impact of the financial crisis on reputation dynamics. Chapters 16 and 17 identify the value of reputation, with the final three chapters showing how to manage reputation against issues and crises.

Andrew Hiles, Kingswell International
Editor

Contributors

Georgia Aarons currently leads strategy and business development for Halpern, one of London's leading communications consultancies. Prior to joining Halpern, she spent six years working as a recruitment and talent management consultant for Wall Street investment banks. Aarons has worked with Professor Argenti and Dartmouth's Tuck School of Business on consulting and training programs for clients such as Shell, Novartis, Freddie Mac, and Citibank. She holds an undergraduate degree from Columbia University and a graduate degree from the University of Cambridge.

Paul A. Argenti has taught management, corporate communication, and corporate responsibility starting in 1977 at the Harvard Business School, from 1979 to 1981 at the Columbia Business School, and since 1981 at Dartmouth's Tuck School of Business. He is currently faculty director for Tuck's Leadership and Strategic Impact Program and its custom executive programs for Novartis. His latest book (coauthored with Courtney Barnes) is *Digital Strategies* and he is currently working on the sixth edition of his *Corporate Communication* textbook. Professor Argenti is a Fulbright scholar and winner of the 2007 Pathfinder Award from the Institute for Public Relations. He has consulted and run training programs for many companies, including General Electric, ING, Sony, Novartis, and Goldman Sachs.

Michael Brown is professor of corporate reputation and strategy at Birmingham City Business School and head of its center for corporate reputation and strategy. He has led the research for Britain's Most Admired Companies survey of corporate reputation, and he has published in several management journals and coauthored, with Paul Turner, the book *The Admirable Company*. He has also provided consultancy services for many of the United Kingdom's blue-chip companies.

Magnus Carter is chairman of Mentor Communications Consultancy, which he founded in 1998. He lectures and coaches in media handling, reputation management, and issues and crisis management. His clients include NHS Blood and Transplant, the Office for National Statistics, Rolls-Royce, KPMG, and the Universities of Bedfordshire, Bristol, Sheffield, Southampton, and the West of England. He is an associate consultant of the Bristol Business School, a visiting lecturer at Ashridge Business School, and an approved trainer for the Chartered Institute of Public Relations. Carter began his career as a newspaper reporter and later gained more than 20 years' experience in radio and TV news, working with the BBC and commercial companies.

William Cox is managing director of Management & Excellence (M&E), a sustainability auditing and rating firm with offices in Madrid and São Paulo. He received his PhD from the London School of Economics, a finance degree from the University of Oxford, and degrees in philosophy and political science from Boston University. M&E specializes in demonstrating the financial returns of sustainability projects and works for several of the largest blue-chip companies in Brazil, the United States, and Europe. Before cofounding M&E 10 years ago, Cox ran his own consulting firm in Germany and was managing director of Hill & Knowlton in Switzerland. He is the author of six books and many professional articles.

John Dalton is director of the London School of Public Relations. He is an established author on reputation management and advises governments and multinational corporations on reputation and allied fields. In addition to teaching and lecturing, John also is an active consultant in the areas of corporate message development, brand reevaluation, and how to conduct reputation audits. He is a member of the International Institute for Strategic Studies (IISS), with a keen knowledge of international relations, and is also a professional biologist, with an interest in biological and radiological terrorism and its risk and crisis implications for governments and organizations. He is currently setting up the London Centre for Issue and Crisis Management, which will specialize in crisis leadership skills.

Daniel Diermeier is the IBM professor of regulation and competitive practice, a professor of managerial economics and decision sciences at the Kellogg School of Management, and a professor of political science at the Weinberg College of Arts and Sciences, all at Northwestern University. He is director of the Ford Motor Company Center for Global Citizenship and co-creator of the CEO Perspective Program (Kellogg's most senior executive education program). Professor Diermeier's work focuses on reputation management, political and regulatory risk, crisis management, and integrated strategy. He was named Kellogg Professor of the Year (2001) and received the prestigious Faculty Pioneer Award from the Aspen Institute (2007). In December 2004 he was appointed to the Management Board of the FBI.

Mark Eisenegger is co-head of the Department of Research into the Public Sector and Society (fög) of the University of Zurich (www.foeg.uzh.ch), as well as chairman of the European Center for Reputation Studies (ECRS) based in Munich and Zurich (www.reputation-centre.org). His research and teaching focus on the sector of organizational and corporate communications, reputation theory and research, and media transformation.

Peter Firestein is author of the book *Crisis of Character: Building Corporate Reputation in the Age of Skepticism*. He serves as strategic advisor to senior corporate managements in all major world markets, helping them to build market value and sustainability by strengthening support among investors and social stakeholders. He is originator of the "Investor valuation analysis/ Open perception study," a methodology for developing market intelligence that reveals how investors make decisions to buy and sell the shares of a particular company. Firestein also serves as advisor to senior executives and boards on strategies for developing sustainable reputations as well as crisis avoidance and management. He speaks and writes widely on these matters.

Leslie Gaines-Ross is Weber Shandwick's chief reputation strategist and one of the world's most widely recognized experts on reputation. She spearheaded the first comprehensive research on CEO reputation and its impact on company reputation and performance. She developed Weber Shandwick's global reputation studies "Safeguarding reputation," "Risky business: Reputations online," and "Socializing your CEO." Her article "Reputation warfare" was published in the *Harvard Business Review*. Gaines-Ross is the author of *CEO Capital: A Guide to Building CEO Reputation and Company Success* and *Corporate*

Reputation: 12 Steps to Safeguarding and Recovering Reputation. She writes a blog on reputationXchange and tweets as @ReputationRx.

Genoveffa Giambona is the deputy director of the Oxford University Centre for Corporate Reputation. After obtaining a degree in English literature and language *cum laude*, Giambona went on to study for a Master's degree in English history, literature, and culture at the University of Southampton. Besides reputation, she is interested in meta-evaluation and in researching how learning mechanisms work in different contexts and cultures. Her research interests are also in the area of leadership development, management studies and learning, virtual teams, and trust. Jeni also has an interest in the application of realist synthesis, narrative analysis, and discourse analysis.

Andrew Hiles is founding director of Kingswell International, consultants and trainers in crisis, reputation, risk, continuity, and service management. He has conducted projects in some 60 countries. He was founder and, for some 15 years, chairman of the first international user group for business continuity professionals and founding director of the Business Continuity Institute and the World Food Safety Organisation. He has contributed to international standards and is the author of numerous books. He edited, and is the main contributor to, *The Definitive Handbook of Business Continuity Management*. Hiles has delivered more than 500 public and in-company workshops and training courses internationally and broadcasts on television, radio, webinars, and podcasts.

Mark Hill founded The Group in 1991 and, with his team, has built the United Kingdom's leading agency providing online corporate communications services and consultancy advice. He has provided strategic advice about digital communications to many UK and international companies for 15 years and involving corporate and not-for-profit in industries ranging from conglomerates to financial services, and retail to utilities.

Joachim Klewes is honorary professor at the Heinrich Heine University, Düsseldorf, and senior partner at Ketchum Pleon, the leading communications consultancy in Europe. In addition, he is the founder of the Change Centre Foundation, an independent think-tank focused on scientific research and concept development in the field of change and transformation in business and society. His consulting expertise covers the fields of strategic communications, including corporate communications, and board/CEO positioning and coaching, crisis and issues management, public affairs, and change management.

Daniel Künstle is CEO of the communications analysis and consulting company commsLAB (www.commslab.com), which specializes in the development and implementation of corporate profiles. From 2004 to the end of 2008 he was chief of staff of the Swiss Insurance Supervisory Authority and member of the steering committee of the Swiss Financial Market Supervisory Authority (FINMA). Before that, between 1994 and 2004, he acted as group spokesman for major bank UBS and its predecessor, the Swiss Bank Corporation, as well as heading the UBS Unit for Corporate Reputation Analysis.

Elliot S. Schreiber is president and CEO of the consulting firm Brand and Reputation Management LLC and is also clinical professor of marketing and executive director of the Center for Corporate Reputation Management at the Bennett S. LeBow College of Business at Drexel University. He is internationally recognized as one of the most experienced and knowledgeable experts on reputation and reputation risk management. Previously he was a senior marketing and corporate communications executive at Du Pont and Bayer in the United States and at Nortel Networks in Canada, and later was managing partner of an international e-business consulting firm. He has a PhD from Pennsylvania State University and has been visiting professor at universities in the United States and Canada.

Jonathan Silberstein-Loeb is a research fellow at the Oxford University Centre for Corporate Reputation. Before moving to Oxford, he was an Alfred Chandler Jr. traveling fellow at Harvard Business School, a fellow at the Newberry Library, Chicago, a fellow of the Lilly Library at the University of Indiana, Bloomington, a Deutscher Akademischer Austauschdienst fellow in Berlin, and a Fulbright Fellow in Kyoto, Japan. He received his doctorate from the University of Cambridge.

Shireen Smith founded Azrights in 2005, having worked as an in-house lawyer at media organization Reuters for five years. She has also held positions at Coopers & Lybrand and Eversheds, and she was a part-time in-house counsel for a small IT company for more than seven years. She has over 20 years' experience as a commercial solicitor and is particularly interested in new technologies, the Internet, and social media. Working closely with Ferreter, an IT business run by her husband Paul, the firm is able to assist clients with the full range of technical expertise required to provide a comprehensive reputation management service to clients.

Andrew Tucker teaches at Brunel University, where he leads the "Trustworthy organization" and "Governance beyond the boardroom" projects. He is co-CEO of Mettle Consulting Ltd, a reputation metrics company. He has published widely on corporate reputation, corporate governance, and organizational trust modeling and measurement. He sits on the board of the Online Reputation Management Association. He previously worked as a political analyst and helped to set up an online health-care company.

Paul Turner is professor of management practice at Birmingham City Business School, having held professorial positions in Cambridge and Nottingham. He was president (Europe, Middle East, and Africa) of the Convergys Corporation, group human resources business director of Lloyds TSB, director of BT, and vice president of the Chartered Institute of Personnel and Development. He has published in business journals and has authored or coauthored *Workforce Planning* (2010), *The Admirable Company* (2008), *Talent* (2007), *Organisational Communication* (2005), and *HR Forecasting and Planning* (2002).

Jon White is a consultant specializing in the application of psychological thinking to the problems of organizational communication, working internationally for clients such as the European Commission and Shell. He is associated with Henley Business School, Cardiff University, and the University of Central Lancashire, and universities in Germany and Switzerland, for teaching, research, and special projects. He has written books and articles on public affairs, public relations, and corporate communications practice, and management case studies for teaching purposes on organizations such as Dunhill, Lloyds of London, AEA Technology, Diageo, and the South

African company Barloworld. He is a fellow of the UK's Chartered Institute of Public Relations.

Philip Whittingham is European chief enterprise risk officer at XL Group, where he is responsible for developing risk management policy and approaches to meet the regulatory requirements of Solvency II and the Bermuda Monetary Authority. He started his career broking general insurance business in the London market before moving into risk management at a large UK insurer. He subsequently has had industry and consultancy roles centered on risk management, including at two Big Four firms, before joining XL in 2010. Whittingham is chairman of the Institute of Risk Management's Solvency II special interest group and is course developer and lead examiner of its risk management in financial services paper. He is a regular speaker on Solvency II and risk management.

Robert Wreschniok is managing director at Emanate in Germany. Before that he was business director at Pleon KohtesKlewes, responsible for reputation management and strategic stakeholder dialog. Together with Joachim Klewes, he is coeditor of the management book *Reputation Capital: Building and Maintaining Trust in the 21st Century*. After completing his MA in international relations at the University of Sussex, he received a certification in strategic foundation management from the University of Basel. He is a board member of the European Centre for Reputation Studies and spokesman of the Private Institute of Foundation Law.

Rupert Younger is founder director of the Oxford University Centre for Corporate Reputation at Oxford University's Said Business School. Dr Younger is also a cofounder and a consulting partner of the Finsbury Group, the financial communications group. He has twenty years' experience, working with major UK and international companies on their financial communications, investor relations, and reputation engagement programs, and he is a specialist in international IPOs and M&A, having led many of Finsbury's major transactions. He is a member of the Royal Company of Archers, a Council member of the Winchester College Society, and a member of the Senior Common Room at Worcester College, Oxford.

How Firms Should Fight Rumors
by Andrew Hiles
Kingswell International, St Georges de Reintembault, France

This Chapter Covers

- ▸ What a rumor is.
- ▸ What makes a successful rumor.
- ▸ How rumors spread.
- ▸ The impact of rumor.
- ▸ Examples and case studies.
- ▸ How to fight rumors: lessons and guidelines.

Introduction: What Is a Rumor?

To understand how to fight rumors, we need first to understand what a rumor is and then how and why it circulates.

There are many definitions of "rumor," but what they have in common is that a rumor comprises unverified, unconfirmed information of uncertain origin and doubtful veracity that has got into general circulation. It may contain elements of truth as well as unfounded allegations. A rumor may be positive ("This stock is going to rocket—they've struck oil") or negative ("That restaurant serves cat as chicken"). A rumor may be substantively true, such as unconfirmed bad or good news that is being prematurely released by unofficial sources.

The scientist Robert Knapp, who helped the US Office of Strategic Services (OSS) to use rumor as a weapon in World War II, defined rumor as: "a proposition or belief of topical reference without official verification."[1]

Rumor differs from propaganda, which is an organized campaign to promote a doctrine or practice. However rumor may form part of a propaganda campaign.

What Makes a Successful Rumor

The originally secret, since declassified, OSS "Doctrine re Rumors" (effectively a "How To" manual on spreading rumors)[2] described an effective rumor as being "self-propelled." It described five characteristics:

- ▸ *It is easy to remember.* It is vivid, and contains local color, concrete detail, often a slogan, and humor.
- ▸ *It follows a stereotyped plot.* It recalls the history and folklore of the target group and is an old story dressed in new clothes.
- ▸ *It reflects the momentary interests and circumstances of the target group.* It interprets some current event and fills a knowledge gap. It contains some verifiable element of fact and appears to be supported by other events or rumors.

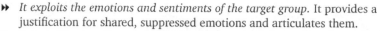

>> *It exploits the emotions and sentiments of the target group.* It provides a justification for shared, suppressed emotions and articulates them.

>> *It is challenging.* It contains "inside information" that cannot be verified directly and is "neither too plausible nor too implausible."

How Rumors Spread

The OSS manual described the qualities that make a rumor spread as being:

>> Plausibility.
>> Simplicity.
>> Suitability for task—for example, slogan rumors can be short and simple, building on existing situations or beliefs. New "information" may need more narrative.
>> Vividness.
>> Suggestiveness.

The OSS "Doctrine" suggested spreading rumors by designing different, apparently independent supporting rumors in different places.

Long before the Internet, Mark Twain saw the force of rumor: "A lie can travel halfway around the world while the truth is putting on its shoes," he wrote. Sadly, the truth travels (or at least is acknowledged) somewhat more slowly, against the tide. Rumors are spread by word of mouth at informal meetings over coffee or round the water cooler (referred to as the "watercooler effect").[3] A team of scientists and mathematicians at Rochester University has come up with dynamic social impact theory[4]—a model to calculate the spread of rumor. One of the motivations for spreading rumors is the kudos which the spreader gets from apparently being on the inside—"knowledge" is power.

With the advent of social media, rumor can be spread farther, quicker, and with more devastating effect. Wikipedia lists over 300 social networking sites,[5] ranging from the well-known (Facebook, with more than 640 million subscribers; Myspace, 100 million plus; Twitter, over 175 million; LinkedIn, over 100 million) to specialist sites and blogs with a few thousand subscribers. Another source lists 750 "top" sites.[6]

Increasingly, rumors are being spread by email and SMS. Viral emails can spread globally within hours. In March 2011, an email and SMS about a nuclear radiation rain shower were reported to be spreading panic across the South East Asian region, including countries like the Philippines that are close to Japan.[7] In Kyrgyzstan, Skype groups were reportedly validating rumors of ethnic disturbances. Skype currently handles 30 million concurrent users. The threat is serious enough to have made the Securities and Exchange Board of India (SEBI) issue an advisory that said intermediaries (brokerages, etc.) must have in place an internal code of conduct; ensure that employees, temporary staff, and even voluntary workers do not circulate unverified information; restrict access to blogs, chat forums, and messenger sites; and keep logs of such blogs.[8]

Dynamic Social Impact Theory (DSIT)

DSIT states that beliefs and attitudes are based on:

➤➤ *Strength of influential sources:* You are more likely to believe a rumor told by a friend or family member.

➤➤ *Immediacy of influence:* Rumors often take hold in close-knit, homogeneous neighborhoods and communities.

➤➤ *Number of sources:* The more people in your network there are who believe a rumor, the more likely you are to believe it.

Based on this, Brooks and DiFonzo developed the "MBN-dialogue model of rumor transmission," where the spread of rumor is based on the motivations (M) for spreading the rumor, the strength of belief (B) in the rumor, and the novelty (N) or newness of the rumor.

The Impact of Rumor

Recent research by Convergys Corp. found that one negative customer review on YouTube, Twitter, or Facebook could cost a company up to 30 customers.[9] Negative *rumors* can hardly have less of an effect.

The impact of false rumors can seriously damage a company's health in many different ways. The most precious asset a company has is its brand value and reputation. Often this exceeds, in value, the tangible assets of the firm. Table 1 presents a 2010 valuation by Brand Finance of the top 10 brands, their brand valuations, and their credit ratings.[9]

Table 1. Brand value: Top 10 brands in 2010. (Source: Brand Finance[1])

Brand	Country	Brand value (US$ billion)	Credit rating
Walmart	US	41.4	AA–
Google	US	36.2	AAA–
Coca-Cola	US	34.8	AAA
IBM	US	33.7	AA–
Microsoft	US	33.6	AAA
General Electric	US	31.9	AA–
Vodafone	UK	29.0	AAA–
HSBC	UK	28.4	AAA
Hewlett-Packard	US	27.4	AA+
Toyota	Japan	27.3	AAA–

Brands and the goodwill associated with a company name have a real value—which is capable of being severely damaged by adverse rumor. As I wrote in *The Definitive Handbook of Business Continuity Management:* "That value is created by many years of advertising and good experience by the consumers of the product or service and it can be quickly eroded. When contamination of Coca-Cola was alleged in France and Belgium a few years ago, the brand value of Coca-Cola was reported to have sunk by $8 billion."[10]

Other impacts can include:

» Loss of share value.
» Loss of sales.
» Loss of customers.
» Loss of credit rating.
» Cash flow problems.
» Vulnerability to predatory and opportunist takeover.
» Loss or delay of the capability to market new products or services under the brand name (brand development/brand extension).
» Increase in public relations, advertising costs, and legal fees to counter negative rumor and recover market share.

Case Study

The Qantas Crash That Never Was

On November 4, 2010, Qantas A380 flight QF32 was bound for Sydney with 433 passengers and 26 crew on board when Indonesian authorities said that there had been some sort of explosion over the island of Batam, just south of Singapore, at about 9.15 a.m. local time. Local eye witnesses found aircraft debris, and pictures on local television showed the Qantas logo on some of this.

The plane defueled and returned to Singapore's Changi Airport after the pilots were forced to shut down one engine, engine two, of its four engines. Qantas said that the airliner landed at 11.45 a.m. local time. The flight landed safely and no passengers or crew were injured.

Widespread and inaccurate rumors spread rapidly through Twitter that the plane had crashed.

Reuters reported that Qantas had told CNBC television that a plane had crashed near Singapore and that it was an Airbus A380. Kompas, a popular Indonesian newspaper, reported on its website that it was "suspected that a Qantas plane exploded in the air near Batam."

On initial rumors of a crash, Qantas shares dived 15 cents, or 3%, to AU$2.82.

On landing, a passenger twittered its safe arrival with a photograph of its damaged engine and wing and Qantas issued a press statement. Shares recovered to AU$2.92.

Case Study

The Impact of Rumor: The Toyota Recalls, 2009–10[11]

In 2009, Toyota was the world's number one car manufacturer, outselling Ford and GM. Rumors spread of electronic control problems, unexpected acceleration, and other defects. From fall 2009 to spring 2010, Toyota recalled 8.5 million cars, 8 million with potential floor mat, braking, unwanted acceleration, accelerator pedal, and steering problems. The recall-affected models make up 58% of Toyota sales. During this time many other manufacturers also recalled cars, but they attracted little publicity.

By March 2010, Toyota had been unable to replicate the alleged electronics failure as the cause of the random unwanted acceleration and had rejected software failure as a cause.

Edolphus Towns, Chairman of the US Committee on Oversight and Government Reform, claimed that up to 39 crash deaths in the United States from 1990 to 2010 may have been linked to accelerator-related problems.

- Toyota shares fell 23% to US$71.78 in the three-week period to February 4, 2010—8% in a single day—and 14%, US$21 billion, in just one week. Before the final recalls, Reuters said that $30 billion had been wiped from Toyota's share value.
- A 35% drop in brand value was forecast by Brand Finance and, depending on which brand value survey is used as a base, this cost between US$9.6 and US$11.7 billion.
- On February 4, 2010, Toyota itself estimated that it would have to spend US$1.12 billion on warranty expenses and would lose as much as US$895 million in lost sales over the recall.
- The cost of a global advertising and public relations campaigns to recover Toyota's tarnished reputation and damaged market share can be roughly estimated, by comparing it with similar campaigns, at about US$300 million initially.
- Toyota closed factories in the United States.
- Toyota saw its US market share fall to 14% in January 2010—its lowest level since January 2006—from 17% for full-year 2009, putting it behind GM.
- To incentivize buyers to kick-start the relaunch is estimated to have cost US$3.1 million in the first year.
- In January 2010 Toyota enjoyed a Standard & Poor's (S&P) AAA– credit rating. Its credit rating dictates the interest rate at which it can borrow funds. Toyota Motor Corp.'s corporate credit rating was reduced by S&P to A-1+. Moody's downgraded Toyota to AA1.
- Toyota has not put a price on productivity losses. Productivity losses caused by factory closure and lower sales may be US$800 million to US$1 billion.
- The value of used Toyotas dropped by around 10%.

In February 2011 the National Highway Traffic Safety Administration (NHTSA) and the National Aeronautics and Space Administration (NASA) report found that the most common problem was drivers hitting the accelerator when they thought they were hitting the brake. NHTSA called this "pedal misapplication." Of the 58 cases by then reported, 18 were instantly dismissed. Of the 40 cases left, 39 were held to have no cause. The rest were deemed "pedal entrapment."[12]

So, while some of the reasons for the recalls remain valid, the key rumor triggering them was simply that: a rumor.

Examples of Rumors
A few examples follow of rumors that have affected firms, their products and services.

- Coca-Cola has suffered continual rumors that the Coca-Cola trademark can be read as meaning "No Mohammed, No Mecca" in Arabic when it is reversed and read from right to left. The Coca-Cola website[13] dismisses this, pointing out that "The Coca-Cola trademark was created in 1886 in Atlanta, Georgia, at a time and place where there was little knowledge of Arabic." It adds that the rumor has been rejected by leading Muslim scholars, whom it quotes. Nevertheless, the rumor persists, and Coca-Cola's sales in the Middle East are negligible. The website also refutes some 27 other rumors.

>> In August 2000 Procter & Gamble (P&G) lost a business-defamation lawsuit against independent distributors of Amway Corp. products, who were accused of spreading, in 1995, a voice-mail rumor linking P&G to Satanism. The rumor may have arisen because Procter & Gamble's president had discussed Satanism on the Phil Donahue program, a nationally televized talk show, some 20 years before. It was also said that a logo depicting a bearded, crescent-shaped man-in-the-moon looking over a field of 13 stars was a Satanic symbol. P&G shares fell 1 3/8 to 62 15/16 on the New York Stock Exchange. After appeal, the case was finally settled in 2007 with an award of US$19.25 million to P&G.

>> In the 1980s it was rumored that Mexican employees urinated into bottles of Corona beer to be exported to the United States. The rumor was traced back to Luce & Sons, distributor of competing Heineken Beer. Corona sued and won, but reportedly spent US$500,000 in public relations and related costs to recover the damage.

>> For more than 30 years a rumor has claimed that McDonald's restaurants use earthworms in their hamburgers, another that they used cow eyeballs. McDonald's countered this by stating that they met the stringent standards set by the US Food and Drug Administration and by the equivalent authority of each country in which they operated. There are more than 100 defamatory rumors circulating against McDonald's. In another case in the United Kingdom, environmental activists Helen Steel and David Morris were sued over a pamphlet against McDonald's. The case dragged on for 10 years, eventually being settled in McDonald's favor. McDonald's said that it did not plan to collect the £40,000 award. Although McDonald's won, the case generated a great deal of adverse publicity.

>> In September 2004, the Kryptonite bicycle lock company suffered from an Internet rumor that some of its cycle locks could be picked with a Bic ballpoint pen. They responded by supplying more than 380,000 replacement locks to customers worldwide.

Summary

Rumors can come from any direction, at any time. They are frequently a mix of fiction and fact, but they may also be unconfirmed fact that has escaped control. 360 degree environmental scanning is essential to provide an early warning. A predetermined strategy is needed to ignore or to combat them. A rebuttal needs to be quick and comprehensive.

How to Fight Rumors: Lessons and Guidelines

Here are a few lessons, suggestions and prompts, learned the hard way, by companies that got it wrong.

Be Prepared

>> Create a bank of goodwill by acting transparently, ethically, and socially responsibly. Court opinion influencers, analysts, and the media. The strength of your brand and reputation is the front line of your defence.

- The bigger they are, the harder they fall. How big are you? Who would like to see you fall? Why? What can you do to eliminate these reasons or to create a soft landing?
- Carefully analyze your product, its contents, and its packaging and promotion. What could be misinterpreted and lead to adverse rumors? In the 1960s fish fingers commonly included a deep-sea fish that was in plentiful supply. This fish was colloquially known as "rats tail." When this was brought to the notice of Birds Eye, it quickly opted to use alternative fish. Indeed, the "fish finger" has been replaced in some markets by "fish stick." Plan for the worst and hope for the best.
- Identify your partners, allies, and adversaries. How could they cause you problems? Sweatshops, child labor, unethical practices? Choose your suppliers carefully.
- Consider security: what hacking, internal emails, mail or trash-can contents could set off the rumor machine? What is kept on laptops or USB memory sticks that could be lost or stolen? Control them.
- Develop or review your crisis management and product recall plans to reflect rumor management aspects.
- Develop a rumor management plan that includes social media.
- Actively monitor social media for adverse mentions of your company as well as monitoring the traditional media.
- Don't just hear; listen! Don't go into denial: face the issues. See a rumor from the perspective of your customers. Remember the Ford Explore/Firestone issues in 2000–01 when Ford vehicles fitted with Firestone tyres were crashing. Ford insisted that it was a tyre issue. Wrong. It was a Ford issue—*they* fitted the tyres.

Take Prompt Action

- Act quickly. A fire doubles in size every few minutes, and it's easier to extinguish a match than an inferno. Know the deadlines for local, national, and international trade and general press, radio, and television and prepare appropriate material in time for each news cycle. And remember, social media never sleep. A few clicks, and another million people can hear the rumor.
- Expect heavy traffic on your website. Drop images, videos, Flash, that consume bandwidth. Plan for upscaling—traffic could increase on your website, Facebook, and Twitter outlets by 1,000%. Minimize inbound traffic by using self-help and voice mail—and update information regularly and frequently.

Get—and Keep—On-Message

- Pull your advertising on any products or services that are at risk from the rumor (at least until you have a rebuttal plan). Advertise other services or products instead.
- Your spokesperson should stay calm, collected, and logical in the event of a rumor, no matter how outrageous it may be. Emotional outbursts give the impression of bluster and lack of control. BP CEO Tony Hayward's remark at the time of the BP Gulf of Mexico oil spill was a classic example. He said he wanted "to get my life back." Fisherman Mike Frenette's riposte was killing. He said: "I want mine back, too. He's ruined it."

7

➤ Choose a credible spokesperson to represent you. A PR person or the CEO are not as trusted as doctors or an employee whom the rumor target can identify with as being "someone like me."

➤ Try to avoid reinforcing minor rumors by repeating them in order to deny them.

➤ Silence is not always golden—it might be interpreted as proof of guilt. Avoid "No comment" responses. Rumors thrive on uncertainty. Remember, at least some of the rumor circulators may be trying to establish the truth by circulating it for verification or rebuttal within a peer group.

➤ On the other hand, there may be times when ignoring a rumor—taking the moral high ground—may be appropriate, especially if the rumor is trivial.

➤ Pre-empt potential rumors and rebut the current rumor by publishing explanations and facts that undermine its credibility. A strong, vivid rebuttal may change public perception and actually improve a company's image. Sometimes it can be effective to take a high-profile stand, publishing a strong rebuttal that's supported by facts. Examples are the Coca-Cola[14] website and President Barack Obama's Fight the Smears website.[15] Both list false rumors, with explanations and rebuttals.

➤ The soccer saying "Play the man as well as the ball" holds true. Take the battle to the enemy. Attack may be a good defense. But think hard before trying to undermine accepted authorities, especially if they are respected and independent.

➤ Communicate, communicate, communicate. Counter the rumors with explanations and facts. Spread a tsunami of good news stories about the company. It takes three positives to overcome one negative. Consider all stakeholders, including employees and regulators.

➤ Use video where practicable: it has greater impact than statements.

➤ Make sure the entire organization is on-message: communications to customers, suppliers, employees, the public, and the media have to be consistent.

➤ Communicate acceptable priorities: life, health, and environmental concerns need addressing before issues of profitability and supply.

Minimize Scope for Error and Misunderstanding
➤ Treble-check all facts.

➤ Do not speculate.

➤ Consider cultural differences and their impact on how your advertising, packaging, and marketing slogans may be interpreted. Avoid unintentional offence and address those differences.

➤ In interviews, make sure that the nonverbal language matches the words. More is communicated nonverbally than verbally, and inconsistency is easy to spot. Be positive and confident—but not arrogant. Avoid negative implications. Remember that humor may be inappropriate or misinterpreted.

➤ Identify and actively target the likely audience(s) for the rumor.

➤ Don't deny the truth—it might take time, but the truth will always out. The earlier denial will come back to haunt the firm.

Protect Your Market and Share Value

▸▸ Act to protect your share price: prepare and deliver statements to stock exchanges if appropriate.

Take Responsibility

▸▸ If at fault, don't play down the impact of problems—these may be a serious matter to the customer. Avoid arrogance. Show humility and repentance. Show care, empathy, and compassion.

▸▸ Avoid the blame game. It might be a problem with your suppliers, but as far as the customer is concerned, if they buy from you, it is down to you to accept responsibility. You can sue the suppliers later.

▸▸ Never, ever, ever, lie to the media.

Make Restitution

▸▸ If at fault, make restitution—quickly. Take prompt action to remedy a product or service defect, like Kryptonite. Simply changing the product packaging may help. In 1992 Snapple, a US beverage manufacturer, was rumored to support the Klu Klux Klan (KKK) because the picture of a ship on the Snapple label was said to be a slave ship and the "K" on the label was said to indicate support for the KKK. Snapple redesigned its label to make it clear that the ship showed the Boston Tea Party and the "K" stood for "kosher pareve" (food without meat or dairy ingredients). In 1998 Wall's ice cream changed its logo when it was claimed that the original, when read upside down, was defamatory to Muslims.

Call in the Cavalry

▸▸ Let someone else defend you. Refer to respected, independent experts to refute the rumors. Toyota chose NASA.

Get It Out, Get It Over, Move On

▸▸ If there is bad news, get it out—all of it. Rumors will persist like a chronic illness if bad news drips out a drop at a time. And try to publish it at a time when more important news is making the headlines.

Be Cautious About Lawsuits

▸▸ Think carefully before taking legal action, especially if it is against a little guy and your firm is a big guy. The media love "David and Goliath" stories. Besides, legal action is expensive, time-consuming, distracting for senior management, and can create a steady, debilitating drip of news stories that reiterate the rumor as the case drags on—maybe for many years—through judicial processes that may include repeated appeals.

More Info

Books:

DiFonzo, Nicholas. *The Watercooler Effect: A Psychologist Explores the Extraordinary Power of Rumors*. New York: Avery, 2008. For the psychology of rumor. (Paperback subtitled *An Indispensable Guide to Understanding and Harnessing the Power of Rumors*.)

Doorley, John, and Helio Fred Garcia. *Reputation Management: The Key to Successful Public Relations and Corporate Communication*. New York: Routledge, 2010. For responses to rumors.

Hiles, Andrew (ed). *The Definitive Handbook of Business Continuity Management*. 3rd ed. Chichester, UK: Wiley, 2010. For case studies on Toyota and BP, and detail on marketing protection.

McCusker, Gerry. *Public Relations Disasters: Talespin—Inside Stories and Lessons Learnt*. Philadelphia, PA: Kogan Page, 2006. For detail on the Procter & Gamble and BA vs Virgin rumors.

Notes

1. Brand Finance. "Brand Finance global 500 2010." March 2010. Online at: tinyurl.com/6c5gnho
2. Knapp, Robert H. "A psychology of rumor." *Public Opinion Quarterly* 8:1 (Spring 1944): 22–37. Online at: www.jstor.org/stable/2745686 2. Office of Strategic Services Planning Group. "Doctrine re rumors." June 2, 1943. Online at: www.icdc.com/~paulwolf/oss/rumormanual2june1943.htm
3. DiFonzo (2008).
4. Dube, William. "Deciphering the watercooler effect." *Research at RIT* (May 2010). Online at: www.rit.edu/research/other_story.php?id=23
5. List of social networking websites from Wikipedia: en.wikipedia.org/wiki/List_of_social_networking_websites
6. List of the top 750 social networking sites and tools from e-crm: tinyurl.com/yfw9un3
7. Kumar, Manish. "Nuclear radiation rain email, SMS rumor spreads panic in Philippines, India." *ForestLaneShul* (March 15, 2011). Online at: tinyurl.com/4zhtsln
8. Raman, Kripa. "Keeping a tab on staff spreading rumours is difficult: Marketmen." *Hindu Business Line* (March 25, 2011). Online at: www.thehindubusinessline.com/markets/article1571507.ece
9. Shannon, Sarah. "One bad Twitter 'tweet' can cost 30 customers, survey shows." *Bloomberg* (November 26, 2009). Online at: tinyurl.com/ygqsul2
10. Hiles (2010), ch. 5.
11. For the full story of the Toyota recalls, see Hiles (2010), Appendix A1-AC, p. 597 ff.
12. National Highway Traffic Safety Administration (NHTSA) and National Aeronautics and Space Administration (NASA). "NHTSA–NASA study of unintended acceleration in Toyota vehicles." February 8, 2011. Online at: www.nhtsa.gov/UA
13. Coca-Cola Company—Middle East rumors: tinyurl.com/64xxrh3
14. *Ibid.*
15. Fight the Smears: www.fightthesmears.com

Governance and Reputation Risk[1]

by Andrew Tucker

Mettle Consulting, London, and Brunel University, Uxbridge, UK

This Chapter Covers

» Why governance is a key reputation risk.
» Governance beyond the boardroom.
» Aligning culture and strategy.
» A practical way forward.
» Summary and further steps.

Introduction: Why Governance Is a Key Reputation Risk

Reputation risk is diminished when corporate culture and strategy are closely aligned but heightened when they are divergent.[2] In this context, the role of corporate governance is to produce and enforce rules and structures to align a firm's operating procedures and strategy to produce superior performance. Therefore, ensuring that corporate governance arrangements are optimum are a key aspect of managing reputation risk.

However, in recent years corporate governance thinking has not kept pace with developments in the corporate world. The result can be seen in the number of catastrophic failures of corporate governance that have been found behind recent major corporate reputation crises. From the Royal Bank of Scotland's subservient board—which provided little oversight to the CEO's debt-fueled expansionist plans—to warning signs from mid-management being ignored at Northern Rock and HBOS, corporate governance rules and regulations were followed but stretched far beyond their intended purpose. Yet, as the Organisation for Economic Co-operation and Development (OECD) concluded in 2009, "the financial crisis can be to an important extent attributed to failures and weaknesses in corporate governance arrangements."[3]

Outside the banking sector, the 2010 Gulf of Mexico oil spill exposed BP's weak governance of safety arrangements, the 2008 bribery scandal at Siemens came from bribes being perceived by mid-management as common business practice in winning contracts, and the ongoing phone-hacking scandal at News International provides mounting evidence of an absence of governance oversight by the parent company and an absence of governance practice by the News of the World's management (see Case Study). Again, these firms claimed that corporate governance rules and regulations were followed and expressed surprise at the subsequent reputation damage they suffered.

These examples all show how the firms' corporate governance arrangements failed to align operating procedures with strategy and resulted in massive reputation damage. The Royal Bank of Scotland pursued an aggressive expansion strategy in its global footprint but claimed that its loan book strategy was actually conservative to counterbalance risks elsewhere in the business. However, senior managers (with

11

the tacit acceptance of major shareholders) actively withdrew the counterbalancing checks by promoting risk-taking investment bankers to board positions that required a wider view of the firm's reputation risks. According to BP executives, they had learned the lessons from the 2005 Texas City refinery explosion and had put in place safety arrangements across the firm. However, this safety consciousness did not extend to the group's aggressive strategy of deepwater exploration. As a result, a safety culture with clear awareness and appreciation of safety concerns did not permeate the operating procedures that were drawn up by BP's commercial partners in the Gulf of Mexico.[4]

What is missing from these examples is an understanding of the role of corporate governance beyond a bureaucratic box-ticking exercise—senior executives interviewed at the Royal Bank of Scotland and BP after their respective crises claimed that their organizations had "ticked all the boxes."[5] Corporate governance is taken less as "how we do things around here" and more as "the minimum bureaucracy required." As a result, governance rules and structures are designed not to impede strategy rather than to help deliver it. This, in turn, increases reputation risk because corporate governance is not seen as an effective means and method of exerting operational control.

Reputation Risk and Corporate Governance

Can reputation damage be avoided by focusing on corporate governance issues? Whereas a reputation crisis can strike seemingly without notice, failures of corporate governance take years to build and establish the corporate culture within which reputationally risky behavior becomes the norm. In other words, corporate governance is a leading indicator of reputation risk. Given the abruptness of reputation crises and the enormous resources required to deal with them, it therefore makes operational sense to monitor developments in corporate governance for warning signs of impending reputation damage.

Case Study

News International and Phone Hacking

Sub-agents, in the shape of private investigators, reporters, and management, played a central role in the catastrophic failure of corporate governance at News International (NI). The parent company, News Corporation (News Corp.), has well-known corporate governance weaknesses—preferential voting rights on restricted stock, the elevation of family members to senior positions, opaque reporting, and an ineffective board—that have led to a "Murdoch discount" of around 12% on the company's share price relative to its competitors. Despite this, News International was on the verge of acquiring the remaining 61% stake in the UK satellite broadcaster BSkyB until the role of NI newspapers in long-running phone-hacking practices was exposed by The Guardian newspaper in 2011.

NI had long been planning to fully own BSkyB for clear commercial reasons. BSkyB's full-year results for 2011 showed revenue up 16% to £6.6 billion, operating profits up 23% at £1 billion, and free cash flow up 51% at £869 million. These profits far outstripped the meager profits (and often losses) of NI's newspaper stable. Moreover, even the profitable News of the World newspaper contributed less than 1% of News Corp's global revenue.

From 2008 industry rumors circulated that News Corp. would divest itself of its newspapers once chairman and CEO Rupert Murdoch finally relented. At the same time, increasing management pressure was put on the newspaper editors to produce ever more impressive scoops to redress the general market trend to declining circulation figures. Caught between these twin pressures, newspaper senior staff at best turned a blind eye, or at worst actively colluded in the illicit practice of intercepting the voicemail messages of people in the public sphere.

When two News of the World journalists were jailed for the practice in January 2007, NI claimed that this was a case of rogue journalists (sub-agents) pursuing a story too vigorously. This defence was proved false when police discovered a list of 4,000 possible targets at one of the journalists' homes. Despite this, NI executives, editors, and other employees were able to limit the reputation damage to a small number of out-of-court settlements by using three strategies:

- ▸▸ controlling the reputation damage by successfully presenting people in the public sphere as "fair game";
- ▸▸ influencing the London Metropolitan Police not to fully investigate the wider allegations;
- ▸▸ in effect, blackmailing policymakers not to investigate thoroughly for fear that their private lives might be exposed in NI newspapers.

This successful reputation strategy finally collapsed in mid-2011 when evidence emerged that News of the World journalists had also hacked the phones of a murdered teenager, the parents of murdered schoolgirls, and the relatives of dead British soldiers and terrorist victims.

The BSkyB deal was withdrawn weeks before it was due to be approved by the UK regulatory authorities. The immediate cause was the potential failure by NI senior management to satisfy the "fit and proper persons" test required by the regulator. This resulted in significant reputational damage in the form of share price loss, the resignation of several senior NI executives, and the establishment of the Leveson Inquiry into the phone-hacking scandal. The longer-term cause can be traced to governance failures that had bred a culture of criminality and disdain for the rule of law at the now defunct News of the World. As News Corp's 2011 annual report noted a few weeks later: "It's possible that these proceedings could damage our reputation and might impair our ability to conduct our business... Any fees, expenses penalties or judgement related to the allegations could affect the results of our operation and financial condition."

Governance Risk

Governance risk is those risks faced by a firm as a result of its current governance approach failing to align its culture and its strategy. For example, the 2010 Gulf of Mexico oil spill exposed BP's weak governance of safety arrangements. Key among these governance risks is reputation risk. At a granular level, governance risk includes oversized bonuses demanded by key staff, bonuses paid against short-term and opaque criteria, underskilled and underperforming board members, the prevalence of "black box" methodologies that only a few employees understand, responsibility devolved across the firm but not matched by managers' skill in wielding power responsibly, and innovative and entrepreneurial teams objecting to oversight.

Governance Beyond the Boardroom

Since the Cadbury review (Cadbury, 1992), corporate governance has been commonly taken to be the "system by which companies are directed and controlled." As such, corporate governance is seen as a matter for company boards that is somehow set apart from day-to-day management concerns (see recent endorsements by the Financial Reporting Council, 2010a, and Walker, 2009). However, this focus ignores the key groups of decision-makers that are termed "sub-agents." Sub-agents are nonsenior management staff who may have the opportunity and motivation to pursue their own interests and potentially cause significant losses in the process. Sub-agents are only lightly referred to in current regulatory codes, yet they have played a key role in recent catastrophic corporate governance failures and reputation crises. For example, sub-agents directly caused the collapse of AIG from its "rogue" credit default swaps department in London, the Alder Hay organ-removal scandal, and the Parmalat fraud and money-laundering debacle. In the services sector, sub-agents include customer advisors, analysts, brokers, and insurance underwriters. In the manufacturing sector, sub-agents include internal product and quality inspectors, supply chain managers, and purchasing agents. In the health care sector, sub-agents include care quality managers, hospital consultants, and pharmaceutical R&D managers.

Corporate governance has implications not only for boards (including their nonexecutive directors), but also for a much wider "executive" community. Faced with the intensity of technological change and a challenging competitive environment, firms are constantly adjusting and transforming their ways of doing business with customers and a variety of partners and stakeholders. At the same time, nonboard employees are ambitious to take on responsibility, which top management encourages through empowering policies and structures. This "democratizing" can boost both performance and motivation, but it also broadens the scale of the "theater" in which risk has to be managed.

Therefore, many people beyond the board need to be aware of the implications of their actions and behaviors, not only to deliver commercial performance, but also to comply with business assurance needs in order to foster the long-term resilience of the entity. Organizational effectiveness and compliance are, thus, becoming intricately bound up with each other.

To understand the dynamics of governance beyond the boardroom, we need to supplement the traditional economic model of principal–agent relations. This well-established model helps to explain the issues that arise under conditions of asymmetric information when a principal hires an agent to pursue the principal's interests. One example of this is when the shareholders of a listed company (the principal) hire the board (the agent) to deliver the best possible return on an investment. Ever since research on corporate governance emerged in the 1970s, it has focused on the firm as a nexus of legal contracts.[6] This tradition has elevated principal–agent problems to be of central concern and generated much research around the relationship between shareholders and managers.[7] More recently, this tradition has attracted increased critical analysis,[8] but it had not been challenged substantially before the credit crunch. The principal–agent relationship has recently been redefined by the Financial Reporting Council's (2010b) stewardship code. This code "aims to enhance the quality of engagement between institutional investors and companies to help improve long-term returns to shareholders and the efficient exercise of governance responsibilities by setting out good practice on engagement with investee companies to which the FRC believes institutional investors should aspire." The agent–principal relationship is guided by the board recommending to the shareholders an appropriate balance of risk and return when setting corporate policies by which the firm will be managed.

In the context of reputation risk, a third party must be included in the principal–agent model—the sub-agent (see Figure 1). We call this the principal–agent–sub-agent or PASA model. The A–SA relationship is guided by a contractual agreement to deliver a service, supplemented by a bonus dynamic where the sub-agent's superior performance is rewarded in financial or promotional terms, but little account is taken of his or her losses beyond the threat of dismissal. The SA–A relationship is guided by the demonstration of professional management skills and capacity.

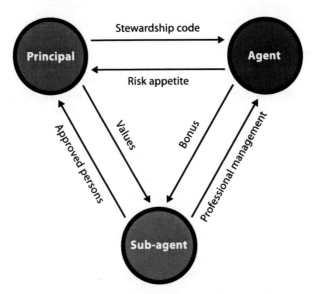

Figure 1. Principal–agent–sub-agent (PASA) model

The P–SA relationship is guided by the principal insisting that sub-agents abide by the corporate governance metrics of the principal, over and above simple legal and regulatory constraints. An example is fund managers setting up "ethical funds" where firms are only invested in if they can demonstrate commitment to the relevant ethical framework. This commitment must be demonstrated throughout the firm rather than simply in its public statements. As part of this same dynamic, regulators are now asking for data on managers' professional competencies further down the management chain than just the board. For key operational employees, the financial regulator now requires data on "honesty, integrity and reputation; competence and capability; and financial soundness."[9]

The SA–P relationship is inherently weak, because there is no point in a principal employing an agent to pursue his interests if the principal then has to actively manage the sub-agent. The SA–P relationship is pertinent when SA becomes, in effect, a junior

P through the granting of stock options. While As have long been tied to P's interests through stock options with longer-term vesting periods as a core part of As' compensation packages, this mechanism is often only employed with SAs in mature firms as part of their bonus arrangements. Stock options are frequently granted as part of SA's core package in start-up companies to manage initial cash flow problems. However, this model presumes a near-term initial public offering (IPO) or equivalent in order for the SA to benefit from the deferred payment. In many other sectors, this is seldom the case. As a result, whereas the A–P relationship is actively managed by A through investor conference calls, quarterly updates, and roadshows, SAs seldom even know the identity of P.

To show the explanatory potential of the PASA model, we can apply it to the most egregious recent example of corporate governance failure driving reputation risk—the financial crisis of 2008–09. Here, the link between the principal and sub-agent failed, and the link between the agent and sub-agent also came under great stress. A number of insights emerge from understanding where the PASA model buckled.

- ▸▸ Bonuses linked to the size of trades rather than profitability and with little corrective function aligned A and SA against P.
- ▸▸ If the SA does not share P's values, he or she will make no effort to understand the implications of his/her actions for P's long-term success. This lack of understanding is exacerbated by the absence of an industry standard definition of "alpha"—the outperformance of the market based on SA's skill rather than general movements of the market.
- ▸▸ A's lack of professional management skills is manifested in SA's lack of interest in understanding the firm's risk appetite as set by the board, with catastropic consequences.
- ▸▸ Sustained and high profitability leads both A and P to adopt the SA's short-term focus.
- ▸▸ The greater the complexity of the products, the more the SA gains effective independence.[10]
- ▸▸ Larger banks are so complex, global, and multidisciplinary that they are forced to adopt a subsidiary model that puts pressure on A to manage professionally and effectively.
- ▸▸ Control aspects of governance break down in innovative, entrepreneurial environments.
- ▸▸ The fragmented nature of the banks' shareholders and shareholding structures worked against P's control of A.
- ▸▸ Where the SA and A relationship breaks down, it is easier for A to "pay off" SA rather than to manage the situation to a mutually acceptable resolution. This practice is known as "checkbook diplomacy."
- ▸▸ Differerent SAs belong to different cultures—the cultural differences between investment and retail banking traditions are especially marked.
- ▸▸ The absence of a widely recognized professional management standard for A.

Many of these issues have been recognized before at a micro level. For example, many financial institutions have tried to design bonus arrrangements that reward long-term profitability rather than size of trades.[11] However, efforts to tackle these issues in isolation are defeated by an absence of systemic thinking that joins up as many of the issues as possible as part of a dynamic whole. Using the PASA model to make progress here means that these issues can be addressed in context, especially with regard to corporate culture and corporate strategy.

The Principal–Agent–Sub-Agent (PASA) Model

This new model explains the relationship dynamics between principals (shareholders), agents (board), and sub-agents (operational heads, salesforce, IT managers, etc.). It helps to highlight potential risks that arise when a firm's culture is misaligned with its strategy.

Aligning Culture and Strategy

Recognizing the role of sub-agents highlights the requirement for firms' corporate governance arrangements to align their corporate cultures and strategies. This is a complex challenge, but some progress is being made. Reviews of the 2008–09 financial crisis concluded that corporate governance is more than the implementation of mechanistic systems and controls. The revised principles of the Basel III Accord, against which financial institutions are to be regulated in future, require a "demonstrated corporate culture that supports and provides appropriate norms and incentives for professional and responsible behaviour is an essential foundation of good governance" (Basel Committee on Banking Supervision, 2010).

This broader approach to governance follows the Walker review's conclusion that it is more important to develop "an overall culture of good governance" than to create additional rules and regulations, which may do little more than "attract box ticking conformity" (Walker, 2009, p. 31). Rather, there is a key behavioral/cultural element to effective governance, where even the most technically advanced governance arrangements can fail without factors such as board/senior management buy-in, effective internal training and communication, and a properly aligned performance management framework. As the present UK Chancellor George Osborne said in 2009, "The banks should be using their profits to rebuild their balance sheets, not to hand out huge bonuses while the rest of the economy picks up the pieces for the follies of finance. But the change of culture needs to go far deeper than bonuses."

To understand governance and reputation risk fully, we need to understand that governance must be managed as a cultural phenomenon. Culture is a slippery concept that is often characterized in one-dimensional or simplistic terms. For a working definition, we follow Edgar Schein's well-known description: "Culture is a pattern of shared tacit assumptions that was learned by a group as it solved its problems of external adaptation and internal integration, that has worked well enough to be considered valid and, therefore, to be taught to new members as the correct way to perceive, think, and feel in relation to these problems."[12]

The Economic and Social Research Council's (ESRC) project "Governance beyond the boardroom"[13] examined these issues with particular attention to the UK financial services sector. Two implications can be drawn immediately from recognizing the role of sub-agents in culture and governance. The first is that the definition of governance is broadened—from the rules and processes that ensure a reasonable return on investment for shareholders, to the rules, processes, and behaviors that ensure: a reasonable return on investment for shareholders; sustainable business; and constructive relationships with stakeholders.

The second implication is that culture is firm- and sector-specific. From our qualitative survey group, we can isolate the following informally expressed "definitions" of culture in the UK financial services sector. Culture is:

» "the way we do things around here";
» "the bonus culture...the culture of greed";
» "teamwork and long hours";
» "how you behave when you think nobody's looking";
» "what people do when they think they are alone";
» "we are a team—we don't tolerate stars";
» "I need my team members to come to me when they know there's a problem."

Working with these definitions, the project adopted a qualitative approach using standardized open questionnaires, with interviews conducted on-site. Ten questions were derived from the hypotheses outlined above.[14] Interview candidates were selected from across the UK financial services sector. The interviewees included: three chairman/company secretary of top UK banks, two mid-level regulators, two general counsels, five senior/mid-level operational heads, three mid-level analysts, one junior trader, one senior nonexecutive director, and four mid-level policymakers. Contemporaneous notes were taken by both interviewers. A combination of manifest and latent content analysis was employed to examine the qualitative data. The analysis revealed 10 clusters of factors that drive governance beyond the boardroom. These factors were marked by the interviewers for frequency of occurrence and magnitude. A mean score was then calculated per driver to identify the relatively strongest drivers per cluster (see Figure 2).

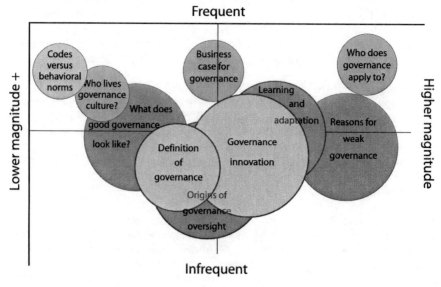

Figure 2. Drivers of governance culture in UK financial services sector

The 10 clusters of governance culture that were identified are listed below.

1 Reasons for governance weakness. This cluster hightlights weak management skills and poor-quality senior management. As a regulator said when interviewed: "There is a major issue when there is a disconnect between operation management and strategy at the board."

2 Definition of governance. This cluster describes the conflict between oversight and frontline functions and problems in the free flow of information around a business. As a general counsel said when interviewed: "How do you get the relevant information? Governance is about the architecture linking the board, reporting functions, people and strategy."

3 Governance innovation. This cluster describes the willingness of the firm to restructure current reporting functions if they now longer effectively link board, people, strategy, and risk.

4 Business case for a stronger governance regime. This cluster specifically addresses how strong governance is a reputational advantage in the market in that there is a direct relationship between having a reputation for strong corporate governance and commercial advantage. As a director of a large fund said when interviewed: "Corporate governance pays off and will be a material factor over a period of time."

5 Who lives governance culture? This cluster describes how the board sets the tone of governance and company culture. It also questions whether corporate governance issues are a specific board-level issue. As a senior nonexecutive director said when interviewed: "Good governance occurs where there is the courage to intervene early and stand up to the optimism bias of ambitious people. The board is a process, not a performance."

6 What does good governance look like? This cluster describes the form vs. substance debate around governance structures. In particular, it asks how good are existing governance metrics. As the chairman of one of the top four UK banks said when interviewed: "I am obsessed by culture, more about the how than the what of operations and bank's focus."

7 Origins of governance oversight. This cluster describes the varying levels of importance that the firm attaches to different origins of governance oversight, like nonexecutive directors, investors, regulators, or strong compliance functions.

8 Learning and adaptation. This cluster focuses on how the firm as a whole learns and adapts new forms of governance as its situation evolves. In particular, it looks at the relative level of importance given to staff ownership of the firm's governance arrangements.

9 Codes vs. behavioral norms. This cluster looks at the relative importance attached to internal and external behavioral codes as opposed to internally generated behavioral norms.

10 Who does governance apply to? This cluster describes how governance is often perceived as just an internal audit and risk management issue. It also recognizes that an employee's attitude to compliance depends on where he sits. Last, the cluster recognizes that governance culture should be embedded across the firm. As a veteran banker said when interviewed: "Entrepreneurial departments see compliance as a pain to be endured and avoided if possible."

A Practical Way Forward

The regulatory debate around reforming the financial sector has stalled recently because regulating behavior is seen as impractical and unrealistic, while at the same time banks are not trusted to self-regulate. Following on from the research outlined above, a more productive and sustainable approach is being developed from the ESRC-funded research. This approach is to roll out a toolkit that can facilitate the assessment and management of such behavioral/cultural factors. The toolkit that is being developed will primarily be delivered via online outlets using a range of spreadsheets, handouts, and decision-making tools. The main components of the toolkit are as follows.

- A process tool that highlights the essential stages and decisions associated with the implementation of effective governance arrangements.
- An audit tool that allows institutions to compare themselves with identified examples of good practice and to assess the gaps in their own practice.
- A suite of recommended metrics (both qualitative and quantitative) that are used to monitor the performance of new or existing governance arrangements. This will include metrics that allow institutions to assess their governance culture.
- Case studies to illustrate good practice.
- Face-to-face training sessions and bundled e-learning modules.

Analysis with the toolkit concentrates on three process-oriented questions.

- *How to show employees that cultural change is not difficult but does require thinking in a different way.* For example, would your firm be prepared to dismiss employees who meet their targets but who do so only through unethical practices? Many firms currently monitor outcomes, but they do not monitor the drivers of those outcomes, or whether those drivers can be isolated and monitored. Many organizations employ a Six-Sigma approach whereby inputs and processes are manipulated to produce desired outputs, and the analysis prompts thinking about how this approach can be applied to your firm's sector.
- *Being more conscious of what organizations measure.* Many organizations collect data that could populate the toolkit but which need to be reorganized for this purpose on a simple dashboard for boards and managers. The goal is not to collect large amounts of fresh internal data, but to make better use of what has already been collected.
- *Making plain the transitional steps that are involved in moving from a benchmark analysis to a future culture.* In other words, a benchmark analysis involves asking: "What does good governance look like for us and how far away from that are we today?" This involves degrees of organizational self-awareness and an understanding of what metrics are currently collected internally. A future culture analysis involves asking: "By comparison, where do we want to get to? Are there case studies we can use to chart the forward path?" This may involve collecting different internal metrics and establishing a long-term commitment to promoting good governance practice through training, key performance indicators, recruitment, and promotion policies.

Summary and Further Steps

▸▸ There is a real and significant link between reputation risk, corporate governance and culture, and strategy execution. If one of these core management areas is misaligned, the effort required to deliver any of them is increased.

▸▸ Effective corporate governance is a leading indicator of reputation risk. In other words, since pride comes before a fall, it makes sense to monitor pride levels to avoid a fall.

▸▸ Management needs to answer two related questions: Does your corporate culture help or hinder achieving your strategy? Do you have the right governance approach to achieve business objectives?

▸▸ Your firm's culture is the key to understanding and analyzing governance risks. These come in many shapes and sizes—from the lone trader blowing up the business by chasing a big bonus, to offering bribes to corrupt foreign officials, to covering up substandard production practices. Use tools to diagnose your firm's culture to help to shape strategy.

More Info

Article:
Kirkpatrick, Grant. "The corporate governance lessons from the financial crisis." *Financial Market Trends* 96 (2009/1). Online at: www.oecd.org/dataoecd/32/1/42229620.pdf

Reports:
Ashby, Simon. "The 2007–2009 financial crisis: Learning the risk management lessons." Financial Services Research Forum, University of Nottingham, January 2010. Online at: tinyurl.com/6gq4e9x

Ashby, Simon. "Picking up the pieces: Risk management in a post crisis world." Financial Services Research Forum, University of Nottingham, and Financial Services Knowledge Transfer Network, 2011.

Basel Committee on Banking Supervision. "Principles for enhancing corporate governance." Bank for International Settlements, October 2010. Online at: www.bis.org/publ/bcbs176.htm

Committee on the Financial Aspects of Corporate Governance. "Report of the Committee on the Financial Aspects of Corporate Governance" (Cadbury Report). London: Gee, December 1, 1992. Online at: www.ecgi.org/codes/documents/cadbury.pdf

Financial Reporting Council. "The UK corporate governance code." June 2010a. Online at: www.frc.org.uk/corporate/ukcgcode.cfm

Financial Reporting Council. "The UK stewardship code." July 2010b. Online at: www.frc.org.uk/corporate/investorgovernance.cfm

More Info

Sants, Hector. "Do regulators have a role to play in judging culture and ethics?" Speech to Chartered Institute of Securities and Investments Conference, London, June 2010. Online at: tinyurl.com/369s2ry

Sants, Hector. "Can culture be regulated?" Speech to Mansion House Conference on Values and Trust, London, October 2010. Online at: tinyurl.com/4ycclz7

Senior Supervisors Group. "Risk management lessons from the global banking crisis of 2008." October 21, 2009. Online at: tinyurl.com/3ebc7n5 [PDF].

Walker, David. "A review of corporate governance in UK banks and other financial industry entities: Final recommendations" (Walker Review). HM Treasury, November 26, 2009. Online at: www.hm-treasury.gov.uk/d/walker_review_261109.pdf

Notes

1. The research for this chapter was supported by the ESRC Business Engagement Fund (RES 185-31-0108).
2. Dowling, Grahame. "Reputation risk: It is the board's ultimate responsibility." *Journal of Business Strategy* 27:2 (2006): 59–68. Online at: dx.doi.org/10.1108/02756660610650055
3. Kirkpatrick (2009).
4. National Commission on the BP Deepwater Horizon Oil Spill and Offshore Drilling. November 1, 2011. Online at: www.oilspillcommission.gov/final-report. Especially chapter 1.
5. National Commission on the BP Deepwater Horizon Oil Spill and Offshore Drilling (2011); and Tucker, Andrew, Greg Spiro, and Elizabeth Nicholson. "Governance beyond the boardroom." Birkbeck, University of London, and SpiroNicholson, 2010. Online at: www.business.bbk.ac.uk/news-and-events/governance-beyond-the-boardroom. (Copyright © Birkbeck, University of London, and SpiroNicholson, 2010).
6. See, for example, Jensen, Michael C., and William H. Meckling. "Theory of the firm: Managerial behavior, agency costs and ownership structure." *Journal of Financial Economics* 3:4 (October 1976): 305–360. Online at: dx.doi.org/10.1016/0304-405X(76)90026-X; and Fama, Eugene F., and Michael C. Jensen. "Separation of ownership and control." *Journal of Law and Economics* 26:2 (June 1983): 301–325. Online at: www.jstor.org/stable/725104
7. See, for example, Eisenhardt, Kathleen M. "Agency theory: An assessment and review." *Academy of Management Review* 14:1 (January 1989): 57–74. Online at: www.jstor.org/stable/258191; Sebora, Terrence C., and Michael J. Rubach. "The duty of fair dealing: Board judgement in management led buyouts." *Journal of Business Ethics* 17:1 (January 1998): 7–13. Online at: dx.doi.org/10.1023/A:1005705626695; and Shleifer, Andrei, and Robert W. Vishny. "A survey of corporate governance." *Journal of Finance* 52:2 (June 1997): 737–783. Online at: www.jstor.org/stable/2329497
8. See, for example, Miller, Gary. "Solutions to principal agent problems in firms." In Claude Ménard and Mary M. Shirley (eds). *Handbook of New Institutional Economics*. Berlin: Springer, 2005; pp. 349–370; and Fligstein, Neil, and Jennifer Choo. "Law and corporate governance." *Annual Review of Law and Social Science* 1 (2005): 61–84. Online at: dx.doi.org/10.1146/annurev.lawsocsci.1.041604.115944
9. See the Financial Service Authority's "approved persons" regime and its ARROW 2 framework on governance, management, and culture.
10. As Alan Greenspan said on the CNBC program "House of cards" in February 2009: "I've got some fairly heavy background in mathematics. But some of the complexities of some of the instruments that were going into CDOs bewilders me. I didn't understand what they were doing or how they actually got the types of returns out of the mezzanines and the various tranches of the CDO that they did. And I figured if I didn't understand it and I had access to a couple hundred PhDs, how the rest of the world is going to understand it sort of bewildered me."
11. In this debate, hedge funds claim that their institutional structures give them sounder governance arrangements than investment banks. See, for example, Boyson, Nicole M., and Robert M. Mooradian. "Corporate governance and hedge fund activism." *Review of Derivatives Research* 14:2 (July 2011): 169–204. Online at: dx.doi.org/10.1007/s11147-011-9065-6
12. Schein, Edgar H. *Organizational Culture and Leadership*. San Francisco, CA: Jossey-Bass, 2004.
13. Tucker *et al.*, *op. cit.* 5.
14. These hypotheses were as follows. H1: Corporate governance issues significantly impact outside the boardroom as well as inside. H2: The Board is not the sole guardian of corporate governance issues. H3: Using a risk management analytical approach to governance fails to understand the interdependent dynamics of governance issues. H4: Governance is better understood and managed as a cultural phenomenon.

The CEO's Role in Reputation Management
by Leslie Gaines-Ross

Weber Shandwick, New York, USA

This Chapter Covers

- ▸▸ The importance of the CEO in the reputation management of his or her company.
- ▸▸ Why the CEO's role is of paramount importance for the reputation of the enterprise.
- ▸▸ How the CEO can manage reputation.
- ▸▸ The rising focus on corporate reputation in an age of unprecedented reputation risk and the CEO's increased responsibility as steward of this reputation.
- ▸▸ Five recommendations for CEOs who recognize their accountability in safeguarding their firm's reputation. Each is based on extensive research conducted by the author over the course of two decades.

Introduction

"Our reputation is more important than the last hundred million dollars." Rupert Murdoch, Chairman and CEO of News Corporation

Corporate reputation matters more than ever, as Rupert Murdoch would be the first to admit today. An increasingly complex business environment, marked by higher standards of corporate governance, citizen journalism, a more cynical public, and emerging special interest groups, places ever more pressure on leadership to protect corporate reputations. In fact, after financial risk, loss of reputation is the biggest risk cited by corporate board members in a recent study by accounting consultancy EisnerAmper LLC (2011). Even annual reports are recognizing the magnitude of reputation as a factor in business health; companies such as Goldman Sachs and AIG are now reporting "adverse publicity" as a risk factor in their 10-K filings.

One statistic often gets the attention of chairmen and CEOs. More than four in 10 of the world's most respected companies lost reputational status in *Fortune's* World's Most Admired Companies survey 2011. This is the "stumble rate" that we at Weber Shandwick study closely, which is based on the performance of companies that lose their no. 1 most admired status in their respective industries. As Virgin Atlantic founding CEO Richard Branson confirms about the loss of reputation: "Your reputation is all you have in life—your personal reputation and the reputation of your brand. And if you do anything that damages that reputation, you can destroy your company … and it's going to be very difficult for that brand to ever recover."

Not surprisingly, 100% of CEOs report that they think frequently about their company's reputation (Gaines-Ross, CEO *Capital*, 2003), and almost six in 10 believe their company's reputation to be under threat. CEOs have taken the reins as guardians of reputation for their organizations. They know that, ultimately, they will earn credit when their companies are doing well, and get all the blame when reputation is in jeopardy. Executive recruiter Korn/Ferry has quantified this sense of CEO responsibility.

In a survey of global executives, the CEO was cited most often as the person directly responsible for risk management (Korn/Ferry Institute, 2010). Similarly, Weber Shandwick's "Safeguarding reputation" study with KRC Research found that 60% of senior global business executives blame the CEO when companies lose reputation after a crisis. The proverbial buck stops with the CEO.

Before recommending different ways that CEOs must take responsibility for any reputational risk that their companies face, one thing cannot be overstated enough— that reputational risks are often the result of ethical lapses in the culture or leadership of an organization. The CEO has tremendous influence on setting the tone and, consequently, the destiny of the company. Recognition of how leadership behavior and actions are perceived has a disproportionate effect, both positive and negative, on how employees behave.

So, what can a chief executive do to manage his or her company's reputation? Based on numerous studies of reputational best practices and years of monitoring global corporate leadership, five ways are recommended that CEOs can follow when seeking to safeguard their company's most valuable intangible and competitive asset.

Monitor, Monitor, Monitor

Executives who systematically examine the ways risks silently emerge and proliferate can foresee and prepare for reputation threats more effectively. CEOs need to know the risks that lurk around corners. Without a rigorous risk assessment process, the CEO can be caught unprepared for addressing a reputational threat. The CEO must not only ensure that his or her team is monitoring for danger, but also grant sufficient resources for the structuring of these systems.

Importantly, reputation monitoring should be broad and deep, not only keeping a watchful eye on competitors, regulators, vendors, NGOs, and the major media, but also scrutinizing all information sources to understand the business environment. Also key is the development of systems that can connect the dots between seemingly innocuous and unrelated issues that can converge and erupt into reputational threats or even crises.

One example of a successful monitoring system comes from a document services firm listed on Fortune 500. The entire board of directors is held responsible for risk management. More than 60 risk categories are assigned to an "owner" within the company's executive ranks, who then reports on that risk to a committee on the board. Committees are developed based on expertise and experience among the directors. The head of enterprise risk management at the company was quoted as saying: "Directors have told me that if you join a board today and you're not doing risk, you're crazy ... when directors come on board, they come by my office and ask for the latest copy of the risks."

Over the years, CEOs have been adding chief risk officers to their executive teams. Responsible for leading risk management practices, this burgeoning executive position has grown 140% according to data from Liberum Research (Nash, 2008). In some companies, these risk or compliance officers report to the board. CEOs should recognize that managing risk is not just about compliance with regulations, but also about ensuring that all employees and activities related to the company are doing the "right thing" at all times.

Companies are also using "reputation dashboards" to monitor traditional and online media for reputation threats. Services from companies such as Nielsen BuzzMetrics, Radian6, Biz360, evolve24, and Cymfony can identify issues of concern from millions of blogs and other social media. In addition, there are online sites where employees can post opinions about their workplaces and reveal festering problems that deserve greater attention. Although it is best to hear about these issues directly, such "smoke signals" can be addressed before it is too late if a CEO or his or her team is vigilantly monitoring. The Internet is especially important to monitor, as the Weber Shandwick/ KRC Research (2006) "Safeguarding reputation" study found that online sources often contain distress signals that should concern companies. Measurement systems can also come in the form of ongoing surveys of customers, employees, and other stakeholders.

Some risk managers engage in the study of "near misses," calculating the chances that something will go wrong. Nuclear power and aviation companies are big fans of this practice. NASA, for example, used to put the chance of any shuttle mission ending in disaster at 1 in 89. The concept of assessing a company's near misses is appealing for reputation management. If a company regularly tabulates and reviews its near misses, it might be able to prepare for improbable events and develop strategies for when a crisis arises. Hospital professionals have been known to meet monthly to review near misses where things could have gone much worse for patients or other members of their medical facilities. The regular discussion among hospital staff sensitizes them to how human error can raise the daily risks they face, and makes them more alert to problems that might surface. If more companies engaged in regular near-miss reviews, we might have fewer reputation scars and slower CEO turnover.

It is the responsibility of CEOs to place reputation monitoring front and center on their strategic agendas, as well as to provide the resources described here, enabling their companies to track, report on, and prepare for potential threats.

Keep Your Door Open

Monitoring systems are not enough without CEO leadership that listens and is open to different points of view. It is critical for a successful reputation steward to be known as someone who will listen and listens first. British Petroleum's (BP) 2005 refinery explosion in Texas City was partly attributed to poor internal communication channels that allowed safety procedures to weaken. As one Texas City refinery employee told a *Fortune* reporter: "The values are real, but they haven't been aligned with our business practices in the field. A scream at our level is, if anything, a whisper at their level" (Schwartz, 2006).

One way to keep the door open is to request data on a company's problems within a certain period of their occurrence. The chairman and CEO of a Fortune 200 company did exactly that. He received red transparent folders of "situation alerts" for any issue his company faced within 24 hours of it transpiring. Everything from employee injury to a competitor's price change was reported in these folders. The CEO ensured that he had a handle on large and small issues that could topple his company's well-led organization.

CEOs, like presidents and prime ministers, are often isolated. They become siloed and lose track of the context in which their business is operating. Anita Dunn, former US White House communications director, described to a meeting of communications officers in 2011 what the world looked like when she departed. Dunn recalled how reading the news on one's smartphone eliminated all context on how the general public outside the capital was actually absorbing the news. She noted that capturing the news of the day on a small screen without seeing or hearing what else was making headlines and what other stories were rising to the top led to extreme "tunnel vision." Dunn said that she has since implored her communications colleagues at the White House to make it their business to abandon smartphone myopia and get the full screen, the full view, of the pulse of average citizens with all the context it deserves. Like presidents, CEOs must force themselves to move outside their limited boundaries and immerse themselves in the daily workings of their employees, customers, and publics to stay truly informed of potential reputational issues.

Another way to demonstrate openness to what is working and not working in a company is to tear down the walls. Some CEOs work out of cubicles or have glass doors or walls to their offices. They model their offices as newsrooms where there are no hushed sounds but where everyone is in the thick of the hustle and bustle. Without hearing what others are saying and seeing what others are doing, CEOs can easily lose their reputational touch points. Other CEOs make the point that reputation management is their job by seating their communications executives nearby on the same floor. These types of symbolic actions signal that reputation is always on the mind of the CEO, that communications inside and outside the organization are mission-critical, and that all ears and eyes are open to the company's reputational well-being.

Other CEOs have been known to "walk the halls," hold town hall meetings with employees, travel to customers, and solicit feedback from stakeholders via email. As Xerox's ex-CEO Anne Mulcahy noted, "My title should be Chief Communication Officer, because that's really what I do. When I became CEO, I spent the first 90 days on planes traveling to various offices and listening to anyone who had a perspective on what was wrong with the company. If you spend as much time listening as talking, that's time well spent."

Visibility is important, as is the ability to demonstrate that the door is open. CEOs who publicly disclose solutions to problems they've uncovered with the help of employees, customers, and others who speak up signal the value they place on collective vigilance against reputation risk.

Learn From Every Crisis

Once a reputational crisis has been successfully dealt with, leaders should step back and start asking questions. By studying one's own mistakes and those of others, companies can avoid repeating or encountering even larger problems that may lie ahead.

Some CEOs request a "root-cause analysis" to determine how the company got itself into a quandary in the first place. This type of analysis enables companies to direct corrective measures at the underlying causes of a problem, rather than merely addressing symptoms or repairing damage.

Other institutions apply similar investigative principles to minimize the recurrence of problems in the longer term. For example, the US Army conducts "after-action reviews" to study errors in judgment after battles have concluded. Increasingly, CEOs are establishing task forces to identify problems that have led to issues that jeopardize their company's reputation. In the engineering profession, it is becoming more prevalent for senior management to form quality audit teams that assess completed projects and prepare "lessons learned" memos which are disseminated to all engineers at the company working on similar projects. By sharing these lessons with a cadre of employees, a consensus for change can develop. Just as companies form audit committees, so too should there be reputation committees, focusing on past missteps and how to avoid them in the future.

And not only is it important to learn from mistakes, but companies should also catalog what they did right when a problem arose. After all, it is easier for employees to accept change if they are presented with positive as well as negative information. One rule that CEOs shouldn't forget is to celebrate and commend people when things go right. Reputation management sometimes comes down to one-to-one or one-to-many communications by the CEO.

Socialize the CEO and Prepare

Julian Assange's release of confidential embassy cables on WikiLeaks is one of the better known examples of how an individual or small group can inflict reputation damage on an institution. One of two world-class companies in a Weber Shandwick/Forbes Insights (2011) study cited WikiLeaks' confidential releases as increasing the level of online anxiety about reputation threats among global senior officers. As reputation insurgency intensifies over the Internet, it will be increasingly important for corporate leaders to consider adopting the tactics, if not the tools, of their online critics.

Chief executives—though not many—have started to expand their use of and participation on the Internet to enhance their companies' reputations. Some CEOs blog, tweet, maintain a Facebook page, or communicate using videos on their corporate websites. Examples of social CEOs include Marriott International's Bill Marriott, Best Buy's Brian Dunn, and Virgin Group's Richard Branson. Even President Barack Obama has personally started tweeting. As of Father's Day 2011, when he reflected on his paternal role, any message on the @BarackObama Twitter account signed "-BO" will be written by the President himself, rather than a staffer.

However, not enough CEOs are becoming digitally "social." Research conducted by Weber Shandwick (2009) found that only 36% of major corporate CEOs communicate through company websites or social media channels in any way. And when these CEOs do venture beyond traditional communication vehicles, the largest proportion go social by posting messages on their company websites (28%) or are featured in videos or podcasts (18%). Instead of using the latest media to convey their messages, CEOs of major companies choose traditional methods; during the same year 93% were quoted in the business press, delivered keynote speeches, or participated in business school forums.

CEOs could take note of the example set by Domino's Pizza US president J. Patrick Doyle. When faced with declining sales after an employee posted a video on YouTube of a colleague defacing food as it was being prepared, Doyle chose the same medium to address the issue. Within two days of the original video's release, Doyle posted a company apology on YouTube and outlined steps he was taking to safeguard Domino's products. His quick response and chosen venue became a bigger story than the original, unappetizing video.

Obviously, traditional forms of communication are also important, so executives should get inline by getting comfortable using all media assets when devising reputation communication strategies. Not only do a company's stakeholders want to read CEO opinions in the *Financial Times,* they also expect to see them online, in the "social" ways that are especially compelling today. Critical to this multimedia solution is a preparedness strategy. How can the senior executive and his or her team effectively respond to reputational threats? At Weber Shandwick, we recommend a new media drill called FireBell (Weber Shandwick, 2010), which simulates the company's response to corporate crises such as reputational attacks on Twitter, product recalls, or leaked documents. Preparedness comes from having diverse systems at the ready, executive knowhow before the crisis happens, and knowing how to execute the systems when the need arises.

If a Crisis Hits, Address It Head On

As I have devoted an entire book to the topic of reputation recovery (Gaines-Ross, *Corporate Reputation,* 2008), it would be remiss of me not to offer a few words of advice on the CEO's critical role in times of crisis.

Corporate chieftains should be prepared to act quickly, decisively, and transparently when navigating reputation upheaval. Strategic advisors Rory Knight and Deborah Pretty of Oxford Metrica have explored the relationship between leadership and reputation recovery. In their research, they found that "honesty, transparency and effective communication have a clear and fundamental financial value…Management must respond honestly and rapidly in a non-defensive way." (Knight and Pretty, 2001). As this chapter was being written, UK Prime Minister David Cameron was returning to the city from his vacation in Italy to head up an emergency meeting on the London riots which have upended the country and damaged the city's reputation. This quick action demonstrated the importance of managing a reputational crisis and taking charge.

First and foremost, CEOs should be accountable for defusing a reputational crisis. A straightforward apology approach has been adopted by several corporate leaders over recent years, and has been quite effective. In fact, research from Stanford's Graduate School of Business has found that higher share prices generally follow corporate apologies within one year.

Apologies should be sincere and honest, with care given to choosing the appropriate channel for this important moment. For example, an email to employees can be less effective than a form of communication that allows them to see and hear the emotion behind genuine regret. Goldman Sachs' CEO sent a voicemail to employees worldwide encouraging them to maintain their focus when civil fraud charges were brought by the US Securities and Exchange Commission against the company in 2010. Harris Interactive's Reputation Quotient survey of US consumers demonstrates the value of honesty, as it found that communicating from the top, from where communications often originate with accurateness, sincerity, and consistency, correlates highly with corporate reputation. (Harris Interactive, 2011).

CEOs should also swiftly announce specific actions that their company will take to fix the problem when their corporate reputation is at risk. Indeed, 76% of global executives cite this solution as the best way to start reputation recovery after a crisis, according to the "Safeguarding reputation" study by Weber Shandwick. And when answering questions about a corporate problem, admitting what is still unknown is acceptable in the early stages of a company's recovery phase. The important thing is to demonstrate that the company's leadership, particularly the CEO, is taking the appropriate steps to get to the root cause of the problem, and then fix it.

And finally, it is the CEO's role to communicate tirelessly during reputation renewal. Employees, customers, the financial community, and other stakeholders regain confidence after uncertain times when provided with consistent communications. In the aftermath of Hurricane Katrina, an energy company faced the daunting task of evacuating employees who were separated from their families and relocating the company's headquarters. The CEO frequently emailed employees, launched a special website, printed all his communications for line and remote workers, and visited field operations. He shared his compassion and concern on a regular basis and received attention from the national media for his hands-on approach to the crisis.

Summary and Further Steps

There are many other ways in which today's chief executive can help to burnish the reputation of his or her company, but those outlined in this chapter are critical in demonstrating the character of the organization, its high ethical standards, its transparency in doing the right thing day in and day out, and the rewards of foresight and preparation. The most important advice to impart is that reputation is more important than ever, and it will continue to become increasingly complex as ever more social networks emerge and reputation activists are emboldened. In the end, preparation is key, and the CEO's role will continue to be paramount. As *Fortune's* editor Geoff Colvin said, "We've long heard that reputation is the new currency of corporate success, and 'reputation economy' became a fashionable word a few years ago. The News Corp. affair may be looked back on as the moment that companies broadly became believers."

More Info

Books:

Gaines-Ross, Leslie. *CEO Capital: A Guide to Building CEO Reputation and Company Success.* Hoboken, NJ: Wiley, 2003.

Gaines-Ross, Leslie. *Corporate Reputation: 12 Steps to Safeguarding and Recovering Reputation.* Hoboken, NJ: Wiley, 2008.

Article:

Colvin, Geoff. "Behind the Murdoch scandal? Scandalous governance." *Fortune* 164:3 (August 15, 2011).

Eccles, Robert G., Scott C. Newquist, and Roland Schatz. "Reputation and its risks." *Harvard Business Review* (February 2007). Online at: hbr.org/2007/02/reputation-and-its-risks/ar/1

Favaro, Ken, Per-Ola Karlsson, and Gary L. Neilson. "CEO succession 2010: The four types of CEOs." *Strategy+Business* 63 (Summer 2011). Online at: tinyurl.com/3l5eqbt [PDF].

Gaines-Ross, Leslie. "Reputation warfare." *Harvard Business Review* 88:12 (2010): 70–76. Online at: tinyurl.com/3ckwlxl [PDF].

Gaines-Ross, Leslie. "Reputation stumble rate still high." *ReputationXchange* (April 29, 2011). Online at: tinyurl.com/3b9n3hb

Korn/Ferry Institute. "Korn/Ferry survey notes that risk management is an increasing priority for corporations." *Korn/Ferry Institute website* (August 11, 2010). Online at: tinyurl.com/2com94h

Krakovsky, Marina. "Admitting missteps may boost stock prices." *Stanford Graduate School of Business Research News* (August 2004). Online at: tinyurl.com/6ks48bq

Lafley, A. G. "What only the CEO can do." *Harvard Business Review* (May 2009). Online at: hbr.org/2009/05/what-only-the-ceo-can-do/ar/1

Nash, Jeff. "Risk climbs to top of corporate to-do list." *Financial Week* (April 28, 2008). Online at: tinyurl.com/3o2g43j

Schwartz, Nelson. "Can BP bounce back?" *Fortune* (October 31, 2006). Online at: tinyurl.com/3ctdzv3

Reports:

EisnerAmper. "Concerns about risks confronting boards. Second annual board of directors survey 2011." 2011. Online at: tinyurl.com/3c3q65m [PDF].

Harris Interactive. "The 2011 Harris Interactive annual RQ summary report." April 2011. Online at: tinyurl.com/3dh8uww [PDF].

Knight, Rory F., and Deborah J. Pretty. "Reputation and value: The case of corporate catastrophes." Oxford Metrica, 2001. Online at: tinyurl.com/2b6e4em [PDF].

Weber Shandwick. "Socializing your CEO: From (un)social to social." 2009. Online at: tinyurl.com/5rzs9cf

Weber Shandwick. "Meet FireBell: Weber Shandwick's social crisis simulator." 2010. Online at: www.webershandwick.com/firebell

Weber Shandwick and Forbes Insights. "Socializing your brand: A brand's guide to sociability." October 2011.

Weber Shandwick and KRC Research. "Safeguarding reputation" survey. 2006. Executive summaries online at: tinyurl.com/44u5wld

Websites:

Ethics Resource Center: www.ethics.org

Fortune world's most admired companies 2011: money.cnn.com/magazines/fortune/mostadmired/2011/

Online Reputation Management—Risky Business: Reputations Online, presenting research by Weber Shandwick in cooperation with the Economist Intelligence Unit: www.online-reputations.com

Reputation Institute: www.reputationinstitute.com

ReputationXchange, the author's blog: reputationxchange.com

Framing Reputation: Vague Concept or Measurable Business Asset?

by Rupert Younger and Genoveffa Giambona

Centre for Corporate Reputation, Saïd Business School, University of Oxford, UK

This Chapter Covers

▸▸ A way of thinking about reputation that differentiates it from brand, image, and identity.

▸▸ A challenge to the traditional notion of reputation management, instead proposing a more nuanced narrative focused on behavior and influence strategies.

▸▸ The role played by high-status reputation intermediaries.

▸▸ An argument in support of the idea that companies in fact have multiple different reputations and that understanding and addressing this is a key task for leaders.

▸▸ A way to answer the question "Can reputation be valued or measured?"

▸▸ What managers can learn and apply in their workplaces.

Reputation

"One can survive everything, nowadays, except death, and live down everything except a good reputation." Oscar Wilde

Everyone has their own favorite reputation quote. The most often cited in business is that attributed to Warren Buffett, who reportedly said: "It takes 20 years to build a reputation and five minutes to ruin it. If you think about that, you will do things differently." But *what* can you do differently? And is it possible to construct and implement a reputation management strategy that delivers the specific reputation you want?

Type the word "reputation" into Google, and you get over 600 million results. That is more than double the result for wealth, and more than three times the result for happiness. Why is there so much interest in this concept? Quite simply, because it matters. Concern about reputation is not just a modern thing. History provides us with many wonderful examples to illustrate how reputation has played its part in the life and times of the human race. 50 years ago, Groucho Marx, the American wit, filmstar, and comedian wrote to his club with the now famous words: "Please accept my resignation. I don't want to belong to any club that will accept me as a member." 150 years ago Abraham Lincoln, the 16th president of the United States, stated that "Character is like a tree and reputation like its shadow. The shadow is what we think of it; the tree is the real thing." 400 years ago Britain's William Shakespeare, in Othello's famous scene, has Iago speak of reputation as "an idle and most false imposition; oft got without merit and lost without deserving."

It is not only literature and history that provide evidence of the fact that reputation has provenance, impact, and authority. A big business in reputation analysis is emerging. Reputation surveys have multiplied—from *Fortune* magazine's Global Most Admired

Companies to the annual Delahaye Best US Corporate Reputations Index. Newspaper and other media headline writers now regularly include reputation in print articles—in headlines as well as in the main body of the text. And reputation has become a major buzzword in corporate publications—not just in reports on corporate responsibility and sustainability, but in mainstream corporate annual reviews. There can be little doubt that corporate reputation is in the spotlight. But, despite all this attention, reputation is a term that is too often loosely applied and too often confused with media relations or corporate social responsibility.

Defining Reputation

When considering how to manage your reputation—as an individual or as a corporation—you first need to understand the concept of reputation as distinct from other, related concepts.

Consider the following series of questions: Is reputation the same as image? Or brand? What about identity or legitimacy? Or status?

Scholars and practitioners disagree about many of these concepts, but on one point there is almost universal agreement. Reputation consists of perceptions—whether true or false—held by others about you. Extending this further, it seems reasonable to agree with economists who frame reputation as expectations about a firm's future behavior or performance based on *perceptions* of past behavior or performance. Taking this as our starting-point, it becomes clear how reputation differs from some of the concepts mentioned above.

In one sense, image is similar to reputation. If you take image to be an impression of a company at a point in time, then it is perception-based. But it tends only to relate to snapshots of a corporation at any given moment. The corporate brand, by contrast, tends to relate to what the corporation wants to be and how it tends to differentiate itself from competitors, rather than what it is actually seen as being. Corporate brands—the brand of a corporation rather than its products—are also created to a greater extent by management action than by external perception. Take some of the United Kingdom's major banks—their corporate brands are going to reflect to a great extent the advertising that defines them. The black horse for Lloyds TSB, the blue eagle for Barclays.

Identity also tends not to be perception-based. Various scholarly definitions exist around this concept, but one of the most commonly cited and used is that put forward by Albert and Whetten (1985) and Whetten (2006) who, in seminal papers, propose that identity is what you are as an organization, as defined by what is central, enduring, and distinctive (CED). This has been one of the most cited definitions of identity in the literature on reputation, and it is helpful as a way of distinguishing it from reputation and also in defining how it relates to the formation and destruction of reputation.

Legitimacy, by contrast, has been generally defined as generalized perceptions or assumptions that the actions of an entity are desirable, proper, or appropriate (Suchman, 1995). However, it differs from reputation in that it tends to be a bipolar concept, as opposed to a more nuanced concept of reputation. According to Deephouse and Carter, "legitimacy emphasizes the social acceptance resulting from adherence to social norms and expectations whereas reputation emphasizes comparisons among organizations" (2005: 329). It would seem clear that a corporation or industry can be legitimate but have a poor reputation—take the telesales industry, for one. Perhaps more interesting is the fact that a corporation can be illegitimate but still have a good reputation—consider the illegal file-sharing industry, whose reputation with consumers remains high despite the efforts of the music industry to highlight the damage done to the creative industries as a result.

And, finally, status. Is this the same as reputation? Paraphrasing Podolny's (1993) belief that status is the perceived quality of a producer's products in relation to the perceived quality of that producer's competitors' products, we can say that status sees organizations or industries being ranked as high, medium, or low—or any point in between—giving a clear definition of status as a ranking system that places organizations in some form of hierarchy.

Unlike all the above, reputation is the relationship between a set of expectations about a firm's future behavior or performance based on *perceptions* of past behavior or performance.

Defining Reputation and Similar Concepts

▸▸ **Legitimacy**: Most often a bipolar measure, based on *conformity* with social or organizational norms.

▸▸ **Status**: A socially constructed and accepted competitive measure involving *ranking*.

▸▸ **Identity**: What you *are* as an organization, and what is *central, enduring,* and *distinctive* (CED).

▸▸ **Brand**: Your *consumer*-facing image, or your corporate brand as espoused by corporate advertising and other related activity.

▸▸ **Reputation**: Expectations about a firm's future behavior or performance based on *perceptions* of past behavior or performance.

Who Owns It?

So, to our second question. If a corporation's reputation consists of perceptions held by others, who owns that reputation? It seems clear that reputation cannot be "owned" by the corporation if it consists of perceptions held by others. But that does not mean that an organization cannot have a degree of control or influence over its reputation. While it cannot command people to perceive it in a certain way, it can try to influence perceptions through the actions it takes, and through the ways in which it communicates these actions directly and to those in a position to influence or shape other external views, such as the media (Rindova *et al.*, 2005).

This is obviously a key point for managers that has important implications. Senior management is used to command and control structures where strategies and objectives are set, and to employees who are tasked with delivering on those strategies and objectives. But reputation, consisting of perceptions held by others based on what they experience *directly* and what they hear about the corporation *indirectly*, does not fit naturally into that traditional architecture of governance.

This leads us to question the way in which corporations are responding to the reputational challenges they face. It seems that the current trend is to recognize the value and importance of reputation by creating managerial posts that have responsibility for it as an output. This might prove problematic. Not only does this silo reputation into one managerial area—most usually corporate affairs or the financial and operational risk committees—but it also reinforces a view at the top that reputation can be managed like any other direct reporting function. Although much has been written on what distinguishes between the good and the not-so-good management of reputation (see for example Bernstein, 1984; Smythe, Dorward, and Reback, 1992; Sauerhaft and Atkins, 1989), we agree with Weigelt and Camerer (1988) when they say that reputation depends on everything the firm does as an entity.

You Won't Own Your Reputation: It Is Owned by Others

- ▸ By definition, reputation is a relational construct. In other words, it is made up of perceptions held by others about you.
- ▸ You do control two things—your behavior, and what you choose to communicate.
- ▸ Behaving well does not automatically guarantee you a good reputation—you will need to communicate your good behavior effectively to the right stakeholders.
- ▸ Communication without the behavior to match what is being said will inflict greater damage on your reputation than simply saying nothing.

Multiple Reputations

What is more helpful is using reputation as a lens through which senior managers can make decisions. As reputation is a relational construct, based on perceptions, it would seem obvious to state that corporations may in fact have multiple reputations with different audiences (see for example McMillan *et al.*, 2005). Consider the finance industry—Goldman Sachs may have a very strong reputation for being a top destination for finance MBAs, but it has a very poor reputation with international regulators.

The idea that corporations have multiple reputations also helps us to understand how it is that companies which suffer crises or reputational damage can not only survive but may also be seen to prosper. Take the finance industry, whose recent implosion made banks and bankers some of the most reviled individuals as seen from the viewpoint of the general public. Not only have the banks and bankers been seen to be the architects of some of the poor lending decisions that created the financial meltdown, but these same banks and bankers have been awarding and receiving bonuses in spite of this public anger. How is it that they have any reputation left? The answer lies in multiple reputations. The general public may well continue to feel revolted by the scale of the bonuses paid to the investment banks for some time to come. But corporations who see bankers' activity up close recognize that certain banks have a well-deserved reputation for being able to provide competitive finance at the right time, in the right place, and in support of the right projects. The fact that they are extremely well paid for this is viewed in a separate light. And consider, for example, the reputation of hedge funds with the general public in the United Kingdom. Any general survey would probably rate them as high-risk, speculative, and dangerous to the financial system. And yet their reputation among UK and European regulators remains strong—and no hedge fund received any bailout funding of any kind during the entirety of the financial crisis.

So any discussion about reputation needs to start by defining what kind of reputation we are talking about, and with whom (McMillan *et al.*, 2005).

Crucially, once management fully grasps this concept, it is not only liberating but also very helpful. Senior managers are faced with daily choices that come with conflicting advice from the various stakeholders involved. Where to invest funds, whether to pursue legal sanction against former employees, which supply chain to invest in and support, and so on. Each of these decisions exists in a gray area rather than the black and white of wrong and right. Managers can use reputation as a tool on which to draw in making such decisions. Take the issue of a supermarket chain deciding on whether to push for further cuts in the supply chain margin. On the one hand, further savings would translate into greater profits for shareholders or better prices for the consumer—or ideally both. But, on the other hand, it will put further pressure on the supplier and possibly create a less dependable and sustainable long-term supply chain. What decision should the manager take?

Looking at this through the lens of multiple reputations can provide some help. What does the company want to be known for, and with whom? (see for example Rindova *et al.*, 2005). If the company sees value in having a reputation for investing in long-term partnerships with its suppliers, then this will clearly be an important factor irrespective of the immediate financial gain. Remembering the definition of reputation that we have chosen to use—namely, that expectations about a firm's future behavior or performance can be based on perceptions of past behavior or performance—a decision to invest in the supply chain will send a clear signal to the supplier and lead to an expectation of fair treatment going forward, which in turn might be expected to deliver value back to the supermarket chain in terms of reliability and quality.

So if we accept that companies can and do have multiple reputations for different things with different people, can these be aggregated into a single measure of reputation? Aggregation becomes immediately problematic. Consider the recent case of BP following the disaster in the Gulf of Mexico. It would seem clear that its reputation for safety in deepwater drilling in the Gulf has been fundamentally damaged with the general public (and possibly others, including investors and regulators). However, its reputation for major project management muscle arguably remains strong within its various industry audiences—as evidenced by the fact that it continues to be awarded exploration licences by oil-producing nations and to be selected as an industry partner for investment projects by other major oil companies. How can these different reputations be credibly pulled together into a single measure—such as the Fortune Global Most Admired Companies? It does not seem possible to do this properly without suffering a major loss of analytical rigor.

Corporations Do Not Just Have a Reputation—They Have Multiple Reputations

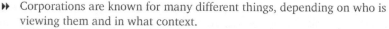

- ▸ Corporations are known for many different things, depending on who is viewing them and in what context.
- ▸ Understanding that you have multiple reputations is liberating, and extremely useful in decision-making.
- ▸ Managers can choose the reputations that they would like to have or promote—and then take decisions accordingly.

Recognizing the existence of multiple reputations helps to explain why and how certain companies can recover quickly from crises, or how they can minimize the damage from a crisis.

Measurement

Aggregation also causes other problems—principally in the area of measurement (Chun, 2005). The reputation industry has often been regarded as woolly, lacking definition, and without any sensible means of measurement. We would disagree. If you accept that corporations have multiple reputations—for something with someone— then we would argue that the value of that reputation lies in the signal that it sends. Consider the example of Goldman Sachs' reputation as a top destination for finance MBAs. What is the value of that reputation? If you consider the signal that this reputation sends, it is clear that Goldman Sachs can measure the value of this signal in cost and revenue terms. Take costs: one could argue that its recruitment costs are likely to be lower than less well regarded firms due to the fact that all it has to do is place an advert on its website and it will attract thousands of the best CVs available. Compare this to the case of a less well known or reputed banking organization which, it could be argued, would have to undertake expensive recruitment fairs and advertisements to attract its candidates. And on revenues: recruiting the best should have a positive effect on revenue generation over and above that enjoyed by others in the industry with lesser reputations. (To read about Goldman Sach's multiple reputations see, for example, Nathaniel Popper's article in the *Los Angeles Times* of April 7, 2010.)

So reputation is better measured when you are clear about which reputation, for what, and with whom it is being measured. Aggregation does not help and, even more unhelpfully, it also reinforces the sense that reputation is a woolly and unmeasurable concept.

Measurement Is Possible—Just Be Clear What You Are Trying to Measure Behavior, Values, and Intermediaries

- ▸ Measurement has been the Achilles' heel of the reputation industry for many years.
- ▸ Managers feel that without a clear means of measurement—and in particular of the value that can be attributed to activity undertaken to enhance reputation— reputation is too difficult an area to deal with.
- ▸ Different reputations can be measured by valuing the specific signals that they send.
- ▸ Aggregations are unhelpful, and they contribute to the lack of clarity on reputation.

Behavior, Values, and Intermediaries

So, consider our three pillars so far. First, reputation is a relational construct that often gets confused with other similar terms but which differs in critical ways. Understanding this will greatly aid your understanding of how to engage with your reputation. Second, you do not own or control your reputation—you only influence it through your behavior and your influence strategies. Beware those governance gurus who advise you to create internal reputation management posts, or those firms that purport to sell you reputation management strategies. They bear false gifts. And third, corporations have multiple reputations for something with someone—and these specific reputations are valuable tools in decision-making and can be specifically valued and measured.

We now need to turn back to the core drivers of reputation itself. It is clear from the narrative above that the actions you take as a corporation will send signals about what can be expected from you in the future, and will contribute strongly to the way in which you are perceived by your various stakeholder audiences.

This in turn is helped by a corporation being clear with its people about what is expected of them when they become a part of that corporation. Nowhere is this more important in the realm of values. Corporate values have, rightly and wrongly in our view, acquired a bad reputation. Rightly due to the fact that most of them seem to consist of the same basic concepts—integrity, dignity, etc.—written up in manuals and stated boldly in corporate materials. But also wrongly because, when properly embedded in the way in which companies operate, they can become an incredibly important and valuable reputational asset.

There are many examples of companies in which strong values exist and where having these is recognized as a fundamental asset—ranging from Standard Chartered in banking, through Marks & Spencer in retail, but as an example we will focus here on the way in which values have played a vital role in the development of the Italian multinational energy giant Eni (see Case Study).

There is one additional important element that needs to be discussed, and that is the role played by high-status reputation intermediaries such as the media and regulators. This is where the reputation management industry in fact plays its part in the creation, maintenance, destruction, and rehabilitation of corporate reputation. Internal roles, and the roles played by reputation management consultants, work on this aspect of corporate reputation. And, put simply, it is not good enough just to be doing the right thing; you have to be able to communicate that you are doing the right thing to your various interested stakeholder groups.

Rightly or wrongly, reputation management in theory and in practice has tended to focus on this half of the reputation equation. Figure 1 is a simple diagram that illustrates the way in which behavior and influence strategies interact to form reputation.

At the heart of reputation lies the area which we have termed "direct experience." This is where your behavior is directly observed—by customers, by suppliers, by regulators, by employees, by investors, and so on. This observed behavior sits at the core of your reputation directly with these audiences because they will ascribe a high degree of accuracy or reliability to this element. If you have observed someone, or a corporation, doing something in particular, then you will trust that to a high degree to signal what to expect from that corporation in the future. In other words, this would lie at the heart of that corporation's reputation for that something with you.

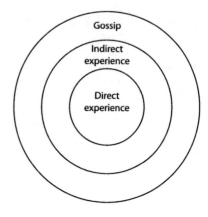

The second circle is the area of indirect experience. This circle of influence is slightly further away from the core due to the fact that you have not directly experienced the corporation's activity. Instead, you have heard about the corporation's activity from someone who has experienced it directly. There will, also, be different degrees of import attached

Figure 1. The three reputation circles

to different people in this circle—you will tend to take note of the views expressed by people you trust and like more than the views expressed by those you distrust or dislike.

The final, outer, circle deals with what we term "gossip." This is the mass of information that is not directly experienced or received second hand—the realm of "someone I know told me that someone they know's best friend was refused a refund," or "I heard that they treat people terribly at that company," and so on. We are all social animals, and we exist in a world where opinions are expressed often without any fact or supportive information behind them.

The reputation management industry deals in particular with some important audiences in this outer group. The obvious examples are the media, whether it is the mainstream media on products, the financial media for investment, or the political media for politics and society; the world of investment intermediaries, whether it be the analysts who advise institutional investors on their investment options, or the wealth managers who advise individuals on where to place their financial assets; and the regulatory audiences, ranging from financial regulators to broader, government-authorized societal bodies. Reputation management is in reality a smarter and more value-laden moniker for media relations, investor relations, and regulatory affairs work.

That is not to say that they are not important—just that they should be seen for what they are, which is vital players in helping corporations communicate what it is that they do. They do not normally play a role in the corporation's fundamental business strategies, although some corporations are very sensibly bringing them much closer to strategy via the role they play in anticipating market and external reaction to corporate decisions.

This leads to a final point on intermediaries and reputation. The main intermediaries mentioned above—media, analysts, regulators—can all accept that mistakes happen in corporate life. Where spin has received a deservedly bad reputation is where what is being communicated is simply not supported by the facts. In other words, dealing with intermediaries has to follow the fundamental behavior of a corporation for reputation to be enhanced; or, to put it the other way around, if corporations try to spin without providing the facts, the reputational damage will be significantly greater than if they simply did not communicate at all.

But what this also means is that you cannot hope to gain a good reputation simply by being good alone. You need to communicate effectively what you are as a corporation and set out what it is you stand for—as an employer, as an investment opportunity, or as a supplier of consumer products.

Case Study

Eni SpA

Eni's unique "Mattei model" is a good example how a corporation has embedded values at the heart of its operations to deliver significant value. The Mattei model has been an operating philosophy since the formation of the company, and it is firmly embedded in a belief that investing in the countries where Eni operates is good for those countries as well as good for business. This is succinctly summed up in the phrase "It is your oil, not ours"—a phrase that was originally coined by Eni's first head, Enrico Mattei, in the 1950s.

All Eni employees are imbued with a proud sense of this operating philosophy from the moment they arrive at the company. Eni has chosen not to place this on its walls as a slogan, but rather to focus the education of all its intake around it as a core operating philosophy. What is communicated by this phrase resonates practically. It reminds all Eni employees that they are guests in the countries where they operate, and that this brings with it a clear duty to behave well and work hard to understand and honor the cultural factors that underpin daily life in often extremely culturally diverse environments.

This operating philosophy has delivered a significant business advantage over the half century that the company has been in existence. From a standing start, Eni is now the largest international oil company operating in the oil-rich African continent. Its success, according to its executives, is largely down to its core values as reflected in strategy, operations, and in all that its employees live up to in their daily activities.

Summary and Further Steps

So, what can managers learn from this? Is it axiomatic that managers who do good things should have a reputation to match? And second, if it is not axiomatic, what are the conditions under which reputational advantage is gained? The best way to look at this is through the double lens of behavior and influence strategies.

Doing the right thing is not only morally right, but is also now expected of business by most, if not all, stakeholder groups. The big trend behind this concerns externalities—the collateral issues that happen as a result of business operations. It has not been acceptable to ignore externalities for some time, but what is newer is the expectation that business will not only identify them in the widest possible sense, but also that it will take responsibility at this broad level. This means that business is faced with multiple, and often contradictory, demands from the different stakeholder groups representing all these different externalities. How can companies navigate through this broader set of responsibilities and deliver reputational advantage?

The first answer is through behavior. What you do matters, as past behavior offers a clear perspective on what to expect from a company in the future. If you are, say, a major energy company that consistently settles all its invoices from a particular supplier within 30 days, it would be reasonable to expect your company to be well regarded by that supplier. But it will not just be your reputation with that supplier that improves—as this supplier talks to others in the industry, word will get out. This is the network effect of good behavior. Responsible behavior has a multiplier embedded in it. As, conversely, does bad behavior.

Equally important is the point that corporate responsibility and sustainability need to be firmly embedded in strategy. This is for two reasons—first, that unless real actions emerge from the rhetoric, it will be seen as "greenwash." Actions must follow words. And second, there needs to be credibility behind any such strategy—and that means that corporate responsibility and sustainability need to be seen to be self-interested, at least in the major part. The reason for this is that such strategies need to be perceived as long-term commitments, not just the latest fad. Reputational benefit accrues when past behavior has enough provenance to be seen as a reliable indicator of future activity.

The second factor then concerns the influence strategies that we have outlined. A company can only get so far in behaving well without communicating well. Only by working strategically with those who influence opinions on the company—media, regulators, investors, NGOs, and unions, among others—will the company be able to gain the network effect essential to generate good reputations with its audiences. These activities are traditionally what the reputation management and communications industries have been focused on, and what reputation management means in practice—the management of the influence strategies that surround an organization.

So, do corporately responsible behavior and good sustainability deliver a good reputation? Yes, if they are core to your business strategy (behavior) and are talked about credibly and with the right audiences (influence strategies). And no if they are the latest bandwagon or fad, and they become tactical PR rather than strategy.

More Info

Books:

Albert, S., and D. A. Whetten. "Organizational identity." In L. L. Cummings and Barry M. Staw (eds). *Research in Organizational Behaviour*. Vol. 7. Greenwich, CT: JAI Press, 1985; pp. 179–229.

Bernstein, David. *Company Image and Reality: A Critique of Corporate Communications*. Eastbourne, UK: Holt, Rinehart & Winston, 1984.

Sauerhaft, Stan, and Chris Atkins. *Image Wars: Protecting Your Company When There's No Place to Hide*. New York: Wiley, 1989.

Smythe, John, Colette Dorward, and Jerome Reback. *Corporate Reputation: Managing the New Strategic Asset*. Century Business, 1992.

Articles:

Barnett, Michael L., John M. Jermier, and Barbara A. Lafferty. "Corporate reputation: The definitional landscape." *Corporate Reputation Review* 9:1 (Spring 2006): 26–38. Online at: dx.doi.org/10.1057/palgrave.crr.1550012

Chun, Rosa. "Corporate reputation: Meaning and measurement." *International Journal of Management Reviews* 7:2 (June 2005): 91–109. Online at: dx.doi.org/10.1111/j.1468-2370.2005.00109.x

Deephouse, David L., and Suzanne M. Carter. "An examination of differences between organizational legitimacy and organizational reputation." *Journal of Management Studies* 42:2 (March 2005): 329–360. Online at: dx.doi.org/10.1111/j.1467-6486.2005.00499.x

Lange, Donald, Peggy M. Lee, and Ye Dai. "Organizational reputation: A review." *Journal of Management* 37:1 (January 2011): 153–184. Online at: dx.doi.org/10.1177/0149206310390963

McMillan, Keith, Kevin Money, Steve Downing, and Carola Hillenbrand. "Reputation in relationships: Measuring experiences, emotions and behaviors." *Corporate Reputation Review* 8:3 (Autumn 2005): 214–232. Online at: dx.doi.org/10.1057/palgrave.crr.1540251

Podolny, Joel M. "A status-based model of market competition." *American Journal of Sociology* 98:4 (January 1993): 829–872. Online at: www.jstor.org/stable/2781237

Popper, Nathaniel. "Goldman Sachs grows stronger even as reputation slides." *Los Angeles Times* (April 7, 2010). Online at: tinyurl.com/3vgou2r

Rindova, Violina P., Ian O. Williamson, Antoaneta P. Petkova, and Joy Marie Sever. "Being good or being known: An empirical examination of the dimensions, antecedents, and consequences of organizational reputation." *Academy of Management Journal* 48:6 (December 2005): 1033–1049. Online at: www.jstor.org/stable/20159728

Suchman, Mark C. "Managing legitimacy: Strategic and institutional approaches." *Academy of Management Review* 20:3 (July 1995): 571–610. Online at: www.jstor.org/stable/258788

Weigelt, Keith, and Colin Camerer. "Reputation and corporate strategy: A review of recent theory and applications." *Strategic Management Journal* 9:5 (September/October 1988): 443–454. Online at: dx.doi.org/10.1002/smj.4250090505

Whetten, David A. "Albert and Whetten revisited: Strengthening the concept of organizational identity." *Journal of Management Inquiry* 15:3 (September 2006): 219–234. Online at: dx.doi.org/10.1177/1056492606291200

Smart Use of Reputation Capital: How to Benefit from Different Reputation Investment Strategies

by Joachim Klewes[a] and Robert Wreschniok[b]

[a] Heinrich Heine University, and Ketchum Pleon, Düsseldorf, Germany
[b] European Centre for Reputation Studies, and Emanate, Munich, Germany

This Chapter Covers

▸▸ The importance of building reputation as the "social capital" of an organization, including its key components *trust* and *credibility* under societal, market, and media conditions of the 21st century.

▸▸ Four strategies for managing reputation capital used in business to increase valuable trust capital and to protect against losses, which should be mastered by every reputation manager.

▸▸ Which strategy to choose according to the type of risk, company, and or time.

▸▸ The fact that today's management essentially consists of (communicative) dealing with crisis and change, and how leadership can contribute to an organization and its employees becoming "crisis-proof" long before a crisis occurs.

Introduction

Today, those responsible for corporate communications are facing tremendous challenges. They are forced to take ever greater risks regarding reputation, and increasingly they are compelled to use more radical methods and messages in the traditional media—above all in advertising communication. This appears to be the only way to catch the attention of consumers and stakeholders.

On the other hand, the new social media, digital networks, and blogs seem to require the exact opposite—i.e. communicating a brand in a way that will allow the brand to be cherished for its own sake. This requires a radically new way of communicating: a dialog instead of the conventional one-way communication from sender to receiver. With this new approach, the core message counts less than the interactions between consumers and a company. The consumer is able to use social media to understand and experience a company and a brand, instead of having to simply believe promises. In this new world where consumer needs are met directly with customized offers, past recipes for success no longer count. Both creativity and wastage are eliminated. Andrew Robertson, the CEO of BBDO, one of the largest global advertising agencies, used strong words to emphasize this when, years ago, Google founders Sergey Brin and Larry Page presented their new advertising concept to him: "Guys, you killed the fucking magic."

In the following article the authors highlight four different approaches—what we call "investment strategies for reputation capital"—that companies can use to boost awareness and trust at the same time.

Reputation and Strategy

Reputation management has experienced much unrest and undergone rapid changes in recent times. A few years ago Warren Buffet was able to say that a good reputation can take 20 years to develop, but that it can be ruined in as little as five minutes. This seems strangely remote now. It might still take five minutes to ruin a reputation, but the idea that anyone might steadily work on and build a corporate reputation over a period of 20 years is rather unrealistic nowadays.

Today, anyone with access to the Internet can form and voice their opinion without depending on classical media. As a consequence, published opinion no longer equates to public opinion. Scandals appear more often and proliferate more quickly than ever before—a development that harbors major risks for companies. But it is not just the channels of communication that have changed; market conditions themselves are also different. The shift in the perceived importance of hard and soft corporate factors—a shift that now increasingly favors intangible assets—has resulted in a heightened risk to reputation.

This took on especially drastic forms during the recent financial and economic crisis. During this time many public companies were hit by a "reputation penalty," and the share prices of some of the leading global players fell as much as 50% below the company's actual market value. Furthermore, the number of companies per industry that are capable of supplying comparable products of good quality and at reasonable prices is growing explosively. Increasingly keen competition in itself can result in an impasse, since these "hard" corporate and product factors of the competing companies have in many cases become only marginally distinguishable. So intangible assets need to be stressed to express the unique selling-point (customer-centricity and satisfaction, user-friendliness, loyalty programs, etc.) to clients and shareholders.

In other words, these are hard times for "relaxed" reputation strategies, since in this dynamic environment you can no longer be sure that the strongest reputation will win in the long run. As a result, more and more companies are turning to reputation strategies whose mechanisms are comparable to those of conventional corporate strategies. Such strategies "actively influence the effects of competition and the speed of change. This lends strategy an essential effect: it shortens time." (von Oetinger, 2003).

Consequently, there are three central questions today for any strategy in the area of corporate communications. The first concerns the resources one needs to implement such a strategy, and how to use these in order to quickly achieve one's goals. The second question is how best to balance effectiveness and efficiency in the process. And last but not least, a reputation manager should aim to find the adequate ratio of reputation risks versus chances in the light of his reputation goals.

Why Reputation Matters

Today, more and more corporate managers and their communications experts ask themselves how they can make their company the customer's first choice in its industry. Or how to make it a company whose excellent reputation precedes it. A company that is the first choice for high-worth job candidates. A company that enjoys a trust bonus from banks and investors when capital needs to be increased or an issue floated to ensure continued growth. Or a company whose advice is sought by politicians during essential legislation processes because they trust its integrity, expertise, experience, and technical competence.

Such companies are the exception, yet they do exist in most industries—much admired, sometimes marveled at, and always keenly watched. Their competitors sense that there are ways they might themselves catch up by making targeted investments in their own reputations. For reputation allows companies to generate added value through favorable exchange conditions. After all, reputation is considered to be the "social capital" of a company, or an indirect catalyst that can amplify a company's social capital. Reputation is a key corporate asset; it can be managed and accumulated, and it can be exchanged for:

- the legitimization of positions of power;
- social respect;
- a price premium for goods and services offered;
- an increased willingness by others to hold equity stakes in times of crisis;
- a willingness to invest preferably in the shares of a company.

The currency in all these exchange activities is identical for all stakeholders of a company: it is called "trust." In times of economic crisis the value of this special capital becomes especially obvious. For, as so often, the true value of something is not recognized until after it has been lost. Today we have almost forgotten what we were reading in 2008 as the real-estate and financial crisis slowly wound its way into public awareness. As early as the spring of that year, similar opinions could be found in economic commentary in the leading international press; these can best be summarized in the following statement, "When the new economic bubble burst at the beginning of the 21st century, money was burned. During the real-estate and financial crisis, not money but trust was burned." Somehow, it was a very comforting message for many readers: "No money is getting burned," the message read, "just trust. So don't worry, it can't possibly be that bad."

In October of the same year, people realized that this was not true; this was the month in which the investment bank Lehman Brothers went bust. Hardly anyone in America or Europe had been capable of imagining that such a bank, with its good name and renowned address, would simply go bankrupt. But when exactly this happened, trust was thoroughly shaken—trust not only in this individual bank, but in the whole banking system. To this day, reputation surveys show that trust still has not been completely restored. The burning of trust—or reputation capital—resulted in the greatest economic crisis of recent decades, and as a consequence, in a gigantic destruction of assets in the stock markets. Trust-engendering company reputation is now fueled primarily by factors that are defined by economic competence; in short, by an intact economic reputation. Therefore, the next economic and financial crisis will also primarily express itself as a crisis of trust.

Four Strategies for Managing Reputation Capital

The authors' consulting experience clearly shows them that, today, the logic and mechanisms of successfully accumulating reputation capital increasingly resemble the rules and investment strategies used in the actual economy for maximizing company assets or protecting them from losses. The growth of capital on the financial as well as on the reputation level follows very similar strategies, which can help to identify existing risks and make them calculable and manageable. Following our observations of the market, we can identify four types of reputation strategy:

▸ hedge strategies;
▸ growth strategies;
▸ value strategies;
▸ total-return strategies.

These are used in business to increase valuable trust capital and to protect against losses. Table 1 shows the differences between the four approaches and explains why not every strategy works with every company, and why organizations will choose one approach rather than another on the basis of the type of risk, the type of company, and/or time.

Table 1. The four reputation strategies

	Hedging	Growth	Value	Total return
Main feature	Monothematic, proactive, target group-focused communication	Focused profile development along carefully analyzed reputation drivers and industry issues	Consciously internalized, structure-oriented reputation building	Focusing on products or services without trying to reinforce them with communication
Investment in communication	High spending for external communication—often also reach-oriented	Investment balanced between internal expenses (e.g. for analyses) and external communication	Clearly higher investment in internal process optimization and measured efforts in external communication	Communication efforts limited to a minimum
Opportunities	High-profile reputation established rapidly	Broadly hedged, well-founded reputation profile with several options available	High multiplication effect from employees and industry circles	Low degree of attention as long as company is not in public crisis
Risks	Words and deeds do not match; public criticism; expectations not met	Low degree of profile development compared to aggressive competitors	Reputation profile not supported by wide recognition	Crash in a crisis as there is no trust buffer. Internally: lack of orientation and support for corporate policy
Especially suited for	Companies in start-up phases	Companies in oligopolistic markets	B2B, hidden champions, large "middle class"	Unsuitable today
Time dimension	Short-term	Medium-term	Long-term	Long-term

How to Benefit from Different Reputation Investment Strategies

Hedge Strategies

Hedge strategies have a high degree of inherent risk, but in the right circumstances they are highly efficient. They focus on achieving goals in as short a time as possible. Essentially, a hedge strategy is about leveraging the use of reputation drivers by focusing communication strongly on one issue or person so that the reputation result will persist for a certain time period regardless of the company's actual situation. Hedge strategies include reputation management approaches that are very closely linked to the company strategy. This is also where the hedging takes place—provided that the business strategy works. If it works in the sense that the projected sales targets are met, or the planned market penetration or market leadership is achieved, this success will satisfy the expectations stimulated by the communications strategy. Meeting expectations is at the core of these reputation strategies, as a bet is being made that a promise made will be fulfilled. Companies and politicians use hedge strategies to establish charismatic leaders and to control high-profile topics on the public agenda in hope that this will result in short-term positive effects on their own reputation. They focus on networking with holders of institutional reputation or opinion leaders in order to accumulate—within a very short period of time—the social and cultural capital necessary for pursuing or securing their goals.

Attempts to implement hedge strategies are not only made by small companies, start-ups, or gamblers. Even internationally active corporations engage in risky reputation-hedging strategies, as in the context of spin-offs, M&A transactions, or even in marketing. For example, much of the automobile industry, which discovered its "green soul" a few years ago, has so far not been able to keep its promises on a large scale. The very same incongruity may be found in energy corporations which project the image of pumping solar energy instead of oil; or the biofoods industry, which has been growing at a breathtaking pace and sometimes creates the illusion of having convinced farmers in China of the benefits of this new way of farming. It does not require prophetic skills to foresee the failure of the hedge strategy in at least some of these fields.

The inherent risk of this type of strategy is exemplified by BP's "beyond petroleum" approach. Its former CEO, John Brown, developed BP's vision as the company of the future, which does business in an ecologically correct manner. In this vision, he focused on more than the short-term benefits for shareholders and drew attention to the positive effects for society. Reality, however, showed that corporate responsibility toward shareholders and long-term responsibility toward the environment and society were incompatible at BP. For example, the company communicated the message that greenhouse gases represent a danger to the planet and heavily advertised ecologically compatible energies. At the same time, nongovernmental organizations pointed out— also by means of massive internet campaigns—what the company's factual reality was, from the Prudhoe Bay scandal more than 30 years ago, to the Deepwater Horizon disaster in the Gulf of Mexico in 2010.

Growth Strategies

On the stock market, a growth strategy tries to identify, ahead of time, markets with future growth prospects. Investors thus select companies that have the highest growth potential for their portfolios. They are less concerned with individual companies, but rather with entire sectors of the economy. A similar approach is adopted by companies trying to understand how specific sector-related issues affect their reputation and that of their competitors. They assume a controlled reputational risk, which they seek to limit through analyses of reputation drivers. This process identifies the areas in which reputation management activities will in fact improve their competitive position. Siemens, for example, is representative of a company that has adopted a growth strategy. With the "Siemens answers" campaign, the company offers answers to the world's toughest questions in the fields of urbanization, climate change, and demographic change, and the company has streamlined all corporate communications around these three key themes.

Growth strategies are all about taking on a controllable reputation risk with the aim of achieving the goal in the medium term, and this is enabled by a thorough analysis at the outset. A company would therefore analyze the effects of dealing with specific industry issues (as in Siemens' three key themes) and determine the effects on itself and its competition's reputations in the opinion market. Using analyses of reputation drivers, the company will then evaluate where new strategies might have a positive effect on its reputation. Identification of reputation drivers is done through stakeholder analyses, which might be based on an opinion poll conducted among the general public or on surveys of specific acceptance markets (politicians, investors, journalists, etc.). These stakeholder surveys collect information related to numerous factors including, but not limited to, a company's trustworthiness, product and service quality, competitive positioning, responsibility, and management leadership qualities.

The impact communication has on the respective reputation drivers is reinforced by means of agenda alignment processes that focus communication on specific industry issues. It is these issues—for example, how well or badly a company tackles the CO_2 problem as a main cause of climate change—that have a crucial impact on the public perception of reputation.

Value Strategies

Value strategies are carefully planned and sustainable in nature, accepting only moderate risks when building reputation capital. An additional characteristic is the claim to long-term and sustainable goal fulfillment. Compared to the other two reputation strategies, this strategy is much more internally focused. Primary target groups are a company's own employees, followed by business partners and customers. It is by these target groups that businesses that select value investing as their reputation strategy traditionally feel more strongly held to high ethical and social standards. As Robert Bosch, the German industrialist, engineer, and inventor, once said: "It is better to lose money than trust."

In its external relationships, a value strategy relies on corporate communications that always emphasize ethical actions. Communications serve primarily to improve perceptions of a company's functional performance (economic reputation) in alignment with the dimensions of its competence and economic performance. Here, however, the focus of reputation management is on minimizing the risk of internal reputation issues impinging on the area of social reputation. In other words, there is a strict focus on not accepting structures or processes within the company that might result in reports that focus on topics other than economics—such as the questioning of matters concerning integrity or of a company's social and environmental standards (social reputation). Furthermore, a value strategy relies on precautionary structural measures within the company and its environment in order to proactively remove any risk of potential scandals.

Typical representatives of successful value strategies can primarily be found among industrial, raw material, and food production companies—though not, however, in retail. In analyses, their economic reputation accounts for 80–93% of their total reputation score. Many examples of value strategies can be found among small and medium-sized family businesses that enjoy an especially good reputation with experts and in specialized industries where some of these "hidden champions" can even be global market leaders without causing a big wave outside their own region.

Case Study

Walmart

Walmart, the US retail giant, attracted global attention when it changed its complete supply chain management by strategically adopting the slogan "going green," which had extensive consequences for its growth, distribution methods, and corporate identity. Walmart declared its sustainability initiative to be an integral part of its future business logic. Tyler Elm, Walmart's vice president and senior director of corporate strategy and business sustainability, put it this way: "We recognized early on that we had to look at the entire value chain. If we had focused on just our own operations, we would have limited ourselves to 10 percent of our effect on the environment and eliminated 90 percent of the opportunity that's out there." (Plambeck, 2007).

Furthermore, Walmart topped its new strategic alignment by announcing a zero-waste program. Through this, the company—which is, after all, the world's largest retail group—intends to reduce its nonrecyclable waste to nil over the medium to long term. In order to achieve this goal, which is both ambitious as well as likely to bolster the company's reputation, Walmart established 14 sustainable value networks comprising renowned experts, nonprofit organizations, and suppliers. They have been tasked with reviewing Walmart's social and environmental standards and identifying both innovations and cost savings. There is no doubt that this approach can result in great gains in reputation, as long as it is pursued with as much perseverance as Walmart devotes to it.

Total-Return Strategies

Total-return strategies are particularly promising and safe. However, the low reputation risk they entail must unavoidably be paid for with a low return on reputation. This strategy has by far the lowest communication-intensity both in external and internal communications. Strictly speaking, total-return strategies tend to invoke the inertia of the "same old" proven methods, rather than being coherent, independent, and future-oriented. This is also the main difference from the value strategies mentioned above. Both are very reserved in their external communications, but in addition total-return strategies see little need to invest in internal communications. Typical statements from companies practicing a total-return approach might be as follows, "We don't need any reputation management or active internal or external communications. We have done very well without these for the last 150 years, and we will continue to do well." Or, "We invest in the quality of our products, and that is a guarantee of high customer satisfaction—which is all that matters to us." Or, "You know, we had our image with the public and in the media examined just last year, and we found that we are almost not perceived at all—and we can live with that very well."

However, such convictions are now colliding violently with the specific societal conditions and market environment of the 21st century. The major difference today is the fact that a well-differentiated media system with a logic of its own has developed that operates on the basis of market criteria and has over the past decades increasingly established itself in society. This has become obvious in the striking acceleration of the quantitative and qualitative spread of publication media that are available in ever-new forms and formats. Furthermore, the publishing of information happens in an increasingly rapid and comprehensive manner, while enjoying growing attention and penetration by the public. This degree of penetration is complemented and reinforced by the Internet, which, after all, is more than just another media channel. Today, anyone who has Internet access can form an opinion outside of the traditional channels of information and leading media.

This dual structural change in the media system—i.e. the increasing involvement of society and the growth of people's information autonomy due to the Internet—has resulted in the problem that the speed of scandal-mongering has clearly increased over the past years. The reputation losses due to scandal-mongering must be borne primarily by economic organizations and institutions—often those practicing total-return strategies, whether explicitly or implicitly. The reason for this is that, during the neoliberal 1990s, the solving of fundamental societal problems was delegated almost exclusively to the economic system. It was denied, for example, that the state had any competence for solving societal problems. And even if, due to the current economic crisis, the state is again accorded more trust, the discussion remains about whose "fault" the current economic malaise is. This has thrust into the limelight those companies which have previously been able to keep themselves out of the media—even if their product quality or other structural company processes have not deteriorated.

This calamity often hits those companies especially hard which have not been able to establish a clear profile with their stakeholder group, something that is essential in a crisis; as a consequence, they will be at the mercy of media interests or of the Internet rumor mill. Issues of good governance, or whether a company treating its employees or external stakeholder groups with social integrity, are subject to controversial discussions by the media and on social networks on the Internet—no matter whether the company concerned exerts an active influence or not. This is one of the reasons why today more and more companies in the business-to-business (B2B) sector, which have for years failed to see any reason why they should build their reputation profile for a wider public beyond their target customer group, must deal with the issue of reputation risk and return. Examples can be found among companies in the pharmaceutical and chemical industries, and also among those active exclusively in the B2B segment, as well as many small and medium-sized companies.

What to Consider When Choosing a Strategy

How should top managers or entrepreneurs proceed when selecting one of the four strategies described? Which strategy suits their company best? What should be taken into account here is not just the company-specific reputation risks and potentials, but also the specific media and societal framework conditions of the 21st century. The causes of reputation risks lie primarily in the attention structures of the mass media and increasingly in social networks. Both these factors are essentially responsible for what will be perceived by recipients, and what may consequently represent a risk to a company's reputation.

What applies more than ever is that reputation is produced by communications—and is exposed to the permanent suspicion of having been orchestrated exactly for this reason. Therefore, active reputation management in the sense of focused risk minimization starts long before an attempt to define the media headlines. And it does so by taking stock of all processes within the company and its environment, however remote they might seem from communications, that can result in relevant perception structures and expectations within the internal and external public. They can be identified and prioritized, for example by using the issue-mapping approach—a prerequisite for being able to adjust or even eliminate them when necessary. This clearly shows that reputation management is more than just communication—it must have a sustainable effect on the reality of the company and its essential decisions. And that is exactly what lies in the hands of top management.

Excellence, backed up by sincere and reliable corporate communications, often remains the best thing companies can do for their reputation. However, attention should be paid to how these communications are delivered, since the traditional form of corporate communications as one-to-many delivery has now itself become a risk to reputation: the unidirectional type of communication can no longer do justice to today's realities of communications. This has to do with the communicative behavior of many stakeholders (such as is obvious in the social media on the Internet) and the resulting expectations that corporate communications policy faces.

This new communicative behavior promotes, for example, growing market transparency and, as explained above, an acceleration of scandal-mongering cycles, which are very difficult to control.

Continuously handling these reputation risks is essential, because the evaluation of individual facts increasingly depends on the zeitgeist; business methods which were considered completely unproblematic only a few years ago may suddenly be seen as morally wrong and worthy of being the subject of scandal-mongering. Issues such as environmental protection, diversity, equal rights, the role of taxpayers, all the way to the controversial discussion of management salaries, emerge and then disappear again.

Reputation Management in Times of Rapid Change

Beyond these issues, there is another more fundamental factor that influences the success or failure of reputation management—the skill of being able to continuously manage crisis and change.

Many communications bosses view their work as ongoing crisis management. And indeed, visiting corporate offices where communications are managed in major international corporations gives the impression that nothing is as common as one crisis following another at a rapid pace.

From product recalls to compliance cases, from US class-action suits to executive misconduct, from mergers to carve-outs, from cost-savings programs to acquisitions (which, due to circumstances, may only be possible during a small window of time), from the issues that blow up almost without warning and escalate rapidly to the more ordinary malfunctions, to drastic fluctuations in share price to an impending takeover. In all these situations, the more strings that are pulled by communications bosses, the more complex, and above all the more international a company or institution is, the stronger is the impression that all that matters is being able to anticipate, prevent, manage, or document any crisis at any time. These are the critical phases during which a company will benefit from the smart use of reputation investment strategies; times during which a company's "good reputation" has to stand the test while under a magnifying glass—indeed, when this reputation may even implode instantly.

Business as usual does not seem to be possible any more—business as usual is crisis and change. From a reputational point of view, it is particularly internal communications that have gained tremendously in importance—especially communications about change. Due to the fact that management nowadays is less and less able to control how the organization is perceived from the outside—because organizations are becoming increasingly permeable to the outflow of information from those within them—all those in charge of communications are well advised to empower their organization's employees to act as loyal messengers.

In times of increasing contingency, during phases of disruptive change, this will not be sufficient for managing reputation sustainably. What good communications managers must be able to do in such cases goes far beyond simply providing employees with the correct messages. Instead, management and employees must be made "crisis-proof." An organization is crisis-proof, in the meaning of this article, if it experiences changes and crises as part of its normal business, and if it can see the creative aspects rather than the threats in these developments.

Of course, from a reputation point of view, leadership is a key factor in these situations. The leader must empathize, provide direction, and dispense encouragement when faced with change or crisis. However, it is equally important to listen to people in an organization in situations that are full of uncertainty, change, and crisis, and to invite them to contribute their share to managing the situation. This means that reputation managers have to act on the following points.

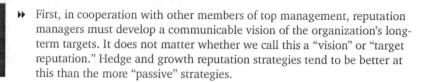

▸▸ First, in cooperation with other members of top management, reputation managers must develop a communicable vision of the organization's long-term targets. It does not matter whether we call this a "vision" or "target reputation." Hedge and growth reputation strategies tend to be better at this than the more "passive" strategies.

▸ Second, reputation managers must ensure that communication does not only work top-down, but also among employees and from employees upward—and that employees communicate well and quickly. This is not only a technology and channel management issue, but rather a question of attitude, practice, and organization. For example, reputation managers should see to it that individual organizational units have, as a rule, no more than 150 employees, because above that number self-regulation and internal communications will barely work.

▸ Third, reputation managers must ensure that any and all employees know that even in a crisis they are not without options to act or to participate, and that they will be treated respectfully when they do.

The result of these deliberations may be surprising. Leadership during change is, so to speak, the linchpin of reputation management—irrespective of the fundamental reputation strategy that is being pursued. In order to solve the three tasks outlined above—whether as an external or internal consultant—you primarily have to work with your management, and do so at all levels.

If reputation management under conditions of almost permanent disruption is analyzed from a perspective that extends beyond the bounds of the organization (i.e. one that includes external communications), credibility turns out to be the foremost factor and a fundamental component of reputation. As a reputation manager, when applying contingency management in such conditions you will have to do the following.

▸ Ensure that the company is recognizable—that the public know whom they should trust. This begins with recognition, and is much more than just the faces that represent the company. (You may guess which reputation strategy will fail in this context.)

▸ Do everything in your power to ensure that nothing is promised which cannot be delivered. As a reputation manager, your primary task is to define the tone in which the organization represents itself externally, on all channels; in particular, on the marketing and distribution channels. This can be a challenge for old-style communications bosses.

▸ Ensure that the messages for and relationships with the different stakeholder groups remain more or less consistent. The challenge here is that "one-voice policies" no longer work in times of WikiLeaks and social media; nevertheless, a certain consistency across channels and stakeholder groups will be very helpful for the organization's credibility.

More than other functional experts, those in charge of communications are in a position to enable the people in organizations to handle contingency and change correctly, thus lowering risks to reputation considerably, or even making reputation sustainable.

Summary and Further Steps

Given the great importance of proper change management for building and keeping a good reputation, reputation managers must be capable of applying all four strategies "by heart." Today it is no longer enough to be a specialist in just one strategy. One could compare this to investment funds that combine elements from different alternative investments; similarly a reputation manager must be able to combine elements of multiple existing strategies, both simultaneously and successively.

The following checklist should help smart reputation managers to improve their own and their company's situation. The checklist is inspired by the strategies we have described and encourages finding the right combination of strategies needed to build a good reputation.

»» Have you examined your competitors' reputation strategies?
»» Have you presented your findings to the top management of your company?
»» What can you learn from your most successful competitor?
»» What are the things you don't want to learn?
»» Have you identified the reputation risks and opportunities faced by your company?
»» Are you monitoring these on a regular basis?
»» Has your top management attended reputation management training that has alerted them to the risks, possibilities, and limits of high-quality reputation management?
»» Have you documented your company's reputation strategy, and has consensus been reached among top management for the full support of this strategy?
»» Are the employees and top management of your company aware of the important factors in a good reputation strategy?
»» Can you describe the reputation strategy of your company in 90 seconds?

If you can answer most of these questions positively, it is likely that your company is dealing competently with the issue of selecting and applying an appropriate reputation management strategy.

More Info

Books:

Bourdieu, Pierre. "Ökonomisches kapital, kulturelles kapital, soziales kapital." In Reinhard Kreckel (ed). *Soziale Ungleichheiten*. Göttingen, Germany: Otto Schartz & Co, 1983; pp. 183–198.

Eisenegger, Mark. *Reputation in der Mediengesellschaft: Konstitution—Issues Monitoring— Issues Management*. Wiesbaden, Germany: VS Verlag für Sozialwissenschaften, 2005.

Eisenegger, Mark, and Kurt Imhof. "The true, the good and the beautiful: Reputation management in the media society." In Ansgar Zerfass, Betteke van Ruler, and Krishnamurthy Sriramesh (eds). *Public Relations Research: European and International Perspectives and Innovations*. Wiesbaden, Germany: VS Verlag für Sozialwissenschaften, 2008; pp. 125–146.

Kim, W. Chan, and Renée Mauborgne. *Blue Ocean Strategy: How to Create Uncontested Market Space and Make Competition Irrelevant*. Boston, MA: Harvard Business School, 2005.

Klewes, Joachim, and Robert Wreschniok (eds). *Reputation Capital: Building and Maintaining Trust in the 21st Century*. Heidelberg, Germany: Springer, 2009.

Markowitz, Harry M. *Portfolio Selection: Efficient Diversification of Investments*. 2nd ed. Malden, MA: Blackwell, 1991.

von Oetinger, Bolko. "Das Wesen der Strategie." In *Das Boston Consulting Group Strategie-Buch: Die wichtigsten Managementkonzepte für die Praktiker*. Berlin, Germany: Econ Verlag, 2003.

Washington, George. *Rules of Civility and Decent Behaviour in Company and Conversation: A Book of Etiquette*. Williamsburg, VA: Beaver Press, 1971. Online at: www.history.org/almanack/life/manners/rules2.cfm

Articles:

Plambeck, Erica. "The greening of Wal-Mart's supply chain." *Supply Chain Management Review* (July/August 2007).

Schütz, Tobias, and Manfred Schwaiger. "Der einfluss der unternehmensreputation auf entscheidungen privater anleger." *Kredit und Kapital* 40:2 (2007): 189–223.

Websites:

Change Centre Foundation: www.change-centre.org/foundation

European Centre for Reputation Studies: www.reputation-centre.org

Engaging Your Stakeholders:
How To Make Allies of Investors and Activists

by Peter Firestein

Global Strategic Communications Inc., New York, USA

This Chapter Covers

» The cultures of corporate managers and investors are vastly different, requiring managers to learn the language of investors to derive fair value in financial markets.

» Systematic research by companies into the perceptions of investors is essential in converting market skeptics into supporters.

» Insularity is the enemy of good decision-making. The airing of diverse perspectives provides the best protection against a management's own excesses.

» The sustainability of an enterprise requires its alignment with the society in which it functions.

» A company's reputation depends on the narrative that it creates through its actions and its communications.

» A company's reputation depends ultimately on its values.

Introduction

No company exists without the consent of widely diverse groups of individuals and organizations. These range from customers to investors to social and civic groups—in fact, to the entire society that surrounds the corporation. It is a mistake—sometimes a fatal one—when any company takes the position that it is free to ignore those who have an interest in its financial health or the impact of its operations. But if the company chooses to take these relationships seriously and implements objective strategies to accommodate the interests of those who consider themselves part of its orbit, it maximizes the chance that it will survive crises and achieve long-term sustainability as a healthy and productive enterprise.

Living in Peace with the Arbiters of Value: Your Shareholders
The Yin–Yang of Companies and Capital Markets

There isn't a company anywhere that is free of dissonance with its shareholders and analysts. That's the nature of life in the equities markets. The market always wants more information, and the company wants the market to be satisfied with the information that it is comfortable giving. Although corporate managers and investors can hardly expect to agree on everything, the distance between them is unnecessary and costly to both.

No management of a public company, regardless of the strength of its financial performance, can consider itself successful without growth in the equity price. Many factors can conspire to prevent price and performance from matching up, including investors' macroeconomic expectations and their view of industry prospects.

But the real disconnect between company managements and equity investors lies in the two groups' wildly divergent cultures. You could say that managers are from Mars and investors from Venus. While both may be reasonable and rational, they often approach a single company with profoundly different ideas on how to create value from its assets.

CEOs often feel victimized by what they see as the refusal of investors and the financial media to accept their views of their own companies. After all, who knows the company better than those who run it? They often remark that the investors who feel so free to offer their criticism couldn't run a public company for one single day. And the investors would agree, but that's not the point. The differences between them are more profound.

Managers go to the office every day with highly evolved ideas about how to create value in the companies they lead. Their professional lives involve the development of strategy, the execution of business plans, allocation of capital, forecasting of product cycles, divining what the competition is up to, and engaging in dozens of other disciplines for which their boards, investors, and employees hold them responsible. Investors, on the other hand, operate in great part from objective valuation models. They can take a more or less mechanical view of the company's past financial performance and, having listened to management's plans and guidance, extrapolate the past into the future. They assess the company's announced strategy and try to read current management's ability to execute it. In many ways, the two groups speak a different language.

Complicating the issue is the absence of serious consideration of investor relations in business education. Despite the fact that investors' understanding of a company is one of the most important factors in determining its market value—and therefore the personal wealth of its managers—the investor relations enterprise has often been regarded as a side issue in the development of capital. "Value paradox" is the term I have coined to describe the weird dynamic by which a company's well-being is determined by investors who seldom come near the company, never sit in on its strategy sessions, and carry on only intermittent communication with those who do.

Giving Investors the Tools to Make Judgments

Investors care about few things more than a company's level of financial disclosure. Whether management breaks out its results by product, by specific geographic areas, by business unit, or by other categories is of crucial importance for at least two major reasons.

▸ First is the information itself. Investors must justify to their own managements and clients their decisions to buy or sell a stock. The level of confidence they have in their future ability to explain their actions— whether the stock price rises or falls—vastly affects their willingness to invest.

▸ The second reason a company's level of disclosure receives so much attention has to do with what that disclosure says about the seriousness with which management regards investors. Other factors being equal, investors will commit to a company whose management they believe will not only tell them the truth, but will also give them the best sense of the business. After all, the investor's ability to succeed in his or her profession depends on the ability to read the company, and you can't read a company whose management you can't trust. So, it is management's obligation not only to run the company well, but also to be believable. One of the most profound difficulties in this relationship lies in the fact that management can only demonstrate past performance, whereas investors only care about the future.

So, how do you turn your skeptics in the market into supporters?

You begin by making yourself predictable. The strongest rhetorical structure through which CEOs can speak to investors is one in which they show that a plan set forth a year ago (or two years or six months ago) was successfully executed and that the results were as forecast—or better.

The best way to get investors on your side is to educate them about the company. Make them experts. With all the technology available, and the sophistication of current valuation models, it is remarkable how well investors still respond to a manager's personal generosity in communicating about the company.

There is almost always a tug-of-war in management's mind about how much information to release. First of all, managers must consider that any information offered to investors may become available to the competition. You can't swear an investor to secrecy, so there is a powerful impulse to withhold information—sometimes to ridiculous degrees.

On the other hand, the availability of information about the company can be a powerful force in raising share value. Managements must consider how much the unnecessary restriction of information is costing them. They can go a long way toward resolving this dilemma by convening regularly to identify the information that must be ring-fenced for competitive reasons. Companies that are realistic about this understand that the criticality of specific information is always changing. Making these regular reassessments allows them to free up information that could contribute to investors' understanding of the business and therefore, potentially, to pay more for the shares.

Diversity of Perspectives as a Safety Net
Avoid the echo chamber. There is a structural trap into which many management teams fall in which they discuss the value proposition and strategies of the company only among themselves without the moderating benefit of external points of view. I believe that many of the decisions by pharmaceutical companies to withhold information on the side effects of drugs resulted from a damaging level of insularity. Managers should understand the importance of allowing the terms by which informed outsiders judge the company to inform their internal discussions.

When applied to capital markets, this principle means that managers must learn to speak the investors' language—to know which parts of the investment story hold value for them, and which do not. The company may be very proud of a technology it has developed, for example. It may believe that its superior design and engineering prove that it will succeed against competitors in the future. But investors may resist paying the company simply for being smart. They are likely to demand information about how the company will monetize its technology. No matter how brilliant it is, they may consider a technology to be a misguided R&D investment and an example of poor management if there isn't a clear payoff.

The Perception Study

Perhaps the best way to go about developing the market intelligence that would avoid such pitfalls lies in what is known in the investor relations world as a "perception study." This is an intelligence-development resource whereby a company authorizes a consultant to act as an intermediary with investors in carrying on discussions about the means by which they judge its share value. These conversations are confidential and candid in a way that would not be possible for the company itself.

The findings of a perception study can be both surprising and highly nuanced. Depending, of course, on the talents of the consultant, company management may learn that specific changes in its disclosure practices will give investors an improved perspective, and therefore the comfort to increase their commitment to the company's shares.

A perception study can impact more than a company's communications practices. Management may be able to identify in investor comments possible changes in strategy that are both reasonable to carry out and capable of bringing investors to a higher estimate of the company's future earnings potential.

A deliberate program of gathering investor intelligence over an extended period of time—say, two years—not only delivers critical market intelligence, but it can also educate management instincts to the extent that executives find themselves capable of anticipating market reaction to strategies and initiatives they have not yet announced—or even decided on. Such instincts can be developed to the point of enabling management to forecast market reaction to M&A transactions which it may only be considering.

While the perception study's purpose is to collect intelligence on investor attitudes toward the corporation, it also provides a meaningful tool of outward communication in demonstrating the company's sensitivity to market attitudes. After all, no investor will be interested in holding a stock unless he or she believes that someone else will come along in the future to pay a higher price. Clear evidence that management is working to achieve this often provides current investors with an additional source of confidence in the company.

The Strange Brew of Numbers and Psychology

The management of a publicly traded company must understand that, although conversations with investors and analysts focus primarily on financial performance figures and descriptions of strategy, investors' private considerations involve much more nuanced and subjective matters. Their observations go to such a personal level as interpreting managers' body language when they speak, assessing their apparent degree of confidence, and, most of all, noting the consistency of what they say over time.

Investors also care a great deal about "bench strength," that is, the talent just below top management that runs business divisions and makes day-to-day decisions. They need to get to know such people through investor conferences which the company may attend or sponsor, or through the participation of these second-tier managers in meetings that corporate leaders undertake from time to time in making "roadshow" trips to visit investors.

Considerations of the talent pool come into play particularly when, as is often the case in these days of rapid turnover, investors concern themselves with a company's leadership succession plan. Is there talent within the organization to replace the current chief? And would that new leader be able to continue to replenish the ranks of management?

In the end, making allies of investors means building their confidence in the company by helping them to understand it in their own terms rather than exclusively in the light in which management wishes it to be seen.

The Value Paradox

The relationship between public companies and investors can be described as a "value paradox." Corporate managers must be administrators, creative strategists, shrewd allocators of capital, and savvy about both customer psychology and industry competition. Investors, on the other hand, are analysts of financial data and, to a considerable extent, psychologists in their assessments of management's abilities and candor. Investors can dissolve the relationship with the company at any moment by selling their stock. Company managements have no such freedom. It is therefore critical that they *learn the language* of investors as a way of keeping them and attracting new ones to maximize market value.

Transparency as a Matter of Survival

The defining reality of the information age is that transparency is no longer a choice. If you don't offer it to the world, the world will impose it on you anyway. Every corporate action, therefore, requires thought along two independent tracks. The first, of course, centers on the value of the action itself. How does it support the company's overall value proposition? The second—equally important and often missed—involves a careful assessment of how the action will play out with the company's various constituencies. Will investors attribute the same value to the action as management? Will resistance among social constituencies divert the company in ways that compromise its original intended value? No conceived action has value until it is accompanied by a strategy to explain and defend it.

Making Allies of Social Stakeholders

In the age of the Internet and 24-hour cable news, it has become virtually impossible for a company to hide anything at all. The age of the fortress corporation—when companies had the ability to act almost exclusively in their own interests and control the information that circulated about them among the public—ended when it became possible for dissident employees and bloggers everywhere to communicate at the push of a computer button. And they not only began to communicate, they quickly became able to organize opposition to a company with surprising ease.

Because of the reputation risk the information age has brought upon us, the influence of investors has been matched by that of nonfinancial stakeholders. These may include governments, regulators, communities in which a company operates, the media that speak to those communities, and activist groups with interests in the environment, human rights, and labor. To an increasing extent, the "buzz" about a company can determine its destiny. So it is nothing more than sensible management these days to assume that any company will run into trouble some day—whether it deserves to or not.

The Time to Prepare for Crisis Is Now

The time to prepare for a crisis is five years before it occurs. Crises seldom approach slowly over the horizon. Most often, they explode in front of corporate headquarters without advance notice. It is the CEO's job to prepare for crisis every day that he or she holds the position. The least of this obligation is to organize the preparation, and continual updating, of a crisis action plan. So, when a significant adverse event occurs, everyone who is involved in the corporation's defense will immediately know his or her specific duties and lines of communication.

Far more challenging is the design and execution of strategies that will attract the support of critical stakeholder groups, which, in a crisis, can make the difference between life and death for a company. Their support often means that the company is more likely than otherwise to receive the benefit of the doubt when things go wrong—when a product is shown to be dangerous to the public, when an environmental mishap occurs, or if it turns out that workers have been mistreated.

When a pipeline bursts, or a product turns out suddenly to be harmful to customers, or improper marketing practices are publicly disclosed, there is a short period of time— often called the "golden hour"—before the press stakes its claim to the event and when the company is able to tell its story, establish the initiative, declare empathy for any victims, and demonstrate that it is the solution, not the problem.

If the company has already established a reputation of trust with influential individuals and organizations, it will find allies in its time of need to resist the impulse on the part of the press, politicians, and the public to assign blame. It is those politicians, in particular, whose carefully developed support may turn critical at a moment when the company's future may hang in the balance.

How does the company establish this support?

A company that wishes to protect itself from a future crisis must undertake two initiatives that are distinct but deeply connected with each other.

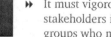 ➤ It must vigorously pursue the development of relationships with crucial stakeholders in government and among regulators, the media, and activist groups who may place themselves in opposition to the company.

> ▸▸ And it must base these relationships on a clear and candid narrative about itself founded on legitimate and clearly defined values. The company should demonstrate day after day, and year after year, that its values are aligned with those of the society around it. This is not easy to do; and it is impossible to fake.

The Communication of Convergence

One of the most creative initiatives a management can take to defend itself against unknown future crises is to engage those groups with whom there is friction and little or no communication. A simple invitation to talk extended to an opposition group can result in a dialog that grows over time. The content of the dialog matters less than the simple fact that it happens. Eventually, both sides become committed to the communication process and develop an interest in seeing it succeed.

One of the results of this "communication of convergence" is that the two sides will begin to develop a shared vocabulary around contentious issues. Over time, the company may begin to hear its own phrases and manner of describing the problem echoed not only by its interlocutors on the other side, but also by that part of the public that adheres to opposing opinions.

The requirement for entering into such a dialog is the willingness to commit to a mutual vulnerability. You can't ask for an engagement by the other side that you yourself do not offer. So, your dialog will also evolve as a result of this interchange.

While the benefits of this process are great, their achievement requires commitment on the part of a senior executive not only to the idea, but also to the task of convincing dissenting voices within the organization that the idea is a good one. The rewards, however, are worth the trouble.

By Your Narrative You Will Be Known

Ultimately, the entire subject of making allies of your investors and social stakeholders comes down to the task of evolving a single narrative by which they identify you.

Coca-Cola's narrative is not "We quench your thirst." Water does that. Coca-Cola's narrative is "We bring the world together."

Like any company, Coca-Cola has to support its narrative in its public actions. So, when social activists and some elements in the international media took note that Coca-Cola was diverting water from parched villages in India to make its soft drinks, it made little difference that the company had a legal contract that allowed it to do so. The company had to take whatever steps necessary to dispel the notion that it was exercising its power for commercial purposes at the expense of powerless people. That's how Coca-Cola— reluctantly at first, but later with great creative energy—became a leader in developing technology to support sustainable water supplies.

It Is All About Your Values

If the requirement for a good reputation is to align with the social norms of the community around you, that community will be asking one question: What are your values? And developing a solid set of values—values that mean something—may be the hardest part of building a strong reputation.

The moral tone of an organization—whether it is a small office or a global enterprise that involves hundreds of thousands of employees—comes from the top, from the single leader. But the great paradox in the matter of corporate values is that, although the leader must lead, he does not create the company's values on his own. The walls of corporate cafeterias everywhere are adorned with lists of corporate values, and they're worth about as much as the attention they are paid by those rushing through their meals. You can mandate strategy, investment, and standards of all kinds. But you can't mandate values. They must come from everywhere within an organization. That's the only way to obtain commitment.

A solid and legitimate set of values not only increases the likelihood that conduct throughout the organization will limit risk, but it also provides a foundation for all important relationships. Values are the language of association—and therefore of survival.

The Values-Based Enterprise

Corporate survival in a world where there are few secrets requires alignment of the enterprise with the norms of the society that surrounds it. Companies will always be defined by the narratives which their actions project. So, achieving the most secure levels of sustainability requires that a company create for itself a deliberate narrative based on an observant understanding of its constituencies. The core of this narrative will always be the fundamental values the company is seen to hold. To maximize the chance of companywide commitment to a set of values, they must be derived from a conversation that includes the whole organization. Values cannot be mandated from above.

Case Study

Chiquita Brands

Management must establish a process of collecting views from throughout the company. Then it-must relinquish control. Chiquita Brands, famous for its bananas, sought a number of years ago to transcend a reputation developed over many decades for exerting excessive power over workers in its Central American plantations.

Among many initiatives, the company drafted a set of corporate values at its headquarters in the American Midwest, then sent the list out for review and suggestions to its employees who work the plantations.

The document returned to headquarters with a surprising addition. The Latin American workers had found a big gap: headquarters' list of values failed to mention the importance of family. Seeing the revised list, the management team at headquarters—whose families were also central to their lives—realized for the first time that for a company's values to be legitimate they had to encompass all important features of the lives both of senior executives in glass towers and of those who cultivated the bananas in the field. And that's how commitment to a discrete and unique set of values came to be achieved in a widely diverse corporation.

Summary and Further Steps

▸▸ The cultures of corporate managers and professional investors are far different from each other. It is management's obligation to understand how investors assign value to the company and to address them in terms that give the company the best chance to achieve the highest reasonable valuation.

▸▸ In the information age, managers must assume that virtually everything they do will eventually come to public light. Transparency is no longer an option, it is imposed. So managers must understand the "optics" of their actions and know that any business planning process must include a strategy for communicating it to financial markets and the public. If you can't explain it openly, you probably shouldn't do it.

▸▸ Long-term sustainability requires alignment of a company's values with its social context. A corporate leader must implement a systematic review of his or her company's standing among its social constituency and invest in senior personnel to assess how the company's practices and policies match up with public norms and expectations.

More Info

Books:

Bennis, Warren G., and Burt Nanus. *Leaders: Strategies for Taking Charge.* 2nd ed. New York: HarperBusiness, 2003.

Dowling, Grahame. *Creating Corporate Reputations: Identity Image and Performance.* Oxford: Oxford University Press, 2001.

Firestein, Peter. *Crisis of Character: Building Corporate Reputation in the Age of Skepticism.* New York: Sterling Publishing, 2009.

Fombrun, Charles J. *Reputation: Realizing Value from the Corporate Image.* Boston, MA: Harvard Business School Press, 1996.

Gaines-Ross, Leslie. *CEO Capital: A Guide to Building CEO Reputation and Company Success.* Hoboken, NJ: Wiley, 2003.

Gardner, Howard. *Changing Minds: The Art and Science of Changing Our Own and Other People's Minds.* Boston, MA: Harvard Business School Press, 2006.

Joiner, Bill, and Stephen Josephs. *Leadership Agility: Five Levels of Mastery for Anticipating and Initiating Change.* San Francisco, CA: Jossey-Bass, 2006.

Larkin, Judy. *Strategic Reputation Risk Management.* Basingstoke, UK: Palgrave Macmillan, 2003. Peters, Glen. *Waltzing with the Raptors: A Practical Roadmap to Protecting Your Company's Reputation.* New York: Wiley, 1999.

Article:

Firestein, Peter. "The investor valuation analysis/open perception study." Online at: tinyurl.com/5uvqf7l [PDF].

Websites:

Author's website: www.firesteinco.com

Author's blog: www.peterfiresteinblog.com

A Holistic Approach to Stakeholder Relations to Build Reputation and Mitigate Reputation Risk

by Elliot S. Schreiber

Brand and Reputation Management LLC, and Center for Corporate Reputation Management, Bennett S. LeBow College of Business, Drexel University, Philadelphia, USA

This Chapter Covers

▸▸ Understanding stakeholder expectations and potential risk.
▸▸ The impact of social media on reputation and risk.
▸▸ Recognizing, assessing, and managing potential risk.
▸▸ The establishment of stakeholder relations councils for managing reputation and risk.
▸▸ A strategic process, called DIFFERS, that helps identify, access, and manage reputation risk.
▸▸ Recommendations for both boards and management.

Introduction

Concerns among boards and CEOs about corporate reputation and the risk to reputation have increased dramatically in the past decade (Economist Intelligence Unit, 2005). According to a study of 551 companies by AON Insurance (Varro, 2009), reputation risk is now the number one concern of senior executives and risk managers globally and is one of the top risk concerns of CEOs.

Senior executives find reputation harder to manage than other types of risks, due to its "amorphous" nature as a "risk of risks" (Tonello, 2007). That is, any risk, whether internal or external, can materialize into a reputation risk. It is troubling, then, that the AON and Conference Board Commission studies found that about 66% of companies have no formal plan in place to manage reputation risk, and that companies are confused about who is responsible for reputation risk and how best to coordinate the issue within the company. Responsibilities for reputation are often fragmented among a number of business managers, leading to poor coordination and continuity, which in turn can undermine reputation and increase risk.

Given the ways that social media have empowered stakeholders, and the growing globalization of companies, reputation risk will only increase for most organizations. Yet there is little guidance that can be found in the professional or business literature that offers advice on how best to manage reputation.

This chapter aims to addresses the gap in business knowledge about managing reputation and reputation risk. The author will provide both an organizational structure that companies can use to manage reputation and reputation risk and a strategic process map, both of which are being used at a variety of international companies and small, not-for-profit organizations.

What Is Reputation?

Corporate reputation is what people generally say about a company's character, performance, or what the company stands for. It is found in stakeholders' familiarity, favorability, and attribute assessments regarding the company as compared to others within a relevant set (for example industry, community, etc.). Reputation translates into the expectations of financial, operational/business, and social value that a range of stakeholders have of an organization, often in comparison to others in the same industry (Korschun, Schreiber, and Andras, 2010). So, for example, for customers value may be a fair price or quality. For employees, it may be a good job, good pay, and good working conditions. For prospective talent, it may be a good place to work. For the community, it might be a company that is a good corporate citizen.

There are several operative terms in this definition of corporate reputation. First, reputation is based on expectations of value that stakeholders believe that they have—or have a right to expect—from the organization. We can define a stakeholder as any person or organization that believes that they have a right to expect some value from an organization, and that are willing and able to act on that expectation, either positively or negatively. For example, employees expect to receive appropriate pay and an acceptable work environment. To the extent that an organization exceeds these expectations, it becomes known as a good place to work, while those that barely meet or fall below these expectations gain a reputation for having a poor workplace environment.

Every stakeholder can either create or destroy value, either directly, or in concert with others. As stakeholder expectations go unfulfilled, there is greater chance of action that can damage reputation being taken against the organization. For example, a nongovernmental organization (NGO) might believe that it has a right to hold an organization to its standards of conduct. If the organization does not meet those expectations, the NGO might "go public" with accusations or demands that could impact the perceptions of the company held by other stakeholders, including employees and customers.

Second, reputation is not monolithic, but rather is stakeholder-group specific. There are often vast differences in the expectations of value across employees, investors or customers, or other stakeholders.

Third, reputation is competitive. Stakeholders judge companies within their industry sectors. In every sector, however, research has found that companies with the best reputations consistently outperform those with poor reputations on every financial measure. There is, then, financial value in reputation, since those with the best reputations enjoy lower cost of capital and credit, attract and retain the best talent, and outperform others in their sector in market capitalization.

Identifying and Managing Reputation Risk

Any incident—internal or external—can become a risk to reputation, which is why reputation can be called a "risk of risks." Some risks can grow within the organization's value chain, whereas others come from external sources. The objective for the company should be to identify and manage these risks before they become full-blown public crises for the company.

Reputation risk occurs when a stakeholder's experience with the organization falls below expectations and the stakeholder takes action that negatively impacts the organization's value (for example revenue loss, market share loss, damage to brand equity, reduced ability to recruit and retain talent, and damage to supply arrangements, among others).

Social media have exacerbated the risk to reputation for every company globally. The rumor mill that has always plagued business is now a "1,440 event" (1,440 is the number of minutes in a day). Customers take part in conversations about companies and their products and services, and many of these conversations include employees, investors, and other stakeholders. Few things are secret anymore, and we must manage reputation risk with this in mind.

Companies have lost a great deal of control over their messages to employees, customers, investors, and others. There have always been disappointed customers and other stakeholders, but now those stakeholders can tweet their displeasure to others worldwide, or create a blog against the company. At the same time, social media have been used by many companies to listen to customers and to engage with them to correct problems before they "metastasize."

Companies too often confuse crisis management with reputation risk management. Reputation risk management is akin to fire prevention management, while crisis management is akin to fire fighting. One knows that there is always the potential of a fire, but one can make changes that minimize fire risks, while also preparing for the event of a fire. The objective is to lessen the potential of a fire, and to minimize the loss to life and property should one occur. When a fire breaks out, one calls the fire department to save people and property. Similarly, when we have a reputation crisis, we fight to save whatever value we can. At the peak of a crisis, the company often is "bleeding out" value, to borrow a medical term. The better we become at identifying and dealing with potential risks early, the more able we are to avoid a crisis, or at least to save the maximum amount of value.

US cable company Comcast faced a crisis in 2008–09 when its reputation was damaged by a blog called "Comcast must die" that was created by a journalist who was upset with Comcast's customer service. The blog generated a series of media stories that sought out other unhappy customers and created a crisis for the company. One disgruntled woman actually took a hammer and damaged equipment at a Comcast installation. Instead of condemning the woman's actions, there was an outcry on social media sites in her support. The company's reputation also was further damaged by a YouTube video showing a Comcast technician sleeping on a customer's sofa while waiting on a telephone hold with his own office.

Comcast's competitors used these situations in a major marketing campaign aimed at attracting customers away from the cable provider. Many inside Comcast thought that they could retain customers by enhancing the technology, lowering the price, or offering new bundled packages to customers. Before taking action, Comcast decided to go on a "listening tour" to hear the complaints of customers. What they heard was that customers were not unhappy with the technology, price, or number of channels—they were unhappy with customer service, and felt that the company did not care about them once they became a customer.

Comcast found that its own compensation systems were contributing to the reputation damage. The company's bonus system for executives was based solely on cash flow, and executives were often cutting customer service to increase profits. To solve the problem, Comcast changed its bonus system to include a customer satisfaction component. The company also became a leader in its own use of social media, reaching out to—and engaging with—displeased customers via Twitter, blogs, and Facebook, to determine their problems and find a solution before the situation worsened. Comcast created its own highly transparent blog called "Comcast cares," which admitted that the company had let customers down and offered to hear and address customer complaints. Comcast's reputation for listening to customers and for customer service is slowly improving. It also has made it more expensive for one of its major competitors to acquire customers, pushing them out of key markets.

The case of Comcast helps us to understand reputation and reputation risk. The company's reputation problems began with customer service, something that is often neglected in reputation management programs. Comcast did not try to address the reputation problem with a traditional marketing communications campaign, but rather addressed it systemically by finding the source of the problem and changing it. It admitted that there was a problem. It reached out to people on social media, and offered to listen and help. Had Comcast followed a traditional approach to its reputation problems, it likely would have created a new public relations or advertising program, which might have damaged its reputation further. Finally, what Comcast learned is what all organizations should recognize: that they need to monitor, identify, assess, and manage their reputation risks before they become crises.

One can think about the process of monitoring, identifying, assessing, and managing risks here as an analogy with cracks in the walls of one's home. If one sees a crack, there are choices to be made. One might determine that the crack requires only some putty and paint (i.e. a major public relations or advertising campaign), or we might investigate to determine if the crack is a harbinger of larger issues. There is a natural tendency to want to avoid thinking about things that "might or might not" occur. We need to have in place a process to differentiate between rational approaches to risk assessment and avoid rationalizing risks. However, because the risks can occur anywhere, inside or outside the organization, we need a structure in place that can become the "eyes and ears" of the organization, with multiple stakeholders and multiple touch points.

 Reputation risk management is akin to fire prevention management, while crisis management is akin to fire fighting.

 One can think about the process of monitoring, identifying, assessing and managing risks here as an analogy with cracks in the walls of one's home.

Stakeholder Relations Councils

A stakeholder relations council offers a good way both to build corporate reputation and also to serve as the primary reputation risk management team. The author has designed and installed such councils at a variety of organizations, both large and small. An example of such a council is shown in Figure 1.

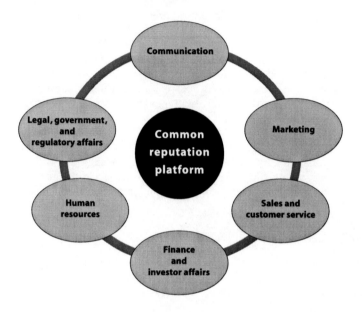

Figure 1. Example of a stakeholder relations council

The stakeholder relations council should comprise those in the organization who have primary stakeholder responsibilities. For example, marketing and sales have responsibility for customers, human resources has responsibility for employees, and finance and investor affairs have responsibility for financial analysts and shareholders.

Some companies have formed what they call "brand" or "reputation" councils. The problem I have found is that these terms conjure up preconceived notions of who should be on the council, and who has responsibility for the issues. It has been the experience of the author that it is easier to get executives from outside of marketing or communications to a meeting about reputation when one "brands" the council as a meeting of stakeholder relations executives. Many people in the organization believe that they "own" a stakeholder relation. Only a few believe they have responsibility for reputation.

The corporate council can help set direction, collect research, and make policy, but in many global organizations a single, corporate-level council is insufficient to reach all the areas where reputation building and risk occur. The councils should be established at the level where decision-making and risk occur within a company. Large companies need such councils within divisions and in various regions of the world, where the country manager or division head can verify that the company is both managing its reputation appropriately for the stakeholder base and also assessing risks, which could well be different from region to region. For example, the risk of an NGO attacking a company for animal testing or genetically modified foods is far greater in the European Union than in the United States. A European council would be much more attuned to that risk than would a counterpart in the United States. Regional councils are also attuned to social, political, and economic differences that should be considered.

Although we may have dispersed risk management, we need to have clear guidelines on what is and what is not acceptable risk. There are different definitions of appropriate behaviors in different regions of the world. My advice is to establish a policy of "one thought, many expressions." That is, the corporate council should establish the parameters of acceptable risk exposure, and the division and regional councils should work within those risk definitions.

The council is there to manage cross-functionally, but someone must be delegated by the CEO to maintain and supervise the council. Typically this will be either the chief communications or chief marketing officer. The person in charge should have the confidence of the CEO, as well as the ability to facilitate collaboration.

Case Study

Stakeholder Relations at a Major Pharmaceutical Company

The case of a major international pharmaceutical company demonstrates the stakeholder councils' work and their value. A regional operation of the company had a number of distinct programs under way. The human resources team had led the development of a new vision and values statement that it was soon prepared to share with employees; the marketing organization had been working on a new customer engagement and segmentation program that was ready to be implemented; and corporate communications was preparing a major corporate social responsibility program. There were no connections between these programs. Each was distinct, separately managed, and had its own message.

The author was asked to visit the company and propose how it might integrate these programs and to build its reputation more effectively. The concept of the stakeholder relations council was introduced. The CEO recognized the value of the approach, and he instituted the council and its members.

Using the process discussed in the next section, the council began by focusing on defining the reputation that was desired by the company and how it would be interpreted by the various functions. As might be expected, there were major differences among the various functions about how the company should be seen and what it should stand for. As the process unfolded, however, the members began to realize how one program impacted on others, and how consistency and continuity of actions and communications were important.

The three major programs were integrated by the council members into a single, focused program. Each council member assumed responsibility for his or her own reputation scorecard (discussed in the next section), and the council had a common scorecard that was reviewed with the CEO and executive committee at each of its meetings.

Of particular interest—beyond the strategic focus the council provided—was the collective sense that developed from the council, and this has been the experience with all such councils. The members, who came to the first meeting as individual representatives of their functions, began to think of themselves as a collective. In fact, the council developed a separate budget, and the chair was later named to a new position as head of corporate reputation management.

Due to the success of the regional stakeholder relations council, one was adopted at the company headquarters and more were established in other regions. The company considered the council to be a major success in helping it integrate its messages, build consistency and continuity in its programs, and gain greater efficiencies.

Measuring Reputation

It is important that the executive team look at appropriate metrics that help them manage reputation risk proactively. There are many excellent reputation studies, but most are "snapshots after the fact," akin to a financial report. One knows how past actions have been judged, but we have little knowledge of how to build future programs.

Some companies base their entire reputation management program on the yearly *Fortune* "Most admired" study. As important as these rankings are, they are simply a snapshot of reputation as seen by directors, officers, and financial analysts in each of the industries surveyed. We cannot extrapolate the results to other stakeholders. We must understand the expectations of value for each.

Managers should avoid looking at reputation studies that provide an aggregate reputation score across all stakeholders. Such studies can potentially mask poor perceptions among one stakeholder that might lead to increased risk.

There are three key areas that I would suggest are important for research, to understand areas of opportunity as well as risk. These are:

- ▸▸ the organization's desired attributes and associations versus the importance of those attributes and associations to the stakeholder;
- ▸▸ the stakeholder's expectations of the organization, its industry, or both, versus their experience;
- ▸▸ the stakeholder's experience with the organization versus a perceived "ideal" or "best-in-class."

The first two topics help the management team to understand stakeholder expectations. The third gives them a perspective of where the company is vis-à-vis the desired expectations of stakeholders. We will know how close we are to the ideal in comparison with our competitors.

At the same time, as we have noted repeatedly in this chapter, the management team needs a set of internal metrics that it can regularly monitor to gauge if risk is growing.

Stakeholder relations councils offer a good way to manage reputation and reputation risk cross-functionally.

The DIFFERS Process: Enterprise Reputation Building and Risk Management Framework

Any council needs a strategic process to guide its work. To accomplish this, I have developed the DIFFERS process, which stands for "define, identify, find, frame, engage, relate, score," as shown in Figure 2. This seven-step process connects the company's business and market strategy, brand, employee engagement, and communications. It was used by the pharmaceutical company in the case study, and has been used by most of the councils as their process map.

The process begins with the council restating the company mission in terms of two to four key attributes that they would want stakeholders to think about "top-of-mind" *(define)*.

The next step is to *identify* how and where the company creates or does not create value in five areas—the so-called "5Cs" (company, competitors, customers, collaborators, and context). The council begins with the company's history, culture, and value chain to see if it is maximizing or squandering value for customers, and how it compares in this with competitors. The council also looks at collaborators that the firm has, or might want to have, that could help it to create more perceived value than it can alone. Finally, the council looks at the social–economic–political–technical environment to see if there are changes under way or expected that might impact the "line of expectations."

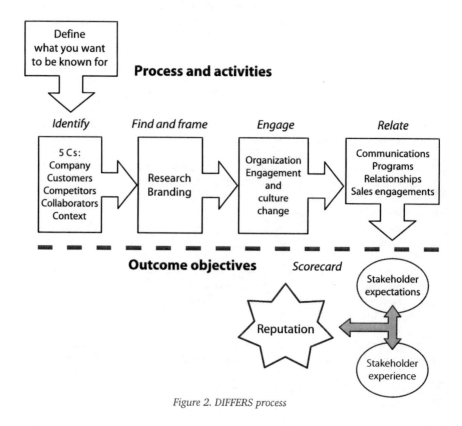

Figure 2. DIFFERS process

Once the council disaggregates the 5Cs, research is conducted (the *find* stage) to determine how key stakeholders perceive the company *vis-à-vis* competitors and where potential risks lie. The three key research topics listed above form a solid framework for such study, and any gaps found in the investigation should be treated as potential risks. For example, at one company, the reputation of the company was found to be excellent with most stakeholders, but one group believed that the company fell well below its expectations versus competitors. On looking into this further, it was discovered that changes in the organizational structure of one division had caused this problem. The issue was quickly addressed, and the risk exposure was avoided.

With the research analysis in hand, the council works to *frame* the promise to stakeholders through a positioning statement. From the research, one should know where one's organization stands *vis-à-vis* both competitors and the "ideal" that stakeholders have. If one is far from both competitors and the ideal in terms of perceived value, this gap must be closed, or the potential for risk from underperforming stakeholder expectations will increase.

The *engage* part of the process is when we begin our engagement with employees, to help them understand the desired perceptions: for example, where the organization stands relative to competitors and the ideal. Many organizations make the mistake of telling employees what the strategic direction is and challenging them to "live the brand." This approach is far less successful than involving employees by asking for their thoughts on how best to enhance perceived value with stakeholders, and where they believe risks exist.

Finally, the council is ready to focus on ways to *relate* to stakeholders, through marketing and communications, including advertising, public relations, social media, and social responsibility programs. As one can see, marketing and communications come at the end of this process, after strategy and research. In many companies, reputation and risk management begin with marketing and communications, which often lead to proposals for corporate social responsibility or public relations programs that are disconnected from strategy and prove ineffective.

The final step in the process is the development of a *scorecard* to provide objectives and deliverables for each member of the stakeholder relations council. The scorecard has as its starting point the baseline information found in the research phase of the process. Objectives are established for building reputation and/or narrowing potential risk areas over a set period of time, with metrics that allow the council to measure and report progress or make needed changes. The metrics in the scorecard should allow managers to understand both how they are creating reputation value and when risk is materializing.

Recommendations for the Board of Directors

The link between reputation and the long-term strategic value for the firm necessitates that the board assume an oversight function. The following are recommendations for consideration by boards.

▸▸ Boards need to pay greater attention to both reputation and reputation risk, since shareholder value is affected.

▸▸ Boards should familiarize themselves with the rationale that management uses to prioritize its various stakeholders, and be persuaded that the relationships are appropriate to the company's long-term business objectives.

▸▸ Boards should regularly review management's assessments of potential risks, and propose how these risks should be managed

▸▸ Boards should consider the establishment of a reputation committee with the same level of importance as other committees of the board. This committee should regularly seek information independent of other reporting methods on reputation risk factors that might impact the company.

▸▸ Boards should adopt the recommendations contained in the Conference Board's 2007 report, "Reputation risk: A corporate governance perspective" (Tonello, 2007) and embed reputation risk into an overall enterprise risk management system;

▸▸ Reputation and reputation risk should be a systematic part of all merger and acquisition analysis, since the reputation of the acquired firm will impact the overall reputation of the acquiring firm.

▸▸ Boards should insist that the company have a stakeholder relations council in place, and that the council report to the board regularly.

Boards should familiarize themselves with the rationale that management uses to prioritize its various stakeholders, and be persuaded that the relationships are appropriate to the company's long-term business objectives.

Summary and Further Steps

▸▸ This chapter has highlighted the importance of reputation to the value creation and differentiation of an organization. · The risk to reputation is increasing, and both boards and senior executive leadership should take immediate action, if it is not already under way, to prioritize and strategize relationships with the company's stakeholders.

▸▸ As a derivative of so many actions and communications of the company, it is difficult—if not impossible—to have reputation management handled by a single function within the corporation.

▸▸ Reputation building and risk management require that the organization define its acceptable risk tolerance, and not only that it be communicated to all employees, but also that proper training be instituted to assure that appropriate standards of behavior and communications are in place at all "touch points."

▸▸ The nature of reputation and reputation risk requires that it be managed cross-functionally. As a guide to organizations, this chapter has provided detail on the use of both a stakeholder relations council and the DIFFERS process, which organizations can use to manage reputation and reputation risk strategically and holistically.

More Info

Books:

Elkington, John. *Cannibals with Forks: The Triple Bottom Line of 21st Century Business*. Oxford: Capstone Publishing, 1997.

Fombrun, Charles J., and Cees B. M. Van Riel. *Fame and Fortune: How Successful Companies Build Winning Reputations*. Upper Saddle River, NJ: FT Prentice Hall, 2004.

Kossovsky, Nir, and Todd A. Miller. *Mission Intangible: Managing Risk and Reputation to Create Enterprise Value*. Pittsburgh, PA: Intangible Asset Finance Society, 2010.

Larkin, Judy. *Strategic Reputation Risk Management*. London: Palgrave MacMillan, 2003.

Low, Jonathan, and Pamela Kalafut. *Invisible Advantage: How Intangibles Are Driving Business Performance*. Cambridge, MA: Perseus Publishing, 2002.

Reichheld, Frederick F. *The Loyalty Effect: The Hidden Force behind Growth, Profits and Lasting Value*. Boston, MA: Harvard Business School Press, 1996.

Sexton, Donald E. *Value above Cost: Driving Superior Financial Performance with CVA, the Most Important Metric You've Never Used*. Upper Saddle River, NJ: Wharton School Publishing/ Pearson Education, 2009.

Articles:

Balmer, John M. T., and Guillaume B. Soenen. "The Acid test of corporate identity management™." *Journal of Marketing Management* 15:1–3 (1999): 69–92. Online at: dx.doi.org/10.1362/026725799784870441

Barton, Dominic. "Capitalism for the long term." *Harvard Business Review* (March 2011). Online at: hbr.org/2011/03/capitalism-for-the-long-term/ar/1

Couts, Andrew. "Apple makes 50% of all handset industry profits, analyst says." *Digital Trends* (July 9, 2011). Online at: tinyurl.com/455wd2k

Eccles, Robert G., Scott C. Newquist, and Roland Schatz. "Reputation and its risks." *Harvard Business Review* (February 2007). Online at: hbr.org/2007/02/reputation-and-its-risks/ar/1

Friedman, Milton. "The social responsibility of business is to increase profits." *New York Times Magazine* (September 13, 1970).

Martin, Roger. "The age of customer capitalism." *Harvard Business Review* (January–February 2010). Online at: hbr.org/2010/01/the-age-of-customer-capitalism/ar/1

Obloj, Tomasz, and Krzysztof Obloj. "Diminishing returns from reputation: Do followers have a competitive advantage?" *Corporate Reputation Review* 9:4 (December 2006): 213–224. Online at: dx.doi.org/10.1057/palgrave.crr.1550029

Porter, Michael E., and Mark R. Kramer. "The big idea: Creating shared value." *Harvard Business Review* (January–February 2011). Online at: hbr.org/2011/01/the-big-idea-creating-shared-value/ar/1

Roberts, Peter W., and Grahame R. Dowling. "Corporate reputation and sustained superior financial performance." *Strategic Management Journal* 23:12 (December 2002): 1077–1093. Online at: dx.doi.org/10.1002/smj.274

Varro, Alex. "Aon announces top 10 global risks." *Insurance Networking News* (April 21, 2009). Online at: tinyurl.com/64h6gwa

More Info

Vergin, Roger C., and M. W. Qoronfleh. "Corporate reputation and the stock market." *Business Horizons* 41:1 (January/February 1998): 19–26.
Online at: dx.doi.org/10.1016/S0007-6813(98)90060-X

Yarrow, Jay. "Apple has 50% of the profits from major phone makers." *Business Insider* (May 2, 2011). Online at: tinyurl.com/3z23tr8

Reports:

Altman, Daniel, and Jonathan Berman. "The single bottom line." June 13, 2011.
Online at: tinyurl.com/6k3ldws [PDF].

Bayer, Daniel Sandy, and Ellen S. Hexter. "Managing reputation risk and reward."
Report no. R-1442-09-RR. Conference Board, March 2009.

Brancato, Carolyn Kay, Ellen S. Hexter, Katharine Rose Newman, and Matteo Tonello.
"The role of U.S. corporate boards in enterprise risk management." Report no.
R-1390-06-RR. Conference Board, June 2006.

Conference Board. "Commission on public trust and private enterprise: Findings and
recommendations." Report no. SR-03-04. January 2003.
Online at: www.conference-board.org/pdf_free/sr-03-04.pdf

Economist Intelligence Unit. "Reputation: Risk of risks." December 2005.
Online at: www.eiu.com/report_dl.asp?mode=fi&fi=1552294140.PDF

Gu, Feng, and Baruch Lev. "Intangible assets: Measurement, drivers, usefulness."
Working paper. 2001.

Korshun, Daniel, Elliot S. Schreiber, and Trina Larsen Andras. "Corporate reputation and
the new stakeholder capitalism." Working paper, Center for Corporate Reputation
Management, Bennett S. LeBow College of Business, Drexel University, 2010.

Schreiber, Elliot S. "A framework and process for aligning the organization to enhance
reputation by maximizing perceived competitive value." 14th International Conference
on Corporate Reputation, Brand, Identity and Competitiveness, Rio de Janeiro, Brazil,
May 19–21, 2010.

Tonello, Matteo. "Reputation risk: A corporate governance perspective."
Report no. R-1412-07-WG. Conference Board, December 2007.

Torok, Robert, Carl Nordman, and Spencer Lin. "Clearing the clouds: Shining a light on
successful enterprise risk management." IBM Institute for Business Value, June 2011.
Online at: tinyurl.com/3peg5df [PDF].

Watson Wyatt. "Human capital index: Human capital as a lead indicator of shareholder
value." 2002. Online at: www.watsonwyatt.com/research/printable.asp?id=W-488

Websites:

Comcast Must Die: www.comcastmustdie.com

YouTube video of sleeping Comcast technician: www.youtube.com/atch?v=CVp7b5gzqU

Managing Reputational Risk: Business Journalism

by Jonathan Silberstein-Loeb

Centre for Corporate Reputation, Saïd Business School, University of Oxford, UK

This Chapter Covers

- ▸▸ How credible commitments can help to mitigate reputational risk.
- ▸▸ Establishing credible commitment, and trust, requires a better understanding of the incentives of journalists, as well as the perceptions of business, both of which are explored in this chapter.
- ▸▸ The consequences of these differing incentives for building trust between journalists and businesses and for company strategy are explored in the final section.

Introduction

It is taken as given that journalism affects corporate reputation. To understand better how journalism about businesses is written and what can be done to contend with the reputational risk that it may present, this chapter seeks to explain how business practitioners and business journalists perceive each other and interact. It is the central argument of this chapter that establishing mechanisms for credible commitment helps to mitigate reputational risk. As there is no formal mechanism for establishing credible commitment between business representatives and business journalists, doing so depends on their respective incentives and corresponding informal constraints, such as career advancement and the loss of reputation. Insofar as journalists must have sources, and sources must communicate with their stakeholders, journalists and corporate decision-makers rely equally on each other, and therefore may be hostages of one another in instances of repeated interaction. The implicit recognition that both parties are beholden to each other may be the most effective mechanism of credible commitment. Behavior that demonstrates an awareness of this codependence helps to establish trust, which is central to effective media relations.[1] Trusting relationships facilitate an understanding of the incentives that undergird credible commitments, which helps to make them reinforcing. Recognizing the importance of credible commitments has clear consequences for the way in which companies develop communication strategies.

Much of what follows is predicated on the preliminary results of an international study of business journalism and corporate reputation that the Oxford University Centre for Corporate Reputation is conducting. This chapter relies on evidence gathered as part of this study in more than 80 informal, off-the-record interviews conducted in England with journalists from major national dailies that publish business sections and with business leaders (see Appendix 1).

The Incentives of Journalists
For Whom Do Journalists Write?

It might reasonably be expected that the audience for business journalism would affect journalists' incentives, but journalists have, at best, an imperfect impression of the reader for whom they write, or who reads their articles. "The general reader" is a phrase that journalists frequently use, but it lacks a clear definition. There is considerable difference among writers at each publication, which makes for little differentiation between publications, although the *Financial Times* is tailored toward the investment community more than the *Sunday Times*. Some business journalists claim to write for the person on the Clapham omnibus, others for the clerk in the City. The public is largely financially illiterate, and journalists are obliged to explain the basics to the general reader, but this duty does not undermine the value that business news holds for specialists. Those business professionals who read the business sections—and most do—do so less for insight than for context.

What Motivates Journalists?

Journalists' motivations affect their incentives. In a survey of American journalists that has been conducted four times over the past 30 years, Weaver and Wilhoit (1996) identified three principal functions among journalists: disseminators of information; interpreters of events; and adversaries of business and government. Throughout the survey period, the dominant professional role of journalists has been "interpretive"—that is, to provide analysis and interpretation of complex issues. Since the 1970s, it has always been the case that only a very small minority of the sample felt that the adversary role was important. The percentage of journalists surveyed who believed that it was extremely important for the mass media to "be an adversary of business by being constantly skeptical of their actions" has always been low, even in the wake of dozens of scandals involving large corporations. The percentage of journalists who believed the adversarial function to be extremely important was greatest among those working for news magazines, and least among those working for radio. Although these data pertain to American journalism, cultural similarities between Britain and the United States, and responses from journalists interviewed in London, provide reasons to suspect that a like study carried out in the United Kingdom would produce similar results.

The motivation of business journalists in part derives from the way in which they perceive the companies about which they report. Opinions vary from journalist to journalist, and journalists change their minds over time. When they believe they are on to a hot story, their approach may be adversarial; when they are covering a diary event, it may be interpretive. The journalists who were interviewed evinced as much a desire simply to "understand how the world works" as to serve an interpretive or watchdog function, although many professed themselves to be skeptical of authority. Regardless of their perceived role, most journalists interviewed believe that they can hold business to account when required. It is broadly the case, and common sense, that business journalists at the *Financial Times* tend to see themselves as serving more of an interpretive function, whereas journalists at *The Guardian* tend to see themselves more as watchdogs of business. Journalists at the *Daily Mail* were also more likely to think it their job to hold business to account. Journalists at other publications are either indifferent, or opinions among them vary so considerably that any characterization by publication is impossible.

How Do Journalists Interact with Business Sources?

Regulations respecting the disclosure requirements imposed on businesses significantly affect the quantity and quality of information available to journalists, but the material divulged in disclosure documents is in the public domain. Such material is unlikely to be newsworthy, especially now that the Internet makes it so easy to search for and share this information. Journalists require scoops, and for this reason, contacts are critical to all journalists, regardless of publication. How journalists develop these contacts varies according to publication, and to style of writing. Breakingviews.com and *The Economist,* for example, as well as columnists at the dailies, need not worry about quoting sources on-the-record. If discussions are *de facto* off-the-record, then journalists have an easier time getting information. The perception of a particular publication, and its perceived audience, among sources is also influential: people in the City are more likely to find time for a chat with journalists from the *Financial Times* than they are with journalists from *The Guardian.* Consequently, those journalists who see themselves as watchdogs find it more difficult to cultivate the sources they require to fulfill this function.

There is irony here that bespeaks a fundamental problem in all forms of journalism. Readers of *The Guardian,* and similar publications, are less interested than readers of the *Financial Times* in the daily operations of big business. Journalists who see themselves as adversaries of business tend to work for publications that circulate among readers with a dislike for big business, or at least only a secondary interest in it. Given their readership, adversarial journalists are therefore less likely than journalists working at business-friendly publications to contact, or be contacted by, the very people whom they seek to hold to account. Journalists waging crusades tend to operate on the margins, and to rely on workers in the third sector for information, rather than the business decision-makers, on whom journalists at business-orientated publications tend to rely. Further, publications tailored for business, such as Breakingviews.com, *The Economist,* the *Financial Times,* and the *Wall Street Journal,* have been more successful than general publications at charging for their online content, not least because the people who read these publications perceive them to be important to their careers. Publications tailored for business audiences have more resources to devote to serving a watchdog function, but perhaps less incentive to do so. The fact that News Corporation owns Dow Jones, which covers day-to-day events, enables journalists at the *Wall Street Journal Europe,* which News Corporation also owns, to devote more time to in-depth reporting, and yet comparatively few journalists at the *Wall Street Journal Europe* see themselves as watchdogs of business.

Regardless of the way in which journalists perceive their role, it is broadly the case that they are concerned to advance their careers—and obtaining scoops, or exclusive news, is an effective way for them to do so. Although journalists may obtain exclusive news either through investigation, which is typically adversarial, or through sources, which rely on relationships, in practice the two often overlap: sources provide leads, which require further investigation, which requires sources. The reality is that journalists rely on their contacts and the strength of their relationships with sources to do their jobs effectively. Whether journalists perceive their function to be interpretive or adversarial will determine the extent to which they are willing to bite the hands that feed them. In an age of WikiLeaks and whistleblowing, journalists will always find someone with a story, but those journalists with a proclivity for provocation are likely to find that their pool of contacts dries up quickly. All journalists must constantly query whether flouting or favoring their sources best serves their interests. If journalists are unwilling to cross their sources, they risk being mere conduits.

Journalists Have a Code of Behavior

To further their careers and to obtain quality contacts, journalists must maintain their credibility, which is achieved through accuracy and consistency. Relationships with sources are built up over years and are based on trust. Maintaining these relationships requires journalists to be accurate and honest. Unsurprisingly, all journalists profess to uphold these standards and to behave professionally. Assuming journalists are committed to doing their jobs well, which may be a large assumption, they will seek to obtain access to credible and authoritative sources, which typically means bypassing PR in favor of speaking directly with executives. They will also attempt to corroborate the facts of a story through a process of triangulation.

The relationship between journalist and source can be a game of cat and mouse, one of tit-for-tat, of "you scratch my back, I'll scratch yours," or a continuous negotiation. Journalists know, and business decision-makers confirm, that without prior relationships journalists will be directed first to PR, although most journalists hope to speak to C-suite executives on every story. Even then, to talk to a company that is not PR-trained is rare. Some sources are more forthcoming than others. Most of the journalists interviewed believe that external PR professionals are better sources than internal communications officers, but it is occasionally the case that company employees are especially well briefed and agency employees are uninformed. On the one hand, to the extent that journalists perceive PR to be a hindrance that must be circumvented, the presence of PR may radicalize journalists; on the other hand, if a PR professional, or any source, is discovered to have lied to a journalist, they will lose their credibility as a source. Among business journalists, there exist the "good" and "smart" PR professionals who understand this game, and the "bad" PR who "don't get it." A process of name-and-shame in newsrooms generates and promulgates a source's reputation.

The Incentives of Business Representatives

Most companies proactively undertake to conduct, in conjunction with an external financial public relations agency, a series of strategic, staged formal meetings with journalists throughout the year that coincide with annual announcements. Interactions between companies and journalists more frequently take place in informal environments, which, from a corporate perspective, are less orchestrated and strategic, and which consequently have potentially greater reputational repercussions.

Willingness of Business to Engage with Journalists

Willingness to engage with the media varies, but some form of interaction is necessary and important. Saying "no comment" may make it difficult for journalists to write a story, but more often it tends to annoy them, and it rarely prevents them from writing. Few C-suite executives court business journalists, but nearly all are convinced of the importance and beneficial effects of trusting relationships. As a general rule, CEOs tend to interact more with the media than with nonexecutives. Chairpersons only get involved when there is a strategic event, such as a takeover bid or a governance issue. Much of the interaction with journalists tends to focus around the reporting of company results, but executives make efforts to have regular contact with journalists to provide background information. Much of this interaction is conducted under the guise of helping journalists to understand the business, explaining decisions made, or making sure they get the facts of the story straight.

The Importance of Trusting Relationships

Trusting relationships may help CEOs to avoid negative coverage. Creating such relationships with journalists entails interactions outside work-related environments. These informal interactions, typically conducted off the record, may be informative for journalists and executives. CEOs and other executives are convinced that even if they have lousy news to give, they receive more balanced treatment from journalists they know. A "professional relationship," according to many business leaders, helps them to promulgate messages that kill adverse rumors and gossip. Long-term relationships make journalists more receptive to the views businesses put across. It can be dangerous to court journalists, but once a trusting relationship is established, journalists will seek to maintain it through good behavior to ensure continued access to a reliable source. Developing effective relationships with journalists requires honest discussion and exchange. Trade in information does not characterize such relationships. Journalists may grant businesses favorable treatment on negative stories in exchange for off-the-record comments, but this a perilous strategy to pursue. Sustainable, effective relationships rely on a modicum of respect and quite a lot of patronizing. Trust is critical, and so is honesty.

Although personal contact creates more credible relations, evidence suggests that the Internet has made the relationship between journalists and corporations more mediated. The personal communication that previously followed the release of statements—and which allowed for clarification—has ceased, making public statements more important. The focus of media relations is now more on preparation than on relationship building. This shift also reflects the fact that traditional media are less important than they once were. Creating a case for a company that meets the needs of all its stakeholders requires waging battles on multiple fronts, and not just in the *Financial Times*. Media fragmentation also makes relationships between journalists and sources less manageable. The permanency, accessibility, and transportability of information on the Internet means that companies must have a clear message.

Creating Credible Commitments to Mitigate Reputational Risk

Journalists, whether they perceive themselves to be watchdogs or not, require information. To obtain this information, and to do their jobs effectively, journalists must gain the trust of their sources. Corporate decision-makers likewise have an incentive to gain the trust of journalists so that they may effectively communicate important information to the market. At the upper echelons of business and business journalism in London, theory and practice converge more often than not. There is an implicit recognition that both parties require each other.

Decision-makers have information at their disposal that journalists do not, and consequently they are obliged to convey this information to journalists frankly and in such a way that the journalists are satisfied that there has been full disclosure. The uneven distribution of information and the burdensome obligation of disclosure make mistrust and miscommunication likely. Journalists, by dint of their information deficit, are likely to be suspicious of their sources. Decision-makers, confronting such suspicion, are likely to be convinced that journalists are always looking for dirt. If a company is conducted in a strategically sound manner and within the law, it has little to worry about from the media. (Even if it is conducted in an unsound manner, recent history suggests that journalists may be slow to cotton on.) A consistently sound strategy achieves favorable results. Profits are facts on the ground with which it is difficult for even the most biased journalist to argue. If the business is performing poorly, it is only fair, and of service to the market, that this be reflected in the papers.

Yet, the blame game is subjective, and journalists are fallible, so it is reasonable that in the court of public opinion businesses should have advocates as they do in courts of chancery. Even the good have need of an advocate. Although the rules of the game that dictate the behavior of advocates in the court of public opinion are by necessity unwritten, and more informal than those regulations under which barristers labor, adherence to them is as necessary for the orderly distribution of justice, and flouting them is just as punishable. These are the rules that apply to the construction and maintenance of trusting relationships.

Trusting relationships diminish the prospect that rogue journalists will undeservedly lash out at corporations and their representatives. As with capital, during good times business leaders should seek to generate favorable relationships that are resistant to change during less fortuitous periods in the life of the organization. Journalists seek to build trusting relationships by obtaining a reputation for credibility, which is obtained through professionalism. Being credible does not mean being sympathetic to sources—it means being fair. For decision-makers to convey their opinions effectively to journalists, they too must be seen as being credible. The best way to achieve credibility with journalists is for business-decision makers to be open and honest. Of course, journalists may sensationalize a story to augment their own career or to sell newspapers, just as companies may employ strategies of obfuscation and spin, but for journalists opportunistic behavior undermines credibility, and for corporations spin is at best a fallible prophylactic.

A Continuous Process of Negotiation

It is useful to imagine relationships between journalists and corporate decision-makers as a continuous process of negotiation. In an insightful article, Charron (1989) observed that these relationships are "at once cooperative and fraught with conflict." The dual nature of these relationships, wrote Charron, "implies a double negotiation: over the exchange of resources, and over the rules regulating this exchange." Cooperation results from mutual interdependence of the players for resources. Each actor's dependence on the other varies according to the possibility of alternatives. A more adversarial dimension arises from attempts by either journalists or sources to manage this relationship. Charron concluded that collaboration and accommodation are the best strategies for sources, although these strategies entail risks, whereas journalists, when their interests are not directly at stake, will tend to adopt a strategy of avoidance rather than accommodation.

For many years PR professionals have known that "spin" is self-defeating. It is widely recognized that nuance, and presenting both sides of the story, is critical to maintaining the credibility of PR. In the upper echelons of PR in England these enlightened views hold sway. When possible, PR professionals ought to provide journalists with reliable information and facilitate their access to C-suite executives. All journalists recognize that sources will put their version of the story across, and they regard this as reasonable, but anything less than collaboration and accommodation is likely to incur the wrath of journalists and do a disservice to public relations. The power to improve media relations, and to augment corporate reputation, therefore lies with corporations. In the blame game, corporations are both more permanent and more manageable players than individual journalists, whose personality and practice is less readily determined or constrained. Mechanisms, such as professional codes of conduct, however fallible they may be, already exist to dissuade journalists from opportunistic behavior. Any further restrictions on journalistic activity would have an adverse effect on the social benefit they provide to the public. The onus to improve relations lies with business.

PR Should Play a Role in Strategy

Businesses ought to avoid putting those that communicate on their behalf in a position in which they are obligated to jeopardize their relationships with journalists. Instead, the PR function should play a more influential role in developing corporate strategy so that company behavior is justifiable to journalists, and so that sources are able to retain credibility with them. So long as businesses do not oblige sources to deceive journalists, media relations will be predicated on trust, which enables businesses to convey effectively the rationale behind strategic decisions.

During the past decade, there have been indications of a greater appreciation of the role and value of the PR function in management, but it is still seen by many as foremost a communications role. Corporate decision-makers are concerned about how actions will be portrayed on the cover of the *Daily Mail*, but there is little direct connection between PR and strategy. In part, this gradual increase in the managerial role of PR is due to the growing importance of investor relations. As Davis ("Public relations, business news and the reproduction of corporate elite power," 2000) has observed, publicly quoted companies periodically devote resources to government policy-making and institutional regulation, but they are more concerned with institutional shareholders and the wider business community. Such concerns translate into an emphasis on communications with investment analysts, business leaders, and business journalists.

Given the influence that the media may exercise on company reputation, executives must weigh the gains to be had from strategic actions against the losses to be expected from adverse media commentary. If the executive is convinced that the profits to be gained from a particular strategic action outweigh the potential loss to profits incurred from negative media coverage, the executive has a responsibility to carry out the action. If, however, the response of the media may be so adverse as to cause damage in excess of the benefit derived from strategic action, the executive has an equally powerful but opposite obligation to avoid the strategy, to modify it, or to explain it to the media in such a way as to limit losses when the strategy is carried out. The PR function should help in making this calculation. This is not to say that PR ought to be the conscience of the corporation; rather, PR professionals should bring to bear on the process of strategic planning the perspective and interest of different stakeholders whose support is critical to profitability.

When relationships between corporations and business journalists function effectively, they generate transparency and the amount of information about a company available to the media may consequently increase. Transparency enables the market to know what a company does, and why. All things being equal, a greater quantity of information will better ensure that market perceptions parallel corporate behavior. Transparency may compel companies to adhere to social norms and behave responsibly without sacrificing profitability. Having increased the quantity of information available to the media, and by extension to the public, corporations will have more to manage, but this outcome is conducive to the effective function of markets, which is necessary for economic growth generally and corporate growth specifically.

Summary and Further Steps

▸▸ Implicit recognition that journalists and corporate decision-makers require each other leads to a credible commitment that builds trust.

▸▸ Closer cooperation between the managerial and communications functions within firms helps to facilitate trusting relationships with journalists, and consequently to mitigate reputational risk.

More Info

Books:

Weaver, David H., and G. Cleveland Wilhoit. *The American Journalist in the 1990s: U.S. News People at the End of an Era*. Mawah, NJ: Lawrence Elbaum Associates, 1996.

Articles:

Charron, Jean. "Relations between journalists and public relations practitioners: Cooperation, conflict and negotiation." *Canadian Journal of Communication* 14:2 (1989): 41–54. Online at: tinyurl.com/6fg78qd [PDF].

Davis, Aeron. "Public relations, news production and changing patterns of source access in the British national media." *Media, Culture & Society* 22:1 (January 2000): 39–59. Online at: dx.doi.org/10.1177/016344300022001003

Davis, Aeron. "Public relations, business news and the reproduction of corporate elite power." *Journalism* 1:3 (December 2000): 282–304. Online at: dx.doi.org/10.1177/146488490000100301

Notes

1. I am grateful to Dr Paolo Campana for help on this point.

Appendix 1. Interviewees for Oxford University Centre for Corporate Reputation study of business journalism and corporate reputation

Newspapers and journals	Business leaders	
BreakingViews.com	Torsten Altmann	Carol Leonard
Daily Mail	Norman Askew	David Mansfield
The Economist	John Barton	Peter Morgan
Financial Times	Alex Brog	John Peace
The Guardian	Roger Carr	Roger Parry
The Independent	Peter Cawdron	Sir Ian Prosser
The Times	Stuart Chambers	Michael Rake
Sunday Times	Doug Daft	Don Robert
Wall Street Journal Europe	Terry Duddy	Robin Saunders
	Steve Easterbrook	Oliver Stocken
	Andrew Grant	Robert Swannell
	Andy Hornby	John Tiner
	Lady Barbara Judge	David Tyler
	Frederick Kempe	Lucas Van Praag
	Roddy Kennedy	Sarah Weller
	John Kingman	Gerhard Zeiler

How the Corporate Website Has Become the Hub for Online Reputation Building

by Mark Hill

The Group, London, UK

This Chapter Covers

- ▸▸ The evolution of the corporate website from its beginnings as a narrowly conceived investor relations vehicle.
- ▸▸ How some companies are using their websites to influence reputation online.
- ▸▸ How the corporate site no longer simply states a company's values as abstractions but attempts to translate them into a useful experience for stakeholders.
- ▸▸ The vital role the website has to play in responding to new reputational challenges from the users of social media.

Introduction

The Internet is the fastest-growing channel for influencing corporate reputation. It is also, uniquely, where all a company's different stakeholders and audiences converge. Analysts, communities, customers, employees, investors, journalists, NGOs, regulators, and suppliers all turn up, together, in increasing numbers on the corporate website.

So, if reputation is "the net perception of a company's ability to meet the expectations of all its stakeholders,"[1] the corporate website should be understood as the key online location where those perceptions are reinforced or challenged. This means that everything a company does, or fails to do, online has an impact for good or bad on its reputation with these stakeholders, while the experiences they have with a company through its corporate site—including how information is structured, presented, and expressed—act to support or undermine that company's good name.

Companies that do not appreciate this will see their reputation suffer. User expectations across all classes of website have risen sharply, and standards of web design, usability, and functionality have all greatly improved from even five years ago. For many people, going online is now simply a part of their everyday lives; they don't differentiate between the online and offline engagement that they have with a company—it's all part of the same experience. And when they're online, they expect immediate responses, to be entertained (or, at the very least, to find something interesting), transparency, and, with the advent of social media, something personal.

The best of today's corporate websites are effective tools for building, supporting, and enhancing reputation online. Although this is partly a result of the powerful online communications tools now available—from video to social media—it is also due to approach. Supporting the company's online communications goals is a clear priority, but these sites also are user-focused, something which is reflected in the depth and breadth of the content they provide, as well as the links and connections they promote.

They connect with and cross-connect diverse stakeholder groups in ongoing dialog about the company, its operations, beliefs, and interests; they provide content and features that not only meet stakeholders' information needs but offer a values-driven online experience of the company and opportunities to participate in shaping the company's reputation.

In this chapter we will discuss the evolution of the corporate website from its early incarnation as a narrowly conceived investor relations vehicle and see how some companies are using their websites to influence reputation online; we will look at how the corporate site no longer simply states a company's values as an abstraction but attempts to translate those values into useful and positive experiences for stakeholders; and we will address the vital role the website has to play in responding to new reputational challenges that originate in the social media.

The First Corporate Websites

With deeper penetration of the Internet in the mid- to late 1990s, a new front opened up for those involved in building reputation. The corporate website, as a company's first outpost in this online world, was now a significant factor in how a business might be perceived by its stakeholders.

Often little more than a collection of positioning statements, boilerplate copy and financial information, these early corporate sites may have been about the company, but they were not an expression of what the company stood for, nor did they make any real attempt to engage with stakeholders.

In those early days of the Web, investors—who were the main audience—were happy simply to find any usable information at all; whether or not a company was advanced enough in its communications to have one of these bridgehead sites was the main reputational issue.

From Single to Multi-Stakeholder Focus

As Internet use grew rapidly—from 16 million users worldwide in December 1995 to 361 million by the end of 2000[2]—so the early sites bulked up on content and began adding dedicated sections including media, environment, and society (a forerunner of the now standard CSR section), customers, suppliers, and careers (recruitment).

Although these sections tended to be discrete silos of content aimed at specific stakeholders rather than strands of an overall company narrative—as is still the case on too many corporate sites—there was a definite branching out from investor-led communication to a more rounded picture of the company for a broader range of stakeholders. So various elements of the company story were now present, though site users still had to do some work to put it together and the messages that were given were not always consistent.

This process of opening out to the needs of wider audiences has continued to the present day. Figure 1 shows the spread of content consumed across nine FTSE100 websites in one year and gives a sense of how these sites are being used by key stakeholder groups.

The breadth of interest has also been accompanied by an absolute increase in the numbers of people coming to these sites. An index of site visits maintained by the author's company, The Group, for a range of FTSE100 websites shows growth of more than 1,100% in corporate website visits since 2001.[3]

While some companies still have an online presence that resembles the early sites aimed at investors in their limited content and lack of engagement, their varied stakeholders are online in large numbers, seeking quite a lot more.

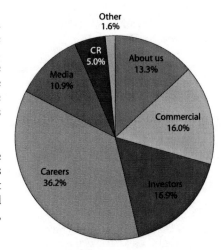

Figure 1. Page views across nine FTSE100 websites from June 2010 to May 2011. (Sites are hosted by The Group)

Articulating the Corporate Story

Companies that understand this are using the corporate website as a means to help build and enhance reputation. They address the needs of their stakeholders by telling the company story through deep, rich, and—most importantly—consistent content, and by offering an online experience that shows people what the company stands for rather than just telling them.

Striving for Consistency

Effective reputation building requires consistency of communication with all stakeholders in terms of factual content and information, and in messaging and tone of voice. In the past, the silo approach to website content often resulted in a fragmented experience for those who chose to go beyond their allotted section and travel through the wider site. The immediate impact was (and in some cases still is) to expose the divergence between the different forms of communication that a company used with its various audiences. On a higher level, it also raised questions about the overall clarity of the company narrative and its ability to develop coherent communications online.

Moreover, corporate communications spawned a range of new websites—for corporate marketing, campaigns, reporting, etc.—that were, by definition, already enmeshed in a web of other commercial and national websites. And the inconsistencies within corporate sites were more than matched by the wider experience of traveling between these different outposts of a company's online estate.

This is a problem that persists to this day. Stakeholder audiences tend to be unruly. Refusing to stay corralled into neat and controllable groups, they move around these online estates, getting confused by inconsistent websites and mixed messages. In the Internet age, companies can and do suffer serious reputation damage by saying contradictory things in different markets—note the 2009 Maclaren baby stroller safety recall in the United States as a relatively recent example.[4] But also, in a less extreme sense, the disjointed experience at a macro, multisite level can result in a fractured sense of company reputation and difficulty forming any deeper "net perception" among all stakeholders.

Owners of the better corporate sites understand, for instance, that analysts will venture out to explore information from subsidiaries, that stakeholders in local markets will seek out information on a parent company, and that the commercial activity of business units is of interest and use to corporate audiences. And from that understanding comes a more coherent approach to website planning whereby shared content and multiple user journeys between sites are given as much prominence as those within the corporate site. In this way, companies seek to enhance their reputation by providing a framework by means of which all elements of their online presence can be navigated and understood.

Ethics and Values: Don't Tell Me, Show Me
Beyond consistency in the technical sense of having appropriate messages, design, and content within and across the company's sites, there is a deeper sense of consistency in how what a company espouses on its corporate site matches what stakeholders actually experience there.

If a website is to express what a company is about, it's essential that this story and what drives it—the company's mission and values—are clearly identified and fully integrated into all aspects of the site.

Expressing what a company stands for takes more than a mission statement. The best corporate websites maintain and enhance reputation by translating company values into consistent and engaging experiences that can become the foundation of stakeholder relationships online. They deliver coherent engagement with stakeholders, regardless of whether they want to invest in, work for, trade with, or just follow the company.

Reckitt Benckiser's website,[5] for example, lists the company's values of achievement, ownership, entrepreneurship, and team spirit in its careers section. However, it not only goes on to explain what those values mean in practice—in a direct and engaging way, not in corporate speak—but it also embodies those descriptions in what the site is saying (content), how it is saying it (tone of the copy), and how the information is presented (design). And this is true across the site, not just in the careers section, where traditionally companies have relaxed their approach.

Though the integration of values and experience across the website represents progress in influencing corporate reputation online, it is not enough. Companies also need to think about what is happening across all their communications and face up to reputation's most notable new challenge: the social media.

The Rise of the Social Media
In communication terms, corporate reputation can be a function of the interplay between what a company says and how it says it, and what others say about that company. Traditionally, when trying to build and enhance corporate reputation, companies relied on a range of specialist stories told by professional storytellers using well-understood channels of communication, including, more recently, the corporate website.

The emergence of social media disrupted those channels and presented a pressing challenge to corporate reputation. First, social media provided technology and tools that helped to turn readers of content into publishers, subverting not only the established communication channels but also the dominant media sources. And second, the communication norms of social media demand the pushing of fewer messages and more transparency, interaction, and dialog.

The rise of the social media has been extraordinary—the numbers tell the story.

▸▸ More than 13 million hours of video were uploaded to YouTube in 2010, the equivalent of 35 hours every minute.[6] By 2008, YouTube had become the world's second largest search engine.[7]

▸▸ An average of 460,000 new Twitter accounts are set up every day,[8] with users sending 200 million tweets a day at the time of writing—up from 65 million just a year ago.[9]

▸▸ Facebook has more than 750 million active users;[10] 47% of people in the United Kingdom visit Facebook on average 68 times a month.[11]

No longer could companies even pretend to control the message (although in fact this claim was always spurious). Online conversation about companies, their products, actions, and performance was now happening off the corporate website. Authority was becoming displaced; the 2009 Edelman Trust Barometer survey found that, for information about a company, "conversations with friends and peers" were what people trusted (40%), with official corporate sources way down the list (26%).[12]

The threats to corporate reputation were (and are) very real. Twitter, in particular, has proved perfectly suited to spreading rumor and misinformation. In the early days, poor governance ruled. Account names went unsecured, opening the door to mischievous cybersquatters. Rogue accounts could even become more popular than official ones—the Deepwater oil spill in 2010 saw the emergence of @BPGlobalPR,[13] a parody account that now has 169,744 followers, easily eclipsing the official account, @BP_America, with 28,737 followers.[14]

As companies struggled to get to grips with what was happening, some saw their reputations holed by the actions of their own employees. We saw a spate of ill-advised tweets and or blog posts from employees' personal accounts; and the word "dooced" entered the vocabulary.[15] It wasn't just what people were writing that was the problem; Domino's Pizza encountered the power of viral video and a severe reputation challenge when a couple of employees shot a video of themselves preparing contaminated food.[16]

Most often, however, the damage to reputation was done by a lack of understanding of how to respond to genuine comment, however unwelcome. That response could be slow (for example Eurostar, slow to use its promotional Twitter account to respond to travellers trapped for hours by poor weather[17]), inept (Nestlé deleting unfavorable comments on its Facebook page), or plain crass (Habitat attempting to promote its sales tweets by incorporating hashtags referencing the Iranian election[18]). These are historical examples; for the most part, the companies concerned have turned their communications around.

But the examples are, nonetheless, indication that consistent, measured communication broke down in face of the social media. And, crucially, the action had very definitely moved away from companies' own turf, the corporate website.

The Irrelevant Corporate Website?

Industry analyst Jeremiah Owyang was the first prominent voice to call out the company website for irrelevance, back in May 2007.[19] The rest of the Web—customer networks, user forums, blogs—was where people were making decisions, he claimed. In 2011, the head of Facebook UK did something similar,[20] suggesting that a Facebook presence meant that there was no need for a company site (you could say that he has a vested interest). But, in truth, the challenges and opportunities of social media give corporate websites a more important role than ever before, particularly in online reputation management.

The corporate site is owned by the business; here, companies have ultimate control of their content. While a presence on Twitter, YouTube, and Facebook may now be increasingly necessary, these are not the company's spaces, however attractively they may be customized. It is the corporate site that is a company's secure online home.

But Facebook, Twitter, YouTube, and blogs allow for an unprecedented degree of engagement between companies and their stakeholders. For those companies that take the plunge, with the security of clear goals, guidelines, and a strategy behind them, it is an opportunity to demonstrate their responsiveness, tell their story, correct misconceptions, and build relationships. Even for those who are not quite ready to fully engage, there are benefits. Simply by listening—by tracking phrases and following key influencers—companies can get real insights into what makes their stakeholders tick.

So, from regarding social media largely as a reputation risk, companies are now also starting to see them as an opportunity—not just for brand marketing, but for corporate communications and corporate reputation management too.

For this to be successful, social media channels must not be treated in isolation but as a part of a company's wider online communications. This is a strategy that has the corporate website at its heart.

Opening Up

Corporate websites were never really as Jeremiah Owyang contended—"an unbelievable collection of hyperbole, artificial branding and pro-corporate content."[21] As we have seen, even at their worst they were far more likely to be dull and flat than hyperbolic.

The real target of Owyang's blog post seems to be not so much corporate sites but brand sites, with consumers the only stakeholders in the picture. Companies may be advised to "fish where the fish are"; the assumption is that audiences are not on the company site. But although, as we've suggested, social media channels are important for corporates, corporate audiences are, for the most part, still coming to the corporate website—over the last three years, our analytics show an average year-on-year growth in website visits of 22% a year for a group of FTSE100 peers.[22]

It is important not to be complacent; social media are clearly not a trend to be ignored. It is also true that audience behavior can and does change—for example, it would be foolish not to heed projections that more people will access the Internet via mobiles than from their desktops by 2015.[23]

What's more, the audiences for the corporate site may be widening beyond the traditional ones. As Keith Weed, chief marketing and communication officer for Unilever, has put it in an interview with Brand Republic (referring to an earlier version of the Unilever site): "I don't think that a lot of company sites have realised that their biggest users now are consumers. And we're guilty as well. Go on to Unilever.com, we're still very corporate. That will change. We're still very corporate in our face to the outside world, because it is positioned to a financial analyst or a journalist. The truth of the matter is over 60% of the people that go to Unilever.com now are consumers and future employees..."[24]

In response, some corporate sites have opened up as platforms for opinion and debate, engaging directly with stakeholders—including the general public. This is taking reputation management to a company's audiences, rather than relying on a reactive, micromanagement approach.

Timberland, for instance, runs a number of blogs on its site, including "Rantings of a responsible CEO"[25] from Jeff Swartz, the company's CEO. At the time of writing, the company is being sold and the blog has not been updated for a few months. However, it has been hugely influential over the years, adding richness and depth to the company's story as Jeff Swartz talks personally and passionately about the sustainability issues that have been at the heart of Timberland's business.

Another example comes from Centrica.[26] The company pulls together blog posts, government consultation responses, video, web chats, and social media feeds on its corporate site, creating an opportunity to talk not just about the business itself but also about wider energy issues (Centrica is one of The Group's clients). This is a long way away from the corporate boilerplate comfort zone. And a responsive and proactive integrated approach is a big part of what makes it work.

The Integrated Website—At the Heart of Corporate Reputation-Building Online

An integrated approach is vital to managing corporate reputation online. As we've already seen, that means a site where corporate values and brand are expressed appropriately through all its sections, to all stakeholders. Such an approach encompasses consistent messaging and a company story that, while anchored from the website, is integrated across all online stakeholder communications. And it's also about how connections are made between the corporate website and the rest of a company's online estate, from social media channels to commercial sites.

The latter can be understood via a hub-and-spoke model, with the website as the central hub and the corporate social media channels and the company's other sites as the spokes. Here, where social media are concerned, an integrated approach allows companies to manage corporate reputation by harnessing the best of both worlds—

the directness, immediacy, and reach of social media, and the space, security, and longevity which the website provide.

Integration with other parts of a company's Web estate—say, a local site or a commercial one—is about guiding people from the corporate site to the content that is most suitable for them, as well as about providing a link back to the corporate context for those who are already there. In this way, companies can help to manage their reputation by providing a framework by which all elements of their presence can be understood.

But an integrated approach to the website and online reputation management isn't only about directing audiences to appropriate content and driving traffic. It also allows companies to raise awareness by playing to the strengths of various online channels. Dell, for instance, has used its investor relations blog, Twitter, YouTube, StockTwits, and Slideshare to announce its financial results,[27] with the information integrated and anchored for the long-term on the investor relations section of its website.[28]

And finally, although the integrated website is not about crisis communications, it can be extremely useful in that context. More than one year on from the Deepwater Horizon accident, BP was continuing to integrate, curate, and develop relevant information on its website.[29]

One question remains. Why aren't more companies taking advantage of the potential synergy between the corporate website and the rest of their online estate—especially social media—to manage their reputation online?

Our research into social media take-up by the FTSE100[30] has shown that adoption is actually on the increase, particularly for Twitter and Facebook. Some companies do still remain wary. We can only speculate why, but a fear of loss of control and legal barriers, along with a siloed approach to communication, may be factors.

Governance and planning are the key issues here, and not just for social media. An integrated online communications strategy, with the corporate website at its center and clear links between different channels, including social media, can help companies to navigate these sometimes choppy waters and emerge with reputations enhanced.

The Hub and Spoke Model of Integration

The relationship between the corporate website and the rest of a company's online estate—in particular, its corporate social media channels—can be understood by a hub-and-spoke model. The website is the central hub and the corporate social media channels are the outlying, but connected, spokes.

The site's role isn't a static one. As the center of communications, it should promote the corporate social media channels and drive a consistent approach to the way the company communicates on each. Each social media channel should also link back to the corporate site (as well as promote the other channels), both in its profile and in the content it publishes.

And so the site comes into its own as a reputation hub, where information can be focused, curated, expanded on, and shared again. The corporate blog, hosted on the company site, has a particularly valuable role to play here as a place where ideas and issues can be taken up and treated in more detail, before being promoted again via social media.

Case Study

SABMiller Responds to Allegations by ActionAid*

In November 2010, charity and NGO ActionAid published a report accusing brewing giant SABMiller of being involved in "aggressive tax planning" in Africa. SABMiller refuted all of ActionAid's allegations and used the blog on its corporate website—as well as Twitter and Facebook—to respond quickly and decisively.

To support its allegations online, ActionAid's activity included video, a Facebook campaign, and spreading the news via Twitter. SABMiller monitored this activity and the reaction to it and responded to the issues raised on its blog and in a number of "Media insider" updates on its site. It also added new information to the site from an independent academic expert that emphasized the major economic contribution, including tax payments, which the company makes.

The blog, written by an identifiable individual and open to comments, allowed the company to take up, address, and expand on specific points raised by the ActionAid campaign. Posts and updates were then clearly promoted on the corporate site—which saw a large increase of traffic—and via the company's social media channels.

SABMiller's measured and timely response demonstrates the merits of putting the corporate website at the heart of reputation management online. Not only did the company mobilize its online channels to respond directly and visibly to the threat to its reputation in real time, but the heart of its response—the extended comment on its website—remains as a clear and findable long-term statement of the company position.

* SABMiller is a client of The Group.

Conclusion

As the reach of social media continues to expand, the more important does integration become. And with the proliferation of application program interfaces (APIs), the opportunities for integration become ever richer. According to Facebook, every month more than 250 million people engage with Facebook on external websites, and more than 2.5 million websites have integrated with Facebook.[31] Jeremiah Owyang, no less, has declared 2011 to be the year of integration.[32]

The corporate website must constantly evolve, staying abreast of this and all future developments. It is not something to launch and forget about, but a business asset that must be managed, audited, measured, and constantly updated.

At its best—integrated, flexible, responsive, and at the heart of the corporate online ecosystem—the corporate website is at the forefront of corporate reputation management online.

Summary and Further Steps

The integrated corporate website has a key role to play in the management of corporate reputation online. It is not a one-off project, to launch and leave, but an ongoing business asset that should be constantly evolving.

▸▸ Establish your online communications strategy, placing the website at its heart.
▸▸ Audit your existing corporate website and online web estate.
▸▸ Integrate your story consistently across your online communications.
▸▸ Explore more flexible online communications channels to complement your website content—blogs, Twitter, YouTube, Facebook.
▸▸ Monitor and measure your online communications; even if your company does not use social media, you should be aware of online conversations about your business and the issues that you are interested in.
▸▸ Set governance processes to guide your ongoing online communications.

More Info

Book:

Fombrun, Charles J. *Reputation: Realizing Value from the Corporate Image.* Boston, MA: Harvard Business School Press, 1996.

Websites:

Brand Republic: www.brandrepublic.com

Centrica: www.centrica.com

The Group: www.the-group.net

Jeremiah Owyang: www.web-strategist.com/blog

Jeremiah Owyang on Twitter: twitter.com/jowyang

SABMiller: www.sabmiller.com

ReputationXchange: reputationxchange.com

Notes

1. Fombrun (1996), p. 37.
2. Internet growth statistics: www.internetworldstats.com/emarketing.htm
3. Gaia Insight study of traffic to a group of FTSE100 corporate websites from 2001–11 (unpublished research).
4. Haurant, Sandra. "Q&A: Maclaren pushchair recall and British customers." *Guardian* (November 10, 2009). Online at: tinyurl.com/y8959os
5. Reckitt Benckiser: www.rb.com/home
6. YouTube statistics: www.youtube.com/t/press_statistics
7. Burns, Matt. "ComScore: YouTube now 25 percent of all Google searches." *TechCrunch* (December 18, 2008). Online at: tinyurl.com/6e5t6et
8. *Twitter Blog.* "#numbers." March 14, 2011. Online at: blog.twitter.com/2011/03/numbers.html
9. *Twitter Blog.* "200 million tweets per day." June 30, 2011. Online at: tinyurl.com/62fvokv
10. Ehrlich, Brenna. "Facebook hits 750 million users." *Mashable* (July 6, 2011). Online at: mashable.com/2011/07/06/facebook-750-million
11. Facebook statistics: www.facebook.com/press/info.php?statistics
12. Edelman "2009 Edelman trust barometer." 2009. Online at: www.edelman.com/trust/2009/docs/Trust_Book_Final_2.pdf
13. BP Public Relations on Twitter: twitter.com/BPglobalpr
14. BP America on Twitter: twitter.com/BP_America
15. Definition of "dooced" on Urban Dictionary: www.urbandictionary.com/define.php?term=dooced
16. Kee, Tameka. "Dominos pranksters done in by crowdsourcing." *paidContent* (April 14, 2009). Online at: paidcontent.org/article/419-caught-by-the-crowd-how-social-media-forces-corporate-accountability
17. Farey-Jones, Daniel. "Crisis-hit Eurostar discovers social media users want more than marketing." *Brand Republic* (December 20, 2009). Online at: tinyurl.com/65u7cdu
18. BBC News. "Habitat sorry for Iran tweeting." June 24, 2009. Online at: news.bbc.co.uk/1/hi/8116869.stm
19 Owyang, Jeremiah. "Web strategy: How to evolve your irrelevant corporate website." *Web Strategy* (May 29, 2007). Online at: tinyurl.com/6ze6vv
20. Shankland, Stephen. "Will Facebook replace company web sites?" *CNet* (March 2, 2011). Online at: news.cnet.com/8301-30685_3-20038242-264.html
21. Owyang, *op. cit.* 19.
22. Gaia Insight study of traffic to the corporate websites of 11 FTSE100 companies from 2008-11 (unpublished research).
23. Mary Meeker, Scott Devitt, and Liang Wu. "Internet trends." Morgan Stanley, April 12, 2010. Online at: tinyurl.com/y8zyet8 [PDF].
24. Durrani, Arif. "Unilever announces crowdsourcing success and a new website." *Brand Republic* (October 12, 2010). Online at: tinyurl.com/68xacel
25. Jeff Swartz's Timberland blog: blog.timberland.com/category/jeff-swartz
26. Centrica : www.centrica.com
27. See the following for a fuller description of this. Jones, Dominic. "Dell Inc. breaks new ground for social media in investor relations." *IR Web Report* (February 16, 2011). Online at: tinyurl.com/645ljuz
28. Dell investor relations: content.dell.com/us/en/corp/about-dell-investor.aspx
29. BP Gulf of Mexico restoration: tinyurl.com/4b6z2tm
30. The Group, resources: www.the-group.net/229-resources
31. Facebook, *op. cit.* 11.
32. Owyang, Jeremiah. "Slides: Social business forecast: 2011 the year of integration (LeWeb Keynote)." *Web Strategy* (December 9, 2010). Online at: tinyurl.com/683voal

Digital Reputation Management
by Shireen Smith

Azrights Solicitors, London, UK

This Chapter Covers

▸▸ The impact of Web 2.0 and social media.
▸▸ Managing reputations: proactively and reactively.
▸▸ Gauging the company's online presence.
▸▸ Handling negative content.
▸▸ Search engine optimization, forums, defamation.
▸▸ Anonymity, enforcement, litigation and jurisdiction.
▸▸ Monitoring conversations, and engagement.
▸▸ Putting in place a strategy.

Introduction

The changes happening in the world with the arrival of social media are having a far-reaching impact on the ways we do business, communicate with one another, and engage with our customers. The impact of social media as a communication channel is apparent when we compare it to earlier developments in society (Table 1).

Table 1. Growth of media formats

Medium	Time taken to reach 50 million users[1]
Radio	38 years
Television	13 years
Internet	4 years
iPod	3 years
Facebook	200 million in 1 year

Yet we are still at an early stage of this revolution in society. In the early days of the Internet, when websites and email addresses were uncommon, we gradually began to see what were then odd-looking address details appearing on people's business cards and letterheads. Nowadays, any business without a blog, Facebook page, and Twitter account is behind the times, and people are increasingly putting their Twitter handles and other social media address details on their business cards.

Key in this new age of instant global communications, where the influence and reach of word of mouth is growing, is effective management of your business reputation. To grow and prosper, companies need to build reputational capital among all stakeholders. Although a company has many different stakeholders, each one reacting to a specific facet of its business (as employee, supplier, financial investor, or client), in fact they are all sensitive to the company's ability to meet the expectations of all its stakeholders.

As there is a link between reputation and share performance, companies are very sensitive about their reputation nowadays and appreciate the need to manage their visibility and actions to maximize reputational capital. How quickly trust in an organization can be lost is evident from the damage to Ratner when its CEO called the jewelry which the company sold "crap" in 1991. After this, and a subsequent comment that Ratner's earrings were "cheaper than an M&S prawn sandwich but probably wouldn't last as long," the value of the business dropped by £500 million, as the share price went from £4 to 10 pence.

Reputation is a judgment from the market that needs to be preserved. Changes in reputation affect all stakeholders. Monitoring reputation is designed to ensure that the behavior and performance of the business consistently meet or exceed expectations. With the growing importance of social media, companies are extending their monitoring to include online discussions.

Web 2.0

As participation in social media platforms such as Facebook, LinkedIn, Twitter, and blogging increases, it becomes necessary to know what is being said about you in order to protect reputation. Whether a company is a web-based business or a bricks and mortar one, it needs to understand that conversations about it will take place online regardless of whether or not it takes part in them.

It's hard to remember a time when only those with specialized skills could post content online. Yet it was only a few years ago that the development of blogging platforms, enabled by Web 2.0 technologies, made it possible for those without specialist web skills to freely communicate online. It is not an exaggeration to say that this change has revolutionized society. The fact that so many people are engaging in discussions on the Web, and are commenting on blogs, forums, and social media sites—sometimes anonymously—is one reason that companies need to keep up with these trends and monitor the digital space.

What makes comments a matter of serious concern is that they can be instantly and indefinitely accessible to millions of people around the world. If a consumer is dissatisfied with a product or service, Web 2.0 makes it possible for them to broadcast their disappointment worldwide. This takes on more sinister significance, as what may have originally been a grumble down the pub heard by a handful of people is captured and remains there for everyone to see, possibly for years.

Even if the original site where the adverse comment was posted has disappeared, the comment may remain cached in a search engine or appear on other websites or blogs. Indeed, it matters a lot on what type of site comments appear. The important point is that whether there is any truth to online smears is immaterial. Once a smear is on the Internet, it's in the public sphere, where it stays. Therefore, as people react more and more to names and reputations, to rumors and word of mouth, and given that so many conversations are taking place online, management of digital word of mouth is more necessary than on any other medium. Being able to respond quickly and appropriately to whatever is discovered is one of the fundamental pillars of online reputation management.

Managing Reputation

There are two ways in which a company's reputation may need to be defended: proactively, or reactively. The best policy is to be proactive and put in place a plan for how the organization will address its reputation management, including its reaction to disaster. The company should be properly prepared in case it is affected by a situation that calls for a fast reaction.

Such situations sometimes arise due to the company's own strategy going awry, as in the case of a campaign by CE Europe to promote its *Resident Evil* video game, which led users to believe that their mobile phones had been infected by the "T-Virus," resulting in panicked telephone calls to antivirus providers.

Proactive reputation management involves taking steps to prepare for deliberate or accidental damage to the good name of the business. Reactive reputation defense is when you've suffered damage and need to put it right after the event.

There are many threats online; however, social media and conversations are the greatest threats to a company's reputation and should be managed proactively at the earliest opportunity.

Gauging the Company's Online Presence

Google accounts for 50% of all Internet searches. Many Google searchers reportedly never look beyond the first 10 links. For businesses and individuals worldwide, this means that their most visible reputation is dictated by 10 blue links and a few lines of text.

If your business is "ABCFashion" and your potential customers are searching for information about you, their first impression is most likely influenced not by your official website, but by the information that comes up when they conduct a Google search. The first or second link might be to the official "ABCFashion.com" site. But what if among the other search results in the top 10 there is one featuring links to a disgruntled review of one of the company's brands, a forum thread entitled "ABCFashion has its clothes manufactured by a company using child slave labor—boycott them," or even a dedicated complaints blog called BoycottABCFashion.com!

It is immaterial whether the comments on the negative sites are inaccurate. The problem is that just like in the offline world, first impressions count. No matter how good your official website, those negative sites are going to sit in the minds of your potential customers and contacts, and will raise doubts. The potential customer could pass over your organization and seek out a company with a more favorable online presence.

There are established ways in which a positive identity for the business may be created and a prominent online presence cultivated. Being active on Twitter—a high-ranking site on Google—is an important way to manage the company's reputation, while also helping it to occupy one of the first 10 links on Google. A good online presence reduces the likelihood of isolated incidents rising to the first page of Google.

Negative Content

If there is negative content found about the company, what can be done? People's first instinct is to want to do everything they can to get the negative content removed. After all, if someone spray-painted something about your business on the wall of your shop, you would want it removed as quickly as possible. Unfortunately, when it comes to online content, having items deleted is not always straightforward. On many occasions, efforts to force people to remove online comment have backfired.

A "softly softly" approach generally achieves a better outcome online than heavy-handedly removing negative content. You could respond by putting across your side in a constructive and positive way.

Examples of mistakes by others include that made by AOL Time Warner when it sent cease and desist letters to a number of Harry Potter fan pages prior to the completion of the official website. This led to considerable animosity in the online community. In response, an alliance of UK fan site owners devoted substantial efforts to alerting the public to what they considered to be the "despicable" actions of AOL Time Warner.

 PageRank is a measurement of the value of a webpage used by Google to order search results. Hundreds of factors contribute, but one of the key elements is the number and quality of other websites that link to a page.

Search Engine Optimization (SEO)

SEO has its place in online reputation management, as it's aimed at increasing your website's performance in the "organic" search results (that is, the results that appear in a search engine because that search engine considers your site to be relevant to the surfer's search terms). It doesn't take long to realize that if your content appears in front of buyers at the time they're searching for products or services, your reputation could benefit by the exposure. Using SEO to build up a strong online presence is an effective way to prevent problems by ensuring that websites with favorable mentions of your company, not negative sites, are the ones that customers see when they search for your product or service. The goal is to make negative content less likely to become prominent, pushing it out of top search results with your own material.

Occasionally, it might be appropriate to engage the services of an SEO company to manipulate the search results with the aim of eliminating negative content. It's important to be clear whether SEO is the correct strategy for *reacting* to negative content, though. For example, if an adverse comment is on a site with a high Google PageRank score (such as the BBC or other news organization), it's not really feasible for SEO to displace that site from the first page of Google. Other strategies would be more effective, and valuable time could be lost by implementing SEO as the solution.

A page with damaging content and a low PageRank score might still appear in normal search results despite an otherwise low ranking. For example, it is possible to appear *above* normal results on page one by using paid advertisements on the company's name for Google's AdWords service. Google's policy on keyword and trademark use has been the subject of a string of legal cases. Discussing these is outside the scope of this article beyond mentioning that it is possible for objectionable content to be promoted with sponsored links.

Even if you decide that SEO is an appropriate way to respond to negative content, it's important to select a company carefully. Certain SEO approaches offer benefits in the short term, that can lead to a website being penalized by search engines later. This would work against long-term goals, as well as potentially impacting adversely on the company's reputation.

Given that many websites are frequented by tens or hundreds of thousands of users irrespective of your SEO efforts (for example, popular discussion forums), SEO is often not appropriate if you discover the existence of adverse comments.

When responding to negative comments, it is important to know what to ignore, and how to deal with the rest. Ignoring a bad review is generally not advisable, but attracting attention or alienating prospective customers with an inappropriate official response is also undesirable. A typical reaction from companies that find negative material online is to try to have it removed by contacting the owner of the website, directory, or forum. The circumstances when it is acceptable to request Google directly to remove content from its index are rare.

Forums

Forum operators are unlikely to be amenable to requests for the removal of poor reviews. The Electronic Commerce Regulations[2] provide some immunity for them and for website hosts, which they lose in certain circumstances, such as when they have been alerted to contentious content on their site. So, for a request for removal to be persuasive, the offending content will likely need to be clearly defamatory or otherwise against the law.

Often, in practice, the only available recourse is to respond to the forum comment. But beware of posting official comments which come close to marketing. They will not be well received, and will often be prohibited by the forum's terms of use.

On the other hand, posting unofficial positive comments using false identities (often referred to as "astroturfing") is one of 31 items in a nonexhaustive list of practices banned outright by the Consumer Protection from Unfair Trading Regulations 2008,[3] and which can attract investigation, prosecution, and a fine. Quite apart from such regulations, responding under false identities could have other adverse consequences. Social media communities value transparency, openness, and engagement, so the company's reputation management efforts are likely to be better received if negative feedback is dealt with in a transparent and nondefensive manner.

Legal professionals who understand branding and reputation management are unlikely to be defamation or litigation lawyers. Yet many litigation law firms brand themselves as reputation management experts on the Web. Litigators are in reality ill-equipped to advise a company's PR or other department on reputation management because the advice should rarely be to take legal action.

Defamation

Many comments that people make, and which could be extremely damaging to a brand, may well not amount to libel. Even if comments are defamatory, whether or not you should resort to litigation is a matter to consider carefully. Reasons not to do so are provided by the number of high-profile instances where a legal or heavy-handed approach online has backfired.

The Streisand Effect

The seminal example of this concerned the publication online of a photograph of Barbara Streisand's residence. On hearing that her villa was pictured on the Internet, Streisand began legal proceedings to have it removed, with disastrous consequences. Rather than having her privacy respected by suppressing the photograph, the action attracted an enormous amount of attention from website operators and eventually the media. The exposure gained would have been difficult to replicate had her intention been to publicize the image rather than hide it.

This episode brought into Internet vocabulary the term Streisand effect, which is now synonymous with any action designed to suppress material online but which has the unintended consequence of amplifying it.

Since then, there have been a number of incidences of this phenomenon, such as the Trafigura scandal. There, an injunction brought to prevent publication of a question asked in the UK Parliament triggered media interest, bolstering public awareness of the report about Trafigura's dumping of toxic waste in the Ivory Coast. This caused far more serious damage to Trafigura's reputation than might have otherwise occurred. Certainly the legal action did nothing to help.

Who Is Responsible, and Where Are They Based?

More recently, in May 2011, the use of injunctions to gag the press led to a "Streisand effect" for the litigant footballer who sought an injunction to prevent the publication of details of his alleged affair. Perhaps predictably, this led to increased media and public interest as more and more people on Twitter took to naming him, in contravention of the terms of the injunction.

Aside from showing how legal action to suppress information can have undesirable consequences, these examples illustrate that, although litigation specialists are key in securing an outcome once a strategy has been decided on, a different type of expertise is relevant when coming to that decision. Litigators, though experts in their field, are inappropriate managers of corporate reputation.

Litigation and Jurisdiction

Two important issues when considering litigation are the enforceability of orders against defendants in jurisdictions beyond the reach of English courts, and whether it will be possible to identify those responsible for posting material online.

Despite the existence of what was initially billed as a "super injunction" to prevent the footballer's identity being revealed, the terms of the injunction were widely breached by Twitter users. Twitter is based in the United States, and the order being enforced was granted by a UK court. Under such circumstances, the subject of an order will not necessarily feel obliged to comply, and due to the global nature of the Internet, an injunction is rendered ineffective.

That is not to say that a UK business cannot take legal action in these circumstances. In contrast to the footballer case, a group of councillors in South Tyneside successfully obtained an order *from a US court* forcing Twitter to disclose contact details and IP addresses of users allegedly responsible for libelous messages by suing in the US courts.

It is worth noting that even where details of the email or user account are disclosed, further information may be necessary to identify the person who is physically in control of that account. This means that sometimes there may be no recourse if there is no authentic name or email address to trace the identity of the person behind the pseudonym or anonymous comment.

A user's IP address does not necessarily identify them. IP addresses are often not fixed, and might be reassigned from one Internet connection to another quite regularly. Also, IP addresses are tied to Internet connections rather than to individuals. The same IP address might be shared between a number of devices and a number of different people. In the case of a wireless network, an unscrupulous next-door neighbor might be hijacking the Internet connection.

So, this is another complex issue to address when deciding what action to take— whether the result will lead to successful identification, and whether the court orders obtained will be enforceable.

Social Media Sites

For businesses, six important services are:

- ▸ Facebook.com
- ▸ LinkedIn.com
- ▸ Twitter.com
- ▸ Quora.com
- ▸ Foursquare.com
- ▸ Ecademy.com

Engaging in Online Conversations

Web 2.0 has spawned social media platforms and online conversations. An effective reputation management program should involve "engagement"—i.e., participating in conversations—alongside monitoring. There is much discussion among social media enthusiasts about the importance and meaning of "engagement." Given the strength of opinion among vociferous sections of the online community about what is "proper engagement," some methods of managing reputation on social media platforms could themselves create a reputational risk.

Understanding the issues before settling your social media strategy, using Twitter, or outsourcing your tweeting, makes sense. It helps to consider in advance what the company will use a platform for. A clear plan of action should be implemented. If the intention is to send out corporate news predominantly via Twitter, the company should be aware that people speak disparagingly of those who "broadcast" promotional messages about their business without listening to what anyone else is saying.

Building some engagement into the plan could considerably enhance how others experience the company.

Therefore, on a day-to-day level, protecting a company's reputation requires active communication and participation in conversations with consumers and others. Many large organizations are using Twitter as a customer service platform, as it is the first place where disgruntled consumers voice their dissatisfaction about a company. By actively listening for negative comments, a company can do a lot to listen, learn, and limit damage to its reputation.

Dell is a good example of a company that had a very poor online customer feedback record but transformed itself by, among other things, creating a number of different Twitter profiles to handle customer service and market its offers. Subsequently, Dell announced that its Twitter strategy had resulted in US$3 million of revenue over two years.

Interestingly, Dell's Twitter accounts, like @DellOutlet, encourage discussion and can be used to provide direct and responsive advice to customers online—for example, where they have difficulties using a website. This approach helped Dell to build a strong community of customer advocates and to quickly respond to community concerns.

Engagement does not come easily to many organizations, especially large ones with different departments that are responsible for distinct aspects of a company's operations. A new dynamic comes into play when the organization is unable to *control* messages about its brand and instead has to *respond to* whatever messages consumers choose to communicate (such as on forums). Corporate reputation boils down to consumer trust, and trust is difficult to control.

Monitoring Conversations

The sheer volume of information makes it difficult to keep track of online comments and to identify which are significant. Therefore, choosing tools appropriate to the size and type of organization is critical, as is the decision about which keywords to monitor.

The development of an emotional commitment to companies by their consumers is now a critical business success issue. Companies may aim to build up this kind of commitment by being part of trusted organizations, trying to create a brand that stands for more than the product or service, or by associating themselves with popular causes, such as green policies.

Employees' and other stakeholders' reputations also have a strong impact on the company's reputation. The degree to which their personal name affects the company name depends on how well known they are, and what role they occupy in the business.

The reputational risks that can impact on stakeholders of a business include incidents like unethical employee behavior, suppliers' business practices, involvement in unpopular conduct (such as that which harms the environment or the safety or security of citizens), having sexist, racist, or similar policies, or backing unpopular causes.

Putting a Strategy in Place

When a company is considering its approach to online reputation management, it is worth bearing in mind the six pillars of global reputation (according to Fombrun, Gardberg, and Server, 2000):[4]

- ▸▸ emotional appeal (trust, admiration, and respect);
- ▸▸ products and services (quality, innovativeness, value for money, etc.);
- ▸▸ vision and leadership;
- ▸▸ workplace quality (well-managed, appealing workplace, employee talent);
- ▸▸ financial performance;
- ▸▸ social responsibility.

Monitoring online reputation is not simply a case of watching out for mentions of the corporate name on Twitter or other platforms. It is also necessary for the company to avoid reputational damage in the myriad other ways in which its reputation could suffer, such as being associated with the wrong partners (those whose activities become embarrassing), having the wrong employees, or backing the wrong causes.

Once such risks to the corporate reputation have been identified, representative keywords should be selected so that the company receives an early alert to possible problems. If the company markets a variety of products or services, it will want to track mentions of the different brand names; it may also want to be alerted when directors and other senior figures in the organization are discussed; it will also likely be interested in what its competitors are doing.

A number of keywords will need to be monitored. In a large company, different departments may have different risk areas which they will want to address by monitoring their own individual keywords.

The most effective reputation management strategy will monitor all six pillars of global reputation mentioned earlier. Successful strategies for the management of reputation risks rely not only on vigilance and staying informed, but also on a readiness to respond quickly and effectively to problems as and when they arise.

Putting a plan of action and an effective team together for online communication is key to success. It is much less possible to control how consumers perceive the business, and all manner of unpredictable events can happen. An effective strategy is to bring together an interdisciplinary team drawing on the skills of various functions within the company which may need to be involved, including the marketing, IT, PR, and legal departments.

Such a team, once put together, should designate responsibilities so that it is ready and able to make swift decisions in a crisis. Only then does the organization give itself a good chance to react instantly to whatever happens, and to develop the know-how to deal with any scenario that arises. With this structure in place, the company will be able to engage with potential and actual consumers while accessing the knowledge and skills of whichever department needs to be involved on a particular question.

Taking a purely legal approach may sometimes be appropriate, as where there is clear defamation. At other times, a cease and desist letter may have its place, and recovery of a domain name may avoid unnecessary expense and aggravation. Other types of response may suggest themselves in some cases. Knowing when to ignore a disgruntled consumer will also be important—it can take a lot of energy to maintain anger, so will it simply burn out?

A well-led team with clear lines of responsibility delegated to members helps the organization to negotiate its way in social media. This may explain why there are so many general counsels on Twitter, and why in-house lawyers tend to be streets ahead of commercial lawyers in private practice when it comes to understanding the risks new media influences represent for corporate reputations.

Free and Paid Reputation Management Tools

Many of the reputation-monitoring tools on the market are designed to measure sentiment following marketing initiatives. A key consideration in effective monitoring is establishing a process for easy access and review of online material, bearing in mind that the volume of discussion to be monitored could be vast. Collecting the data can be quite straightforward, but making them manageable is another issue altogether. A dashboard is the popular approach to dealing with this, and involves constructing an interface that presents new data in one place, and in an accessible way.

The keywords to track should be words or phrases of interest which are not too general. The aim is to flag up interesting material without being overloaded with irrelevant chatter.

There are many paid reputation-monitoring services on offer, with a variety of price plans. Deciding which to select depends on whether the number of keywords to be tracked will increase the charges. If so, the paid services can become prohibitively expensive. Any business with a broad product range, and keywords such as those representing the names of directors, heads of departments, suppliers, investors, marketing campaigns, clients, and competitors, will find it sensible to carry out some in-house monitoring using free tools, even when a paid service is used as well. The company will then be able to monitor more terms, which is desirable for effective reputation monitoring.

Drawing on a selection of the many free tools, such as Google Alerts,[5] it is possible to put together your own monitoring platform and bring the results together in RSS feeds, which can be fed into a dashboard using something like Google Reader. This results in a single webpage that pulls together recent mentions of your keywords from a wide variety of sources for easy access.

However, ensuring that a wide net is cast, so that relevant content is collected from a broad cross section of the web, can be time-consuming to set up, as can arranging this information into an easily digestible format. The optimum combination of paid or free tools will also depend on the keywords chosen and the reasons for monitoring.

Conclusion

It is realistic to expect that, of the hundreds of millions of people online, some will occasionally have a negative comment about the company. It is also useful to know that when something plays out on the social media, it can erupt in a matter of hours. Reaction time can be critical. Therefore, any strategic plan should enable even a large organization to react very rapidly. Situations can creep up on a business all too quickly. Something trivial or which starts off in a minor way can escalate rapidly and catch people and organizations unawares.

Hopefully this article has explained why online conversations pose a unique threat to reputation, and highlighted some of the challenges, both in determining what to monitor, and in limiting the possible impact on stakeholders.

Summary and Further Steps

▶▶ Word of mouth on social media presents unique challenges.
▶▶ Reputation impacts on share price and the company's stakeholders.
▶▶ Businesses need to be alert to online conversations, even if they do not operate online.
▶▶ Freely available tools allow you to monitor reputation in-house.
▶▶ Bringing together an interdisciplinary team for online communication is helpful.

More Info

Books:

Beal, Andy, and Judy Strauss. *Radically Transparent: Monitoring and Managing Reputations Online.* Indianapolis, IN: Wiley, 2008.

Brown. Rob. *How to Build Your Reputation.* Penryn, UK: Ecademy Press, 2007. Includes a valuable foreword by Sir Digby Jones explaining the critical importance of reputation to businesses.

Articles:

Azrights IP Brands blog: ip-brands.com/blog

Distilled blog: www.distilled.net/blog

Mashable, an independent news site covering digital culture, social media, and technology: mashable.com

Notes

1. blog.facebook.com/blog.php?post=72353897130; www.un.org/cyberschoolbus/briefing/technology/tech.pdf
2. ss.17–19 Electronic Commerce (EC Directive) Regulations 2002.
3. These are listed in Schedule 1 to the Consumer Protection from Unfair Trading Regulations 2008.
4. Fombrun, Charles J., Naomi A. Gardberg, and Joy M. Sever. "The reputation quotient: A multi-stakeholder measure of corporate reputation." *Journal of Brand Management* 7:4 (2000): 241–255.
5. Find out more about Google Alerts at www.google.com/alerts

Digital Strategies for Enhancing Reputation

by Paul A. Argenti[a] and Georgia Aarons[b]

[a] Tuck School of Business, Dartmouth College, Hanover, NH, USA
[b] Halpern, London, UK

This Chapter Covers

» This chapter provides an overview on the changing environment for business and the impact recent scandals have had on the public's trust in corporations.

» Understanding the potential value of reputation is a competitive advantage, and knowledge of the potential value of reputation and specific messages can drive communication strategy. Reputation must be measured and managed.

» With the rise of social media, reputation management is more challenging than ever, but those companies that embrace change have an opportunity to reposition themselves.

Introduction: The World We Live In

TMI. Of all the acronyms to enter the hallowed pages of the *Oxford English Dictionary* in 2011, this one may be the most apt in describing the world we now live in. Of the thousands of media impressions each of us faces on a daily basis, it seems that many relate to leaked information and corporate scandal, be it investment guru Warren Buffett's involvement in an insider trading deal, the *News of the World* phone-hacking scandal, or the most illicit, US Congressman Anthony Weiner's sweatpants[1]—TMI, or too much information, indeed.

These headlines underscore a central irony of today's environment: never has trust in business been lower, yet never has it been more important. Beginning most notably in 2001 with the infamous dissolution of Enron, corporate scandals have become ubiquitous in recent years, and trust in business institutions has subsequently dropped. In the 2011 Edelman Trust Barometer, only 46% of Americans and 44% of Britons polled said that they trusted business to do what's right; despite this decline, respondents ranked "transparent and honest business practices" as the second most important factor influencing corporate reputation.[2]

This rise in public scrutiny correlates strongly with the emergence of new digital communications platforms and their widespread adoption. An ever-growing list of interactive tools has given stakeholders the ability to communicate with one another, to disseminate messaging, and, ultimately, to threaten companies' increasingly vulnerable reputations. A third of the world's population uses these tools, or more than two billion people.[3] Where before, messages were created by executives to meet the needs of particular groups, information can now be shared and interpreted by billions of people. For the first time in marketing history, consumers are as influenced by their peers as by the company behind the message.[4] The result is that companies have never been less in control of their messaging. This uneasy reality requires business leaders worldwide to redefine their strategies and brands in the context of these new platforms, and to find a way to use them to their advantage.

This chapter provides an overview of the current business environment and the reputational challenges that have emerged with the growth of digital channels. We will take a closer look at reputation and how it relates to identity, brand, and image, and more importantly, examine why reputation matters. Finally, we will outline the strategies and tactics needed to regain control by exploiting new channels.

Today's Business Environment

Over the course of the last decade, a number of factors came together to catalyze a massive change in the way business is conducted around the world: a decline in trust following the wake of corporate scandals and a turbulent economy; intense public scrutiny of business; disillusionment over excessive executive pay; the growth of digital communications platforms; and the impact of an interwoven "global village."

Corporate Scandal and Credit Crisis Lead to Decline in Trust

Although corporate malfeasance was by no means unheard of in the twentieth century, a stream of scandals began in 2001 that rattled the public's trust in business. Enron was the first major headline; its fraudulent accounting practices were exposed to an already skeptical public, which was still recovering from the bursting dot.com bubble. One could argue that after 2001 the landscape went from bad to worse: in 2002, approximately 81% of surveyed investors "did not have much confidence in those running Big Business."[5] This grim statistic set the tone for what would become a common theme for corporate leaders: the decline in their credibility in the face of increased scrutiny by diverse stakeholder groups.

That many of these scandals occurred during or because of the worst economic recession since the Second World War only exacerbated the existing slide in trust. Beginning in 2007, the global credit crisis shook trust in the financial services industry to its core across all stakeholder groups. One of the major sources of public skepticism about business was compensation within the very institutions that had caused the economic downturn. It seemed that executives were rewarded for failure: the top execs of the seven major financial firms that either collapsed, were sold at low prices, or received taxpayer-funded bailouts were each paid a total of US$464 million in performance pay since 2005, according to an analysis by the *New York Times*. Those same firms lost more than US$107 billion between 2007 and 2009.[6] In total, Wall Street paid over US$144 billion in bonuses at a time when unemployment skyrocketed across the United States and Europe.[7]

Shareholder Activism

Alongside this alarming disparity grew shareholder activism. In fact, activist shareholders had been a driving force in modern investor relations for some time, since corporate scandals, including Enron, Tyco International, and ImClone Systems, Inc., became commonplace in the early 2000s. As financial malfeasance permeated the corporate world, activist investors popped up in droves. When asked what they considered to be the main driver of shareholder activism, 94% of surveyed investor relations professionals cited corporate scandals.[8] With the credit crisis and worldwide attention focused on executive compensation policies, executives found themselves fielding aggressive advances from shareholders demanding increased transparency.

One of the most outspoken was Carl Icahn, who in 2007 was responsible for forcing behemoth Time Warner to restructure four of its divisions and create a share repurchase program.[9] Icahn's website, www.icahnreport.com, has since become a platform for "comment on the desultory state of corporate governance in America."[10]

Rise of Digital Communications Platforms

Icahn's blog—his personal loudspeaker to likeminded investors—illustrates a critical point: while the rising distrust of companies and their leaders may not have been so detrimental on its own, it took place in tandem with another trend, namely the emergence and adoption of new digital communications platforms.

Before the digital explosion at the turn of the twenty-first century, corporations' reputations were shaped by one-dimensional messaging that was pushed down the corporate ladder and disseminated without discussion. But, with an ever-growing list of new tools, stakeholders—companies' employees, customers, or shareholders like Icahn—were suddenly empowered to talk back. Social communities and blogs gave stakeholders the ability to disseminate their own messaging about an organization, and to share and build communities around that information. The rise in corporate scandals and credit crisis, combined with the emergence of these new channels, created a perfect storm that radically altered the business landscape.

The Global Village

This storm occurred on a global level: technology strengthened communication channels around the world to produce what Canadian philosopher Marshall McLuhan foresaw decades ago—the creation of a world so interwoven by shared knowledge that it becomes a "global village."[11] This trend has had a monumental impact on trust in business, particularly over the last decade.

Through the Internet, people have discovered and invented new ways to share relevant knowledge with blinding speed. The data are staggering: by the end of 2010, nearly 80% of the world's population had a mobile cellular phone subscription, and more than 30% regularly used the Internet.[12] As of late 2010, Technorati tracked more than 150 million blogs.[13] Collectively, we created nearly 300 billion gigabytes of information last year.[14] These numbers translate into communications issues that simply didn't exist in the corporate world 10 years ago. The current global connectivity accentuates the volume at which negative feelings can be heard, and makes it difficult for companies to prevent negative—and positive—news from reaching people. Data suggest that these numbers will only continue to increase as consumers assume further control of corporate reputations and communicate with each other in real time, 24/7.

To summarize, the variables that traditionally acted as catalysts in reputational crises have mutated and multiplied exponentially in the face of all the factors discussed above: a decline in trust, a turbulent economy, diverse stakeholder groups' growing influence, the emergence and speed of propagation of digital communications platforms, and an increasingly global marketplace. An understanding of reputation and why reputation matters is more important now than ever.

Enhancing Strategy through Reputation Management

In the changed environment for business, corporate reputation has gained visibility and importance in the eyes of many constituencies. Reputation is now an integral driver in a company's success and credibility, but many managers who have not thought about corporate reputation continue to underestimate its value. This error is partly due to a lack of understanding about what corporate identity, brand, image, and reputation are all about, and what they can do for a business. Skeptics should understand that an inappropriate identity can be as damaging to a firm as poor financial performance. Individuals are seeking trust and transparency, and if perceptions about a company fail to mesh with reality, constituents will take their money elsewhere.

What are Identity, Brand, Image, and Reputation?

A company's *identity* is the actual manifestation of the company's reality as conveyed through the organization's name, logo, motto, products, services, building, stationery, uniforms, and all other tangible pieces of evidence created by the organization and communicated to a variety of constituencies. Constituencies then form perceptions based on the messages that companies send in these tangible forms. If the images accurately reflect an organization's reality, the identity program is a success. If the perceptions differ dramatically from the reality, then either the strategy is ineffective, or the corporation's understanding of itself needs to be modified.

Because identity is the only part of reputation management that an organization can actually create and control, it is critical that it is strategically shaped. One of the key factors that contributes to a successful corporate identity is a careful *brand*: a name or logo that differentiates the goods and services of one seller from those of its competitors. Branding is much more complex and nuanced than a swoosh or a pair of golden arches, however. A brand can provoke an emotional reaction from the consumer; a brand is a promise that sets an expectation of an experience. As marketing expert Kevin Keller explains, "the power of a brand lies in the minds of consumers."[15] A company's value can be considerably influenced by the success of its corporate branding strategy. Coca-Cola, for instance, has a value that far exceeds its total tangible assets because of its strong brand name.

An organization's *image* is a function of how constituencies perceive the organization, based on all the messages it sends out through names, logo, and self-presentation. It is the organization as seen from the viewpoint of its constituencies. But image is in the eye of the beholder: depending on the vantage point of a particular constituency, a company can have many different images. For example, employees will perceive their company's image differently than customers. Even customers who have never interacted with a product will have preconceived notions (just because you've never eaten a McDonald's hamburger doesn't mean you don't have certain perceptions about the company and the product). Large, diversified companies may also struggle to define their images. What is the image for a company as large as Tata, or one as diverse as General Electric?

Reputation is the sum of *all* of an organization's constituencies' perceptions. It differs from image in that it is built gradually, and is therefore not simply a perception in any moment of time. It differs from identity because it is a product of both internal and external constituencies, whereas identity is constructed by the company itself. A strong reputation has important strategic implications for a company, as we shall see.

Why Reputation Matters

The importance of reputation is evidenced by several prominent surveys and rankings that seek to identify the best and worst among them: *Fortune's* "Most Admired" list, *BusinessWeek* and Interbrand's "Best Global Brands" ranking, and the Reputation Institute's Global RepTrak Pulse studies. These highly publicized rankings are evidence of what many business leaders already know: that companies with strong reputations have financial and competitive advantages and experience greater stability.

Reputation is a source of tangible economic value. According to the 2008 Hill and Knowlton Corporate Reputation Watch, more than 90% of analysts agree that if a company fails to look after the reputational aspects of its performance, it will ultimately suffer financially.[16] Reputation does indeed correlate with higher market valuation and stock price, and with less stock price volatility. A comprehensive study by the Munich-based Market-Based Management Institute compared the reputation and stock-market performance of 60 blue-chip companies over the course of five years. The 25% (Top25) of companies with the best reputations considerably outperformed the companies with poorer reputations and, compared to price movements on the DAX 30 in general, the Top25 returned greater yield with lower risk.[17]

The less tangible entities of a strong reputation can also result in competitive advantage. Companies with strong reputations attract and retain the best talent, as well as loyal customers and business partners, all of which contribute positively to growth and success. Reputation "calls attention to a company's attractive features and widens the options available to its managers; for instance, whether to charge higher or lower prices for products and services, or to implement innovative programs."[18] Companies whose corporate communications promote sincerity and accuracy have greater operating leverage and the power to buck negative trends in the economy and in their respective industries. Being able to weather a corporate crisis is a particularly valuable position in an age of skepticism and mistrust, where information travels at lightning speed.

Against the backdrop of the current business environment, organizations are increasingly appreciating the financial and competitive advantages of a strong reputation. How does an organization know where it stands? How does it build trust? Since reputation is formed by the perceptions of all of their constituencies, companies must first uncover what those perceptions are and then choose their reputation strategy accordingly.

Measuring and Managing Reputation

You can't manage what you don't measure. This adage rings especially true when looking at corporate reputation. In assessing its reputation, an organization must examine the perceptions of all of its constituencies. Only when perceptions and identity are in alignment will a strong reputation result.

Many consulting firms, like the Reputation Institute (RI), have developed diagnostics for helping companies conduct this research. Nearly all of these tools require constituency research. The RI's RepTrak Alignment Monitor, for example, conducts extensive internal analysis of employee alignment. Such tools exist because companies run into trouble when they do not practice the values that they promote internally. Walmart is perhaps one of the best examples of a company that has frequently been entangled in contradictions between the values it espouses and its employees' perceptions. The company, which defines its three basic beliefs and values to be respect for the individual, service to its customers, and striving for excellence,[19] has been embroiled in a constant stream of lawsuits, including what would have been the largest employment discrimination class action in US history. However, Walmart has made significant attempts to close the gap that exists between its identity and image in other areas of its business, as we shall later discuss.

Customer perceptions of an organization must also align with identity, vision, and values. On Valentine's Day, 2007, JetBlue learned not only what can happen when this is *not* the case, but also how reputation can be restored by taking bold steps. Since it was founded, in 1999, JetBlue had prided itself on an almost cult-like following amongst its loyal customers. But on February 14, 2007, the airline faced a reputational crisis that put customer loyalty to the test: during a particularly nasty nor'easter, the airline had an operational meltdown that resulted from a combination of bad luck, flawed decision-making, and multiple systematic failures. The airline canceled more than 1,000 flights, incurring millions of dollars in losses and tarnishing its sterling reputation among customers who were stranded at its hub, JFK Airport. Yet, after a publicity nightmare and an enquiry from Congress, CEO and founder David Neeleman was inspired to search for inventive solutions to win back his constituents' loyalty. Some of those solutions, like the industry's first ever customer bill of rights, were groundbreaking, and helped JetBlue to regain, if not exceed, its reputational standing in the eyes of its customers.[20]

The Impact of Corporate Social Responsibility on Reputation

Today, reputational risk transcends simply staying out of trouble; rather, stakeholders are far more proactive in seeking out information about companies, and corporate social responsibility (CSR) now plays a larger role in forming these groups' perceptions. Study after study demonstrates that "good corporate citizenship" directly correlates with the strength of a company's reputation and its bottom line.

Consumers are increasingly preoccupied with the values and reputations of the companies with which they interact: the 2010 Cone Cause Evolution Study, for example, reveals that 83% of Americans want more of the products, services, and retailers they use to support causes. 85% of consumers have a more positive image of a product or company when it supports a cause they care about, and 90% of consumers want companies to communicate to them the ways in which they are supporting causes.[21] Strategically directed CSR programs can be key vehicles for the creation of competitive advantage.

When a company understands what each of its constituencies is concerned about, what matters to them, and what they already think about the company, it is well positioned to structure the right kinds of CSR programs. Walmart is an example of a company that has made significant progress in enhancing its corporate reputation by focusing its CSR efforts on one of the key issues which its constituents have most publicly been concerned about—environmental sustainability. In 2005, Walmart hired a sustainability and energy think-tank to conduct an efficiency overhaul and audit, and then outlined three clear environmental goals: to be supplied entirely by renewable energy, to create zero waste, and to sell products that sustain resources and the environment. The implementation of the plan cost Walmart more than US$500 million, but by talking the talk in its logistics, operations, and sales practices, the retailer has hugely enhanced its perceived environmental impact. In the 2010 *Newsweek* Green Rankings, a ranking of the top 100 global companies based on their environmental impact, green policies and performance, and reputation, Walmart ranked 39th, up from 59th the year before.[22]

To summarize, CSR programs can greatly contribute to a company's reputational capital and provide a distinct competitive advantage in an environment where constituencies increasingly expect responsible and accountable behavior, along with profit. To respond to this demand, executives must manage and measure stakeholders' perceptions, and implement new and creative ways to position themselves.

Reputation Management in a Social Media World

Thus far, we have examined the modern business environment in the context of the profound changes that have redefined the way companies interact with their stakeholders, especially in terms of the two-way conversations facilitated by digital communications platforms. Using examples set by industry leaders, we will now look at strategies and tactics that exploit these platforms and allow companies to regain the control ceded to stakeholders. Those that have embraced social media have successfully adapted to the new environment. Just as digital platforms spawn reputational crises, so too can they solve them.

From Monolog to Dialog

As digital communications have evolved, stakeholders have gained enormous influence in shaping corporate messaging. Whereas corporate communications professionals formerly fed their messaging to stakeholders in a one-way conversation, they now find themselves at the mercy of the people they once controlled, and their organizations' reputations hang in the balance. Those companies that not only embrace this two-way dialog but also recognize that it serves as a source for ideas, opinions, and competitive intelligence will be best positioned.

Dell is an excellent example of a company that has embraced social media as a means of enhancing conversations with the stakeholders it cares most about. Dell learned early on to embrace rather than ignore. Back in 2005, the computer manufacturer's reputation was thrown for a loop when an irate blogger named Jeff Jarvis lambasted the company for poor customer service ("Dell Hell," he called it). Within hours, hordes of customers who were in agreement with Jarvis's claims posted comments on his blog and their own, creating a maelstrom of negative publicity. The company struggled for months as a result of failing to address the criticism, but in July 2006 it launched its own blog, where executives could fat last join the conversation. The blog allowed customers to comment freely on this and later crises, and in February 2007 Michael Dell launched IdeaStorm, a permanent forum in which customers could give the company advice. Metrics showed that the company's customer-service rating rose significantly immediately afterwards.[23] In fact, Dell's communications team estimates that since Dell began using social media, negative comments about the company have gone down by 30%.[24]

Focus on Structure

Dell executives recognized that, in order to remain competitive, they needed to rethink the way they positioned themselves internally to have a positive impact externally. By 2009, IdeaStorm employed a chief blogger and a team of 42 people who worked hand in hand with the broader corporate communications function. Dell evolved its organizational structure to meet changing stakeholder demands, integrating an entirely new division within its communications function and giving it visibility within the company.

This is a critical lesson: at world-class companies, digital communications has morphed from a backroom tactical department to a strategic liaison between an organization and its many stakeholder groups. HP, as well, employed a digital communications team to facilitate conversations between its constituents during a period of incredible change, its 2002 merger with Compaq. Recognizing the challenges behind aligning different cultures and information management systems, HP executives developed @HP, a business-to-employee portal that acted as a gateway to the merging HP and Compaq intranets. The platform served as the infrastructure to communicate messages to all 88,000 plus employees around the globe, and ensured that the right messages were delivered to the right internal audiences. The intranet embodied the new corporate culture.

Focus on Values

As mentioned earlier, the level of concern about corporate responsibility and trust has increased dramatically in recent years, and has been amplified by the ability of digital platforms to democratize access to information. Stakeholders are increasingly demanding value for their money when purchasing goods and services, and are also expecting to see a strong set of values in the companies with which they do business. Once again, companies, like Walmart, that embrace digital tools to engage individual stakeholder groups in the context of their corporate responsibility efforts will prosper over those that run away.

CEO Howard Schultz of Starbucks incorporated an innovative crowdsourcing strategy into his plan to transform the coffee retailer, following years of overexpansion and sliding stock prices. Schultz's challenge was to "rekindle an emotional attachment with customers," and in 2009, the brand created www.mystarbucksidea.com, a forum where customers could literally submit ideas on how to make the brand better. The ideas were categorized, and users could then vote on which they thought should be implemented. Schultz also invested heavily in Starbucks' "shared planet" campaign, which marketed the company's dedication to being "bigger than coffee." Whether these crowdsourcing and CSR initiatives can be directly related to a bump in stock price is difficult to prove, but Starbuck's popularity, at least, has grown in the three years since these programs were implemented: in 2010, Starbucks reported record fiscal revenue of US$10.7 billion.[25,26]

Communicate Online Or Others Will Do It For You

In today's environment, you don't have to search too hard to find stories of corporate giants felled by lone bloggers, or more intimate disasters of celebrities and politicians whose online behavior led to their public demise. The lesson seems to be: tell your story online or have it told for you. In the age of social media, no amount of avoidance can keep crises at bay. The access to information online is staggering, and succumbing to the temptation of sweeping dirty secrets under the rug may come back to haunt an organization's reputation.

During a crisis, the best approach is to provide stakeholders with facts directly on the company's own domain, whether a corporate website, blog, or official Twitter account. Taco Bell's "real beef" campaign is a recent example of how a company can preempt a reputational disaster by acknowledging the truth and then communicating it online. When a lawsuit was announced charging that Taco Bell's taco filling was not 100% real beef, the company realized that the allegations would spread like wildfire online, and it mounted an immediate and aggressive campaign to address the claims. The corporate website had a link on the homepage to a newly created "About our seasoned beef" page with interactive videos, press releases, and statements, and a link to its signature taco meat recipe, which boldly acknowledged the additives in its taco filling. Taco Bell President Greg Creed posted videos on YouTube and messages on Facebook. He then began an online and print advertising campaign, announcing: "Thank you for suing us. Here's the truth about our seasoned beef." Under the gathering storm of public interest, the lawsuit was dropped.[27]

Opportunity to Reposition and Redevelop

Just as many reputational crises spawn from digital platforms, so too can they be managed when the Web is used effectively to regain control. As best-in-class companies demonstrate, harnessing social media actually strengthens relationships and communication. Corporate blogs, for example, open the lines of communication between company leaders and their stakeholders, as we have seen with the examples of Dell and Starbucks. The CEO blog, in particular, is a trend that allows executives to communicate directly with their customers. Twitter is yet another tool that connects brands with their consumers, which can be especially effective during emergencies. Delta Airlines, for instance, learned a thing or two from competitors like JetBlue, and now has a dedicated customer service team that rebooks stranded passengers during storms and other operational crises through Twitter.[28]

When companies empower communities with collaborative skills and tools, they have an enormous opportunity. Facilitating, instead of closing, dialogs with key constituents allows organizations to address emerging problems early. During the 2008–09 recession, Ford Motor Company took advantage of its website and social media platforms to launch live conversations among suppliers, dealers, and customers. These were designed to bring Ford's bright performance—bright compared with the looming bankruptcies and bailouts involving rivals GM and Chrysler—to everyone's attention.

Ford recognized that monitoring influential digital channels, embracing transparency, identifying affected audiences, and customizing communications for each are all critical strategies for survival in what is a new and revolutionary environment.

Conclusion

In the complex modern business environment, organizations' reputations are vulnerable to an increasingly skeptical public and the immeasurable unknowns brought to bear by digital communications platforms. Crises that affect companies today are born of things that didn't exist 10 or even five years ago: a Congressman's misguided photo on

Twitter, a British spy identified by his wife on Facebook, or Time Warner kowtowing to a lone blogger. These are unimaginable circumstances for the business environment of years ago, when information was fed to constituencies in one-way monologs.

The two-way dialog benefits both ends of the conversation, and best-in-class companies have already moved from adoption to anticipation. Brands are starting to catch up with their consumers, and they are increasingly trying to become proactive about understanding how consumers spend time online and where they're going next. Companies have also been establishing sophisticated guidelines and protocols for internal social media usage, and many institutions, like Wall Street investment banks, are starting to allow their employees to set up social media accounts specifically to communicate with clients. Over time, the best companies will learn to have better conversations with their constituents through social media engagement. The net result will be trust, loyalty, and more business.

Summary and Further Steps

▸ Today's manager has to grow and protect value in an extraordinary global economic environment. To do this, reputation must be proactively measured and managed.

▸ Don't forget that corporate reputations are determined by how well a corporate brand is crafted and conveyed to the public; brand, image and identity are all critical components of shaping your organization's reputation.

▸ Embracing social media can help today's leaders develop new ways to communicate and engage with key constituents. If you don't communicate online, someone else will do it for you. Be proactive. Fortune favors the bold.

More Info

Books:

Argenti, Paul A., and Courtney M. Barnes. *Digital Strategies for Powerful Corporate Communications*. New York: McGraw-Hill, 2009.

Keller, Kevin. *Strategic Brand Management*. 3rd ed. Upper Saddle River, NJ: Prentice Hall, 2008.

Aaker, David A. *Building Strong Brands*. New York: Free Press, 1996.

Article:

Argenti, Paul A., James Lytton-Hitchens, and Richard Verity. "The good, the bad and the trustworthy." *Strategy + Business* (November 23, 2010).
Online at: www.strategy-business.com/article/10401?gko=4adb7

Website:

2011 Edelman Trust Barometer: www.edelman.com/trust/2011/

Notes

1. Adams, Richard. "Anthony Weiner photo scandal—As it happened." *Guardian* (June 6, 2011). Online at: tinyurl.com/5spkys3
2. 2011 Edelman Trust Barometer: www.edelman.com/trust/2011/
3. Internet World Stats: Usage and Population Statistics: www.internetworldstats.com/stats.htm
4. Bernoff, Josh. "Introducing peer influence analysis: 500 billion peer impressions per year." Forrester blog (April 20, 2010). Online at: tinyurl.com/y3ko8of
5. Vickers, Marcia, Mike McNamee, Peter Coy, David Henry, *et al.* "The betrayed investor." *BusinessWeek* (February 25, 2002): 105. Online at: tinyurl.com/44o2t93
6. Morgenson, Gretchen. "After huge losses, a move to reclaim executives' pay." *New York Times* (February 21, 2009). Online at: www.nytimes.com/2009/02/22/business/22pay.html
7. Rappaport, Liz, Aaron Luchetti, Stephen Grocer. "Wall Street pay: A record $144 billion." *Wall Street Journal* (October 11, 2010). Online at: tinyurl.com/2cowbqu
8. National Investor Relations Institute. "NIRI activist investor survey—Engage for success." August 27, 2007.
9. Levingston, Steven. "Icahn, Time Warner end fight." *Washington Post* (February 18, 2006): D1. Online at: tinyurl.com/ybnb24
10. Wikipedia on Carl Icahn: en.wikipedia.org/wiki/Carl_Icahn
11. McLuhan, Marshall, and Bruce R. Powers. *The Global Village: Transformations in World Life and Media in the 21st Century.* New York: Oxford University Press, 1989.
12. International Telecommunication Union Statistics: www.itu.int/ITU-D/ict/statistics/
13. Technorati: technorati.com
14. Hilbert, Martin, and Priscila Lopez. "The world's technological capacity to store, communicate, and compute information." *Science* 332:6025 (April 1, 2011): 60–65. Online at: dx.doi.org/10.1126/science.1200970
15. Keller, Kevin Lane. *Strategic Brand Management.* 3rd ed. Upper Saddle River, NJ: Prentice-Hall, 2008.
16. Hill and Knowlton. "Reputation and the war for talent: Corporate reputation watch 2008." Online at: www2.hillandknowlton.com/crw/
17. "How a good name influences performance on the stock market." July 4, 2011. Online at: www.ketchum.com/Reputation_Capital
18. Aaker, David A. *Building Strong Brands.* New York: Free Press, 1996; p. 51.
19. Walmart's 3 basic beliefs and values: walmartstores.com/aboutus/321.aspx
20. Lee, Jennifer 8. "JetBlue flight snarls continue." *New York Times* (February 16, 2007): 7. Online at: www.nytimes.com/2007/02/16/nyregion/16airport.html
21. Cone. "2010 cause evolution study." Online at: www.coneinc.com/news/request.php?id=3350
22. Newsweek Green Rankings 2010: tinyurl.com/3ovelmo
23. Customer Engagement Strategies. "Dell social media snapshot." Online at: tinyurl.com/3ryadvm
24. Odden, Lee. "Dell social media interview with Richard Binhammer." *TopRank* (December 2008). Online at: tinyurl.com/5lkn2g
25. Adamy, Janet. "At Starbucks, a tall order for new cuts, store closures." *Wall Street Journal* (January 29, 2009). Online at: online.wsj.com/article/SB123317714771825681.html
26. Miller, Claire Cain. "A changed Starbucks. A changed CEO." *New York Times* (March 12, 2011). Online at: www.nytimes.com/2011/03/13/business/13coffee.html
27. Jones, Ashby. "'A calculated risk': Taco Bell presses the '88 percent real' campaign." *Wall Street Journal* blog (February 28, 2011). Online at: tinyurl.com/67248b5
28. Eckhouse, John. "How Delta used Twitter to help passengers during a storm." *The Realtime Report* (January 26, 2011). Online at: tinyurl.com/67ynzwk

Long-Term Reputation Effects in the Global Financial Industry: How the Financial Crisis Has Fundamentally Changed Reputation Dynamics

by Mark Eisenegger[a] and Daniel Künstle[b]

[a] Department of Research into the Public Sector and Society (fög), University of Zurich, Switzerland
[b] commsLAB, Basel, Switzerland

This Chapter Covers

- The Memorizing Resonance Reputation Index (MRRI)—a novel measuring procedure for analyzing long-term reputation dynamics.
- The long-term reputation trends of globally active major banks between 2002 and 2011.
- The basis of the study is the reputation-relevant reporting by 24 media from the Swiss, German, UK, US, and Asia-Pacific arenas. Some 200,000 media articles were evaluated.
- The MRRI shows a highly significant correlation between the long-term reputation trends of the analyzed banks and a stock index of comparable composition.
- Moreover, the MRRI shows that socioethical assessments of the banking industry gained quickly in importance after 2009 and led to a massive recasting of social reputation after 2010. Concurrently, economic assessment criteria became less significant.
- To counter the resulting limitation of their economic potential, the analysis suggests that companies in general and banks in particular should shoulder their macroeconomic responsibilities in a proactive way. Since the onset of the financial market crisis, the role of corporate social responsibility (CSR) has become more acute.
- The increased taking on of macroeconomic responsibility by the global financial industry is not only a social obligation, but represents a *conditio sine qua non* for the economic survival of the companies concerned.

Introduction

The financial market crisis of 2007, global economic crisis, and subsequent debt crisis have moved the concept of reputation into the very center of public debate. Ever since the reputation meltdown of the Wall Street banks, insurance companies, rating agencies, supervisory authorities, and entire national economies, there has been a veritable boom around this concept—in the media and scientific discourse, but also in the daily practice of management consultants.

In fact, reputation performs fundamental functions for society as a whole, as well as for the economy. Selective nurturing of the parameter of reputation thus acquires central significance. However, many companies, authorities, and other actors of public life frequently suffer the problem of continuing to depend too strongly on gut feeling in managing their reputation. There is, in particular, a lack of instruments that can validly determine *long-term* reputation dynamics as a basis for a reputation management that benefits the organization.

This chapter responds to this weakness with an approach to reputation that places long-term reputation dynamics at its center. It starts by clarifying the fundamental significance of media-broadcast communications in the process of reputation formation. The novel Memorizing Resonance Reputation Index (MRRI) procedure for determining long-term reputation dynamics is then introduced. Finally, a case study is presented on the effects of the financial market crisis on reputation dynamics in the global bank sector.

Public Communications—The *Conditio Sine Qua Non* of Reputation Formation

Without public communications, and in particular without the permanent background of media reporting, we would be unable to develop a clear idea of society. The media arena is the principal access portal to modern society; we look into this arena and form a picture of our society, the economy, and the companies in the news. The sociologist Niklas Luhmann has described the media arena as a gigantic mirror of society, reflecting its events and processes, and mirroring them back to its members: "What we know about our society, indeed about the world in which we live, we know via the mass media" (Luhmann, 1996, p. 9). The significance of the media arena as an information source quickly becomes clear when we imagine scenarios in which we struggle to find something to talk about, such as in classic small-talk situations. Even if nothing else relates to us, we can converse about the latest news and most current media topics at any time, with anyone, no matter how little we know them.

However, the media arena is more than just a gigantic social mirror. It also forms a communications platform, comparable to an infinitely large stage, which has become further extended with the advent of social media. Not only journalists appear on this stage and express their views and opinions, but all relevant social actors striving for attention, including those from the sectors of politics, economics, science, and society, concentrate their activities on this media platform. Hence, the financial market crisis was turned into a significant communications event merely because it was not only journalists who expressed opinions on the causes and consequences of the crisis in the media, but also prominent politicians and government representatives, economics professors, Nobel laureates, analysts, stock market legends, and leading investors. So it's not enough to reduce media communications to journalists alone. Politicians, scientists, experts, analysts, and nongovernmental organizations (NGOs) bestride the media platform with their topics and events, and, in this way, make it truly powerful.

What, thus, also makes the media arena significant in the economic sector are the circumstances below.

➤ Broad segments of society follow economic events ever more exclusively via the media (media as mirror).
➤ All key economic actors—such as analysts, investors, and economic experts—concentrate their estimates and ratings on the media arena (media as platform).

When rating agencies such as Standard & Poors, Moody's, or Fitch downgrade indebted countries such as Greece, Portugal, or even the superpower United States, we can know this immediately only because these agencies announce their ratings via the media. It is precisely this double function—as mirror and platform—that explains the central significance of the media for the economy: the media arena is the most important information source for economic events, and it is simultaneously the central platform and stage for all those actors who determine how share prices, markets, or business cycles develop. So, it is hardly surprising that empirical reputation research shows a close correlation between reputation curves and share prices. Experts, analysts, and investors observe economic events via the specialist and mass media, and simultaneously announce their assessments via media channels.

Instruments that aim to record key reputation dynamics in the economy and society are consequently obliged to specialize on an analysis of the media arena, i.e. that place where trust in companies and the economy grows or fades. Moreover, such instruments require a long-term perspective. Nothing harms the reputation of an actor more than chasing fast-changing ephemeral trends in an inflationary manner. Reputation management means validly recording the truly decisive reputation dynamics that have grown *over the long term* and harmonizing them in an authentic way with one's own organizational profile. The lack of suitable instruments for modeling the long-term changes of relevant reputation dynamics results in the risk of reputation management overlooking key trends or weighting them incorrectly.

MRRI—The Basis of Long-Term Reputation Management

It is precisely at this point that a novel procedure designed to record the *sedimented* (i.e. long-term) reputation dynamics comes in. The MRRI is used to model the historically grown perception of a company or other publicly exposed actor that is anchored in the public memory (see Sidebar 1). This procedure, developed by commsLAB in conjunction with the Research Institute for the Public Sphere and Society (fög) at the University of Zurich, permits the presentation of long-term sedimented reputation trends.

The MRRI is calculated over time and takes into account—on a daily or weekly basis—the values of the previous period, weighted with a "forgetting" rate. It measures the ratio of resonance (number of media contributions) and media reputation (overall positive or negative evaluation) by considering the corresponding values of the previous period, while adding a forgetting rate. High-resonance events thus determine reputation for a longer period than short-term ones, whose perception produces a volatile reputation effect. The MRRI is expressed on a scale ranging from +100 (exclusively positive resonance) to –100 (exclusively negative resonance).

The method is based on the insight that an actor's reputation is defined not only by current events but—always to a certain degree, and for a certain period of time—also by past events that have caught the attention and interest of the public. Thus, the MRRI does justice to the circumstance that, in the long term, it is above all high-resonance key events (such as the financial market crisis) determine reputation dynamics.

The Method of Long-Term Reputation Analysis

Reputation Relevance

The reputation ratings are calculated on the basis of the media coverage relevant to reputation. The latter is identified as relevant if the companies under review are mentioned in the title, in the lead section, or prominently in at least one paragraph of the text. The measurement of an information-yielding reputation trend consequently depends on substantial public resonance or the relevance of the analyzed actor.

Reputation Ratings

The reputation ratings reflect the value that results from the average rating of all reputation-relevant media reports. The range goes from +100 (all reports positive) to –100 (all reports negative). A reputation value of zero can stand for a neutral or controversial (balance between positive and negative) perception. The reputation ratings incorporate a specific weighting factor, which takes into account the prominence of the company in the respective media report.

Memorizing Resonance Reputation Index (MRRI)

The Memorizing Resonance Reputation Index (MRRI) is used to model the historically developed reputation anchored in the public memory. This method, developed by commsLAB in conjunction with fög at the University of Zurich, permits the presentation of long-term sedimented reputation trends.

The MRRI measures the ratio of resonance and reputation by considering the corresponding values of the previous period, while including a "forgetting" rate. High-resonance events thus determine reputation for a longer period than short-term ones, whose perception produces a volatile reputation effect.

The sedimented reputation thus covers the historically developed reputation anchored in the public memory in a way that is comparatively fixed with respect to time. In metrological terms, it includes the after-effects of reports from earlier periods with a strong impact on public opinion.

Separate presentation of sedimented resonance provides additional evidence by showing how strongly collective memory has been infused with these events, and how their impact has evolved over time.

It is crucial that the MRRIs compiled on a daily or weekly basis be based on a meaningful and stable initial value. As a rule, this requires data covering a period of six to twelve months.

Case Study

Long-Term Reputation Effects of The Global Financial Industry

On the basis of the MRRI, the long-term reputation trends of selected globally active major banks are presented below for the period from 2002 to 2011. We are interested in seeing how the financial market crisis changed reputation dynamics on the public opinion "market" from 2007.

Figure 1 shows the reputation trends of globally active major banks of the United States, Switzerland, Germany, the United Kingdom, and China (gray curve) between 2002 and the end of May 2011 (see Sidebar 2). The graph also displays the sedimented media resonance (number of media articles, shown as the solid gray area) underlying the reputation curve.

The long-term sedimented reputation of all analyzed major banks ("Total MRRI global banks") reached a peak on February 21, 2007. As a consequence of the financial crisis, the reputation of the major banks suffered a massive slump, reaching a low point on March 8, 2009. This was associated with a fundamental rise in the underlying sedimented resonance, i.e. the volume of reporting; although this comprised about 23,000 reputation-relevant media articles per day before the financial crisis, it shot up at times to more than 28,000 articles per day from 2008.

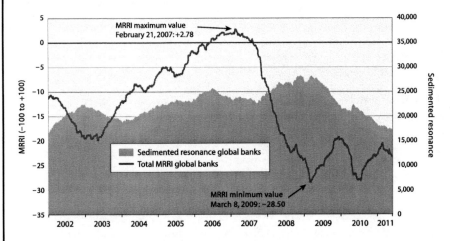

Figure 1. Long-term reputation trends of major global banks. International media sample January 1, 2002 to May 31, 2011

However, even before the financial crisis, the reputation trends of the globally active major banks were subject to large fluctuations from 2007. Thus, at the beginning of 2002, in the aftermath of the accounting scandal at Enron and in the context of the burst dotcom bubble, the discussion of managerial pay that broke out initially in the United States, and subsequently in Europe, proved to be of unparalleled vehemence.

In mid-2002, the discussions about financial scandals, accounting fraud, and the dishonest behavior of individual analysts became more extensive. This resulted in a more fundamental perception of the problems presented by a lack of firewalls around investment managers and a comprehensive debate on the structure and conduct of the large investment banks.

Although excessive managerial pay and stock-option programs, a lack of corporate governance, and the threat of layoffs had already been the focus of the media, the ever worsening economic climate now led to talk of a veritable crisis of confidence with respect to the big financial institutions—with correspondingly negative consequences for the reputation of the globally active major banks.

In an environment that was, in any case, already bedeviled by strong uncertainty (September 11, the war against terror), the call for reforms soon rose to new levels: stirred up by New York State Attorney General Eliot Spitzer, it forced the hand not only of other regulatory authorities, but also of political actors.

Although at its core an economics issue, the debate on the crisis of confidence of the years 2002 and 2003 was by no means limited to the media's economic and stock market columns; in fact, this whole topic diffused widely into the sector of social policy. Thus, the reputation dynamics of the crisis of confidence of 2002 represents a true precursor to the financial crisis that broke out in 2007—although with a decisive difference in the ability of the actors involved to learn from it: it did not cause any immediate economic damage to the major banks and did not limit their growth potential in any way, as we will show in detail shortly.

To the contrary, what followed from mid-2003 to spring 2007 was an almost uncanny increase in reputation that peaked on February 21, 2007, as noted above. The crisis of confidence, and its implied criticism of the global financial industry, appeared more remote than ever, and it was the profits of the investment banking sector in particular—a sector that was widely condemned at the time—which contributed largely to this dazzling reputation.

But the discussions held at that time about accounting fraud, excessive managerial pay, and a lack of corporate governance had by no means disappeared from collective memory. Indeed, they formed the breeding ground for the US subprime crisis—which became acute from mid-2007—to expand quickly into a global financial market crisis, because the global financial industry in particular could no longer rely on any broad-based confidence bonus. It had already lost that in the crisis of confidence of the years 2002–03.

There followed a reputation slump of unequalled magnitude and speed. The financial market crisis led from 2008 to a veritable collapse of the global financial industry's reputation. The international financial services sector was held responsible for the dynamics of this crisis. Short-term shareholder-value thinking, short-term business models, and irresponsible risk policies, as well as the dominance of derivative financial products in whose economic power it was necessary to "believe" in a proverbial sense, were all branded scandalous.

As will be shown, the sedimented reputation curve of the global financial industry reacted significantly more sensitively to the basic impending crisis events than the comparable stock market index.

Analyzed Banks and Description of Data

Table 1. Periods over which reputation data per bank were analyzed

Bank	From	To
UBS	January 1, 2001	May 31, 2011
Credit Suisse Group (CSG)	January 1, 2001	May 31, 2011
Deutsche Bank	January 1, 2001	May 31, 2011
Goldman Sachs	January 1, 2001	May 31, 2011
JP Morgan	January 1, 2002	May 31, 2011
Hongkong and Shanghai Banking Corporation (HSBC)	July 1, 2009	May 31, 2011
Industrial and Commercial Bank of China (ICBC)	July 1, 2009	May 31, 2011
Citibank	January 1, 2002	June 30, 2009
Merrill Lynch	January 1, 2001	June 30, 2009
Morgan Stanley	January 1, 2001	June 30, 2009

Scope of Media Reporting

Reputation-relevant reporting by 24 media from the US, Swiss, German, UK, and Asia-Pacific arenas. The time frame was January 1, 2001, to May 31, 2011, covering a total of about 200,000 reputation-relevant articles (for details see Table 1). Due to the fact that the MRRI has to be based on a meaningful and stable start value, each graph's time frame starts with a one-year delay and ranges from January 1, 2002, to May 31, 2011.

Resonance Strength MRRI on Daily Basis

On average about 21,300 reputation-relevant articles (while including the forgetting rate and a specific weighting factor, which takes into account the prominence of the company in the respective media report).
Start value: 16,706 (January 1, 2002).
Highest daily value: 28,229 (November 28, 2008).
End value: 17,132 (May 31, 2011).

Dow Jones Banks Titans 30 Index (DJTBAK)

The DJTBAK represents leading companies in the global banking sector. The index includes 30 stocks selected based on rankings by float-adjusted market capitalization, revenue, and net profit. The index covers the bank supersector of the Industry Classification Benchmark (ICB). The DJTBAK was first calculated on February 12, 2001.

Finding 1: Long-Term Reputation Effects Correlate Significantly with Economic Development

Figure 2 compares reputation trends of the analyzed global banks (solid gray curve—MRRI) with comparable share price trends (dashed black curve). The comparative parameter here is the Dow Jones Banks Titans 30 Index (DJTBAK), which covers the 30 most important companies from the global banking sector. It can be seen that the reputation dynamics of the global financial industry show a highly significant correlation with the stock market index.

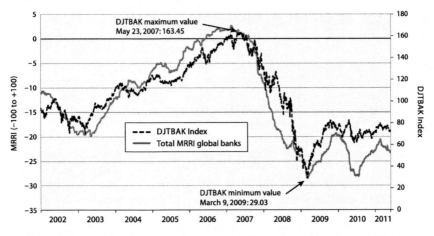

Figure 2. Comparison of the reputation curve and share price of the major global banks. International media sample January 1, 2002 to May 31, 2011

Comparison of the maximum and minimum values of both curves gives a surprising discovery: whereas the lowest values of reputation trends and share prices are effectively concentrated on the same day (March 8, 2009 for the MRRI; March 9, 2009 for the DJTBAK), we see a marked difference at the onset of the financial crisis in 2007: the MRRI reputation, measured over the long term, starts to dip about three months earlier than the comparative DJTBAK reputation (February 21, 2007 as against May 23, 2007).

In other periods of this time series, too, the reputation curve generated a trend early on that was followed, after a lag, by share prices. Thus, the MRRI of the major global banks already foreshadowed the stock market upturn that started in 2004 and, to some degree, clearly anticipated it up to the turning point of February 21, 2007 we have already mentioned.

We see a similar picture in the downturn phase starting in spring 2007; whereas stock market trends recorded sporadic periods of rising prices again in 2008, the MRRI showed a constantly negative development during the same period. Public opinion continued to insist that the problem of confidence in the bank industry had by no means been overcome.

This last observation in particular provides a series of additional explanatory patterns for the interaction between the long-term reputations and stock market trends of the actors featuring strongly in the public eye (cf. previous section).

▸ The coverage of individual companies is embedded in a broader scenario of media reporting, which transports industry-specific, as well as overall economic and business-cycle expectations, to future developments.

▸ Media reporting goes beyond merely reflecting the performance and stock market trends of individual companies. Indeed, media coverage also extends in large measure to sectors such as research and expertise, products and services, and strategy and management, as well as political, regulatory, and, above all, social components. It can be seen, then, that the correlation between reputation curve and share price remains, even when stock market reporting is not considered.

▸ Finally, the reporting is largely permeated by actors originating from subsectors other than the economy. Thus, the media regularly offer considerable space in the public arena to politicians, experts, and other personalities to feed disclosures and developments that are as sensational as possible, with the aim of lending plausibility and credibility to their assessments of the way the economy is heading.

The consequence is the formation of powerful optimistic or pessimistic moods with respect to the economy or individual companies, which have a clearly considerable impact on value-creation indicators such as share prices.

It is perfectly understandable that this plethora of partly contradictory opinions and assessments should lead to a need for simple black-and-white explanations, especially in times of crisis. In view of the increasing complexity of economic and political processes in an age of globalization, however, it is hardly possible to maintain an overview any longer. In addition, even if individual actors were to succeed in achieving such an overview, we must assume that they would be unable to make any headway among the prevailing mainstream and herd instincts of the economy and society, but would, at most, be seen merely as Cassandra voices uttering warnings in the wings.

Indeed, it appears that not only is the mood of the broad mass of the population formed by media reporting, but also that the behavior of powerful actors such as analysts, investors, customers, regulators, and (not least) politicians is oriented to this basic mood relayed by the media. In this context, it is irrelevant whether the perception mediated in this way is really correct. The decisive factor is simply whether it can potentially produce economic or social effects, which must be correspondingly anticipated in the actions of these actors.

To record and map these dominant moods in the economy and society, in their positive or negative tendencies, empirically, and over time, is the core of the approach developed by commsLAB and the Research Institute for the Public Sphere and Society (fög) of the University of Zurich for the measurement of long-term sedimented reputation trends.

Against this background, the question arises as to why the development of sedimented reputation and stock market value, which showed a close correlation up to the end of 2009, increasingly lost this parallel pacing after 2010. As will be shown, from 2010 we can see a fundamental change in the reputation dynamics of the global financial industry which had held true up to that point.

Finding 2: The Recasting of Social Reputation Limits Economic Growth Potentials

Figure 3 compares the social reputation trends of the major globally active banks ("Social MRRI global") with the functional ones ("Functional MRRI global"). At the same time, the respectively assigned media reporting is divided proportionally according to social (dark area at bottom) and functional resonance (light gray area). Whereas social reputation is subject to overall standards of social evaluation and is a measure of ethical integrity, functional reputation is an indicator of technical competence and business success or failure (see Sidebar 3). The overall reputation curve ("Total MRRI global") is also shown.

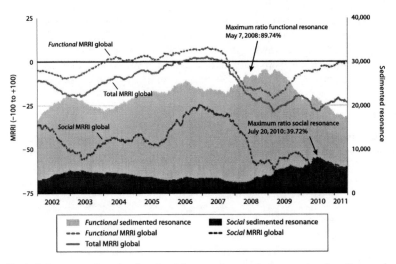

Figure 3. Long-term functional and social reputation trends. International media sample January 1, 2002 to May 31, 2011

An initial comparison of the development of functional and social reputation shows that the consolidation of the global banks' reputations is based essentially on their economic power and expertise ("Functional MRRI global"). The social reputation component ("Social MRRI global") is significantly lower in most cases, but is regularly marked by strong negative effects, especially during major crises, like the crisis of confidence in 2002–03 that has already been noted or during the course of the financial crisis from 2008.

These crises are invariably associated with an increase in underlying social resonance (dark shaded area in Figure 3). This comprised about 25% of the whole volume of reporting during the crisis of confidence, while an escalation could be observed especially from 2010. This peaked on July 20, 2010, with a maximum share of almost 40%—a clear sign that the perception of the major global banks was subject at this time to completely different parameters than at the beginning of the financial crisis, in spring 2008. Thus, the share of functional reporting on May 7, 2008 was still almost 90% (light shaded area). In other words, at the beginning of the financial crisis the reputation trends of the major banks depended almost exclusively on economic factors, whereas from 2010 they were increasingly determined by social assessments. It thus appears that the share of social resonance—i.e. reporting which covers companies in social, ethical, or politicoregulatory contexts—gained in significance progressively from mid-2008 and markedly from 2010.

However, the dimension of social reputation has not only increased quantitatively, its contents have also been exposed to a fundamental change in significance. Against the background of the perspective that the financial market crisis brought national economies to the brink of ruin (Iceland, Ireland, and others), the pressure of expectations is growing not only on banks, but also on companies in general, to assume macroeconomic responsibility. Social responsibility is thus being reinterpreted toward insisting that the primary social responsibility of companies consists of serving their respective economic location or preserving it from harm. This expectation can also be read from the fact that indicators such as tax contributions, dividend payouts, or share price trends (i.e. performance indicators, which benefit both respective economic locations and collective institutions such as social provision funds) have become markedly more powerful reputation drivers.

That the social dimension of reputation—understood as macroeconomic responsibility—is not only desirable, but also very directly influences future economic expectations, becomes clear from the fact that stock market trends unlike during the crisis of confidence of the years 2002–03—are increasingly decoupled from the functional reputation dynamics, which return to positive values from 2009 (Figure 4).

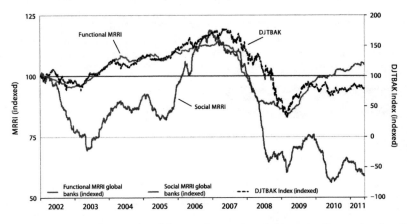

Figure 4. Long-term functional/social reputation trends and share price. International media sample January 1, 2002 to May 31, 2011 (indexed)

Figure 4 compares the development of functional and social reputation with that of the DJTBAK on the basis of an indexed display.

It is striking that the functional reputation and stock market trends for the major global banks were subject to the same dynamics between 2002 and the end of 2009, and thus run a parallel course. But the reputation dynamics start to change fundamentally from 2010. Whereas functional reputation continues to improve from this time, and already stands significantly above its initial values of 2002 at the close of the analysis period at the end of May 2011, the corresponding share price trend stagnates.

The reason for this is that the massive recasting of social reputation shown in Figure 4 after 2010, as well as the extremely low values of social reputation ("Social MRRI" curve), prevent the exploitation of the existing economic potential in the shape of improved share values—or at least greatly limit them.

Three-Dimensional Reputation

Irrespective of which actor we consider, be it a company, a politician, or perhaps a scientist, successful reputation management must always keep the same *three* reputation dimensions in mind (Eisenegger, 2005; Eisenegger *et al.*, 2010).

▸ First, one's own competence and the associated successes must be demonstrated. This *functional reputation*—linked to the performance targets of the respective *function* systems (politics, economy, etc.)—is measured in the economy by how profitably a company is managed.

▸ Second, all reputation-bearers must prove their mettle in the social world, where certain norms and moral ideas apply. This is the field of *social reputation*. It centers on the extent to which an actor is a good citizen.

▸ Third, every actor also possesses an expressive reputation. This dimension is dominated by emotional judgments of taste. Actors with a positive *expressive reputation* appear fascinating and unique.

137

Thus, on the whole the secret of a positive reputation is based on successfully serving certain performance targets (functional reputation), acting responsibly (social reputation), and possessing a profile that marks an emotional difference to one's competitors (expressive reputation).

Summary and Further Steps

▶▶ The assumption of greater macroeconomic responsibility by the global financial industry is not just a social obligation but a *conditio sine qua non* for its economic survival.

▶▶ The instrument used to record the long-term communications dynamics described in this chapter shows that the financial market crisis of 2007 and its aftershocks have fundamentally changed the nature of reputation dynamics. As a consequence of the crisis, functional reputation, which is central to companies and oriented to economic performance criteria, progressively lost importance in favor of more comprehensive social expectations. It became apparent that a tarnished, and simultaneously highly resonant, social reputation prevents the functional reputation from evolving further, a phenomenon that also has a negative impact on share prices.

▶▶ It is, therefore, crucial to ascertain whether, and if so, how, the gap between positive functional and negative social reputation that limits the global banks' share price trends can be closed.

▶▶ In light of this, what is urgently required is to influence the social dimension of reputation in a clearly self-initiated way, by taking practical action that is aligned with the principles of macroeconomic responsibility. For, as we have shown, as a consequence of the financial crisis social responsibility becomes reinterpreted in a direction which indicates that the primary social responsibility of companies consists in shouldering their macroeconomic responsibilities—i.e. by serving their economic locations or preserving them from harm.

▶▶ The concept of macroeconomic responsibility renders social responsibility more acute by insisting that it be linked to the company's core economic competence in order that it appears credible. So, companies must not "somehow" act charitably or for the common good, but rather must apply their own economic performance and competence primarily for the benefit of the national economy, as well as of those countries that act as their hosts.

▶▶ This orientation to national economic principles not only makes sense from the standpoint of reputation, but also promises to deliver solid economic benefits. A gap has opened up between functional reputation and actual prices in the reputation trends of the major global banks since 2010. This is because the dynamics of social reputation have remained strongly negative following the public perception of an insufficient response, particularly by the bank industry, to national economic expectations, which have been recast by regulatory discourse. Thus, the failure of the companies concerned to address their social commitment so far has tended to inhibit their further success. A greater assumption of macroeconomic responsibility can thus represent an effective way not only of consolidating a company's own reputation profile in a sustainable manner, but also of closing this gap and thus redeeming lost economic potential.

More Info

Books:

Eisenegger, Mark. *Reputation in der Mediengesellschaft. Konstitution, Issues Monitoring, Issues Management. [Reputation in the Media Society. Constitution, Issue Monitoring, Issue Management.]* Wiesbaden, Germany: VS Verlag für Sozialwissenschaften, 2005.

Eisenegger, Mark, Mario Schranz, and Jörg Schneider. "*Corporate reputation and the news media in Switzerland.*" In Craig E. Carroll (ed). *Corporate Reputation and the News Media: Agenda-Setting within Business News Coverage in Developed, Emerging, and Frontier Markets.* New York: Routledge, 2010.

Luhmann, Niklas. *Die Realität der Massenmedien. [The Reality of the Mass Media.]* Leverkusen, Germany: Westdeutscher Verlag, 1995.

An Approach to Understanding Reputation Risk in Financial Services

by Philip Whittingham

XL Group, and Solvency II Special Interest Group, Institute of Risk Management, London, UK

This Chapter Covers

- What we mean by reputational risk, why reputation risk is important in financial services, and how it is related to other risks faced by financial services businesses.
- The regulatory drivers that are increasing the pressure on financial services firms to manage reputation risk.
- Some practical suggestions on how reputation risk can be usefully incorporated in the risk management cycle and processes in a financial services business.

Introduction

The Oxford English Dictionary 2010 defines reputation as "the beliefs or opinions that are generally held about someone or something." If we follow that definition, reputational risk must be the potential for loss or damage that occurs to an organization through an adverse impact on its reputation. In other words, something must happen that causes people to doubt previously held beliefs. We assume, of course, that these are "good" beliefs that are being damaged.

Why are these beliefs so important? Well, think about what happens when you move to a new area. Typically you will ask your neighbors if they can recommend a "good" doctor, or dentist, or place to eat, and so on. The same applies to financial services. Our buying decisions—such as our choice to take out an insurance policy or take a mortgage—are very influenced by a number of factors that include price and perception of quality or brand. Indeed, we might pay more for a product which we perceive to provide greater value (as car manufacturers established a lpong while ago). This is why television and media adverts for financial services products are typically geared at building a perception of trust and stability, rather than focusing on the purely financial benefits and product features. Firms invest a lot in building these public profiles and in establishing a reputation to support the profile through the appropriate customer service.

So, how does this link to reputational risk? Let us consider two possible scenarios.

- A well known high-street bank is subject to rumors about its financial security. What happens? There is a sudden increase in customers transferring their accounts or business relationships elsewhere.
- A well-known insurer receives publicity that it is disputing claims. What happens? It loses potential customers.

Are these realistic scenarios? Well, a little research will quickly show that they are indeed based in reality. What they both have in common, though, is that although there is loss, it is not a "typical" loss for the business. Retail banks typically are used to sustaining loss through the credit default of a customer, while insurers (particularly personal lines insurers) are used to losing customers primarily on price.[1] However, in both scenarios a contributory driver or factor in the loss of client trust and declining business volume as a result is loss of reputation.

Case Study

Northern Rock

The story of Northern Rock sits at the heart of the financial crisis of 2007. At the start of the year, Northern Rock was one of the success stories of the UK finance sector. Its pretax profits had risen 27% on the previous year, and the 10 years of growth since conversion to a bank (previously it was a UK building society owned by its savers and borrowers) had seen a year-on-year asset growth of 20%. To do this, Northern Rock relied on wholesale markets rather than retail deposits to fund most of its lending. It bundled its loans together and sold them to investors. However, a reliance on wholesale funding also made the bank vulnerable.

Central bank action in response to a perceived housing bubble meant that interest rates were rising, and this was having an impact on Northern Rock. The initial effect was a fall in share price and a profit warning. The real crunch came in August 2007 with the global liquidity freeze, the timing of which was less than ideal for a cash-starved operation.

Shortly after, the liquidity markets dried up. Northern Rock told the regulator that it was in trouble and a message was passed to the Bank of England. The possibility that the Bank of England might need to act as lender of last resort was raised, but instead it was decided to find a buyer for the bank. A sale fell through on September 10, and it was agreed that emergency funding should be provided. However, news of this leaked out and a public statement had to be rushed out by the government on September 14.

Arguably, the financial community should have taken some comfort at this point. Customers took a different view, though, gaining their facts mainly from press coverage and leaked stories. Alerted to the trouble, the public began to withdraw its funds and a run on the bank commenced that only stopped on September 17, when the government had to announce an unprecedented guarantee for all existing deposits.

There are three key elements to the financial crisis more generally, as highlighted by this story, that are of interest to those learning about reputational risk management, and these are as follows.

▸▸ In part the crisis was probably aggravated by banks not wanting to highlight their difficulties by going to the Bank of England. Reputational considerations would have been at the heart of this.

▸▸ The regulator and the Bank of England had crisis management approaches that did not appear to be adequately coordinated and did not sufficiently address the reputational risk dimension of the case.

▸▸ The public, clearly fearing the worst, participated in a run on the bank that, perhaps, could have been avoided if the messaging had been better.

Causes of Loss Due to Reputation Risk

One of the great debates around reputational risk is whether it is a risk in itself or whether it is an outcome or a consequence of other risks. The latter is easy to explain if we consider the following scenarios.

▸ Because of a breakdown in claims processing (perhaps due to a systems failure), there is a delay in paying claims. This could lead to reputational damage—possibly arising out of unwanted press coverage—leading to loss of business, whether new or existing.

▸ Rumors concerning the financial strength of a bank, perhaps following losses in its investment banking division, result in customers closing their deposit accounts.

In both these cases the underlying cause of loss is an operational (or other) risk event. However, along with a direct financial impact—for example, the cost of rectifying the system failure in the first case—there is also a reputational impact, which typically comes in the form of loss of business. It is driven by the adverse publicity that arises from the operational (or other) failure.

So, for this author, reputational risk is primarily an unintended outcome that is derived from the actualization of other risk types. In other words, it might be deemed to be a "consequential" risk rather than a primary risk. However, while this may be the view on which this chapter is based, there are other aspects that must be considered, including the multiplier effect that reputational risk can have. For example, consider the situation where a bank is rumored to have liquidity problems. Customers start to lose confidence and withdraw their funds, further exacerbating the liquidity problems. This in turn causes further withdrawals by customers who were not initially nervous but now are as a result of the publicity that is starting to emerge. This is an example of what could be termed the "reputational multiplier" effect.

The existence of this multiplier has been examined in a number of studies, one of the first being that by Cummins, Lewis, and Wei (2006), who identified the impact on stock price as being larger than the underlying loss of value because of the reputational multiplier. Further analysis was undertaken by Micocci *et al.* (2008), who examined the impact of operational risk events on reputation through a study of stock price movements following large (in excess of US$20 million) operational risk events. The study, drawing on very well known operational risk losses in the financial services sector (such as the US$9 billion loss of Banco National in South America due to credit fraud in 1995, and the US$2.6 billion loss at Sumitomo Corporation due to unauthorized trading activity in 1996) found significant downward movement in the share price, particularly in the month after the reported losses.

Risk Taxonomy and Reputation Risk

Over the last five or so years, financial services organizations have had to develop a more rigorous taxonomy of risk and a more clearly defined universe of risks. This is essential since the regulators have been asking not just what risks are faced by the organization, but what risks capital is held for. To answer this seemingly simple question requires a firm to define classes of risk very clearly and to make these known throughout the organization so that they can be treated in line with risk management objectives.

Much of the focus to date has been on defining operational risk and, in particular, defining the treatment for so-called "boundary events."[2] However, what firms have perhaps not been as robust in doing is articulating where reputational risk sits in their risk taxonomy, how it should be classified, and whether it is a primary risk, a consequential risk, or just an outcome.

Clearly, given the increasing need to discuss the topic, there is a benefit in agreeing how reputational risk should be described and articulated up front so that all key stakeholders within the firm understand it in the same way. Managing the understanding for those outside the company is more challenging but should not be ignored, and there are plenty of disclosure opportunities for firms to get their message across.

Regulatory Drivers for Reputation Risk Management

As risk managers, we do not wish to suggest that risk management frameworks are implemented just to satisfy regulatory expectations. Nonetheless, financial services is an increasingly heavily regulated sector and we cannot ignore the importance of regulation. What is interesting is that the regulators have identified reputation risk as something that requires addressing. Why might that be? To a great extent the driver comes from the overarching regulatory goals of consumer confidence and financial stability. If firms are seen—or in the particular case of reputation risk, perceived—to be failing, then consumers may lose confidence in the financial market and even in the regulator as well. This is exactly the risk that the regulator has been set up to avoid, and avoiding it is also in the regulator's self-interest. As such, there is increasing regulatory guidance as to what should be done. In other words, even if financial services firms themselves did not recognize the importance of reputational risk, the regulator's own interests mean that it cannot be ignored.

Perhaps the most recent example of the expectation is set out in the Solvency II directive and its related guidance. Solvency II is the new set of regulations for the European insurance industry that comes into force in 2013.

Solvency II, Article 44, level 2, guidance states that the risk management system should be extended to include reputation risk. This is defined as "the risk of potential loss to an undertaking through deterioration of its reputation or standing due to a negative perception of the undertaking's image among customers, counterparties, shareholders and/or supervisory authorities. To that extent it may be regarded as less of a separate risk, than one consequent on the overall conduct of an undertaking." The guidance goes on to state that "The administrative, management or supervisory body of the undertaking should be aware of potential reputational risks it is exposed to and the correlation with all other material risks" and that "the undertaking should pay great attention to understanding and recognizing key values affecting reputation, considering expectations of the stakeholders and sensitivity of the marketplace."

Furthermore, there is a requirement for firms to consider the impact of reputation risk in their Pillar 2 "Own risk and solvency assessment" (ORSA), where the regulators state: "The following risks are examples of risks not considered in the standard formula, but which should be considered in the ORSA, if they are material for the undertaking:

1 Liquidity risk;
2 Reputational risk;
3 Strategic risk."

The Risk Management Cycle and Reputation Risk
Risk Governance
Who owns or is responsible for managing reputational risk? Although we are all familiar with the work of the marketing and public relations function in assisting with the building of a brand, the reality is that it is not solely responsible. In some senses it is all of the business that is responsible, from the board and CEO down. Indeed, we all know from our experience of being a customer that any interaction with an institution leaves an impression that can shape our view of its reputation—be it the receptionist, a salesman, or other.

Indeed, a clear example of this can be seen in the HSBC's published corporate governance approach, where it states that "safeguarding [HSBC's] reputation…is the responsibility of every member of staff." To ensure that this is understood throughout the organization, HSBC trains directors on appointment in reputational matters, and reputation risks are considered at a number of levels including:

- the board;
- the group management board;
- risk management meetings;
- subsidiary company boards;
- board committees;
- senior management.

Because reputation risk is so important, we cannot leave its management to chance. There need to be clear guidelines as to who is responsible for managing that risk (or rather outcome). It may appear obvious that a process owner is responsible. For example, if poor claims service can lead to loss of reputation, then surely the head of claims should be responsible for managing that risk? This may be the case, but in fact there are a number of stakeholders with whom reputation can be lost.

Therefore, one easy way to look at the governance around reputational risk is to do a mapping of stakeholders with whom we might lose reputation (clients, rating agencies, etc.) and to work out who has the primary responsibility for the management of these relationships and the associated reputational risks. Key here is to document and communicate those responsibilities in the same way that it is for other risk types (in terms of reference, for example). A possible mapping of some of the responsibilities in an insurance company is set out in the breakout box.

The roles of the second and third lines of defense in the management of reputational risk (being independent risk oversight and assurance, respectively) are no different. However, it is possible, given the challenging nature of the risk, that the risk function may be called on to provide more coaching, guidance, and advice than with other risks.

Risk Culture

Establishing the governance around reputational risk is, however, only part of the equation. As with all things in risk management, the processes, structures, and risk management tools are only as good as the culture that supports them. Reputational risk is quite esoteric, and the role of culture and its place in terms of people and firms doing the "right thing" is therefore of even greater importance.

Stronger risk cultures propagate themselves better and communicate better, which as we have seen is essential for the management of reputational risk. Firms with a good risk culture understand the consequences for their reputation of good and bad behaviors and do not tolerate mistakes that involve lapses in integrity or which knowingly put the firm's reputation at risk.

A good risk culture reinforces good behaviors, and vice versa. It helps firms to avoid risks for which no returns are expected and ultimately to attract clients who want to avoid surprises in their business dealings and want to trust and believe in the organizations with which they contract.

While the topic of culture is not the subject of this chapter, it is fair to say that strong cultures begin at the very outset, with the HR process of hiring, and continue into compensating people for the right behaviors—and not just for maximizing profit. In firms that take risk management seriously, this should include rewarding people in accordance with how their behavior protects brand and reputation.

Risk Identification and Assessment

In order to successfully manage reputational risk, we need to have a process for its identification. This process needs to be a dynamic one that looks at existing risks but which also considers new, emerging risks. Causes of reputational damage may vary over time. For example, with more trends driven by the green agenda, firms now have to demonstrate greater corporate social responsibility than they might have 20 years ago. Those firms that are not perceived to be good corporate citizens, or "green," might increasingly see their reputation damaged. In fact this is explicitly addressed as a reputational risk impact by the HSBC when it considers "environmental, social and governance" risks and their link to reputation.

As such, the identification of reputational risk is an ongoing task. Typically, firms consider this at two levels.

▸ *Level 1*: Within core business processes, when the question has to be asked about any major decision whether there is a potential reputational impact of implementing it; an example might be moving a call center offshore.
▸ *Level 2*: Within the risk management processes that are overlaid to give further assurance that risks are being treated correctly. Within these, there are two tools that stand out for consideration: stress-testing and the risk register. Internal capital models used by firms, on the other hand, are not as useful since it is hard to quantify the risk in a way that lends itself to modeling.

Thus, two key tools for identification and assessment are emerging around reputational risk. The first is the risk register, a tool that has been around for a while now. The second is a specific form of stress-testing known as reverse stress-testing.

Risk Registers

Risk registers have become a standard tool for risk identification and quantification in the financial services industry. Typically, these involve scoring risks on a predefined matrix of impact and probability. In the past the outcomes have been measured in terms of financial impact. However, there is an increasing trend to use the risk register as a device for the quantification of potential reputational impact. This is done by extending the impact matrix to include a range of reputational impact outcomes that can occur either alongside or instead of the financial impacts. These might range from an incident that is known and communicated internally through to things that lead to national press coverage, or perhaps even rating agency action. The purpose is to help firms to understand the range of outcomes that are possible, not just the financial impacts. This can then drive appropriate risk treatment.

Reverse Stress-Tests

The purpose of the reverse stress-test (which is mandated by regulators in Europe but is also gaining wider traction with other regulators worldwide, for example in Bermuda) is different from that of most stress-tests. Most stress-testing work considers an event and looks at the impact of that event on the business and the achievability of the business plan. Typically the outcome is couched in financial terms (for example impact on earnings, impact on capital held, and sometimes impact on liquidity).

The reverse stress-test is different because it works back from the failure. In other words, we know the outcome of the stress-test (failure), but we do not necessarily know what causes it. In the most extreme cases, reputational risk can lead to business failure. Indeed, it is difficult to overestimate the importance of perception in business. The financial crisis in 2007–08 showed us just how the views of stakeholders—ranging from customers, the rating agencies, through regulators, governments, and others—could adversely affect the future of once seemingly sound institutions.

Therefore, it does not take a big leap to establish that once we have realized that a primary cause of failure can be loss of reputation, we should undertake scenario analysis to understand how this might manifest itself.

Risk Treatment and Response

What is the appropriate treatment for reputational risk? Clearly, a number of the controls in place for the management of reputational risk are also those linked to the underlying risk (certainly in the case of operational risk). So, we have controls to prevent IT downtime, and through that reduced likelihood of IT downtime we are mitigating our reputational risk.

However, it is not straightforward as that. If we consider the situation where we do have IT downtime (resulting from fire, for example), the typical response is to implement a business continuity plan that gets the business up and running again. However, another reputational risk mitigant could be a communication to key stakeholders that says: "Yes, there is a problem, but it is under control." Even more importantly, there should be agreement on what the message should be. It would be less than ideal for the CEO to be communicating one message to a journalist in a telephone call while a preapproved press release tells a different story.

In the days of the Internet, Twitter, and other social media, bad news moves very quickly and therefore firms need to have a defined response plan depending on the nature and level of the "bad news" that they need to manage against. Furthermore, firms need to accept that they will often be defending themselves against stories that might not be 100% accurate but are spreading nonetheless. Experience is increasingly showing that, unless the story is just not true, the best defense is an honest one that accepts what has happened, apologizes for it, and articulates what is being done to control it. Indeed, a rule of thumb should be to be fast, to be honest, and to be complete in one's response rather than drip-feeding incremental responses.

In fact, this is where, again, a use can be found for reverse stress-testing, since the typical approach will look at what contingency plans are in place and what management actions might control how the scenario develops. A good analysis of reputational risk will allow firms to develop communications and crisis management plans, along with other, more scenario-specific tools of mitigation.

The other question we should consider is whether a firm should hold capital as a mitigant for reputational risk. In the main, firms are not going down this route. However, the study by Micocci *et al.* (2008) suggests that, at a 99.9% confidence level, the reputational value-at-risk (VaR) is 1.08% of shareholder's value (for a monthly event window). Given the increasingly numerate analysis of reputational risk impacts, it seems likely that at some point in the future firms may be pressed to hold capital by the regulators, notwithstanding the controls the firm puts in place to avoid consequential losses.

Risk Reporting

Given the nature of reputational risk, much of the risk reporting that might take place around it could be linked to other types of risk—using primarily the same indicators that tell the firm if there is an emerging operational risk issue. However, of equal importance is reporting on the status of the contingency and communication plans. So, in the same way that business continuity plan testing would be reported, consideration should be given to the reporting of weaknesses in reputational risk management contingency plans.

Mapping the Ownership of Reputation Risk

Clearly identifying who "owns" a risk is good practice, and the same applies to the reputational dimension of risk. Some examples of the stakeholders with whom we might need to manage the risk and the relevant internal owner are set out below for the example of an insurance company:

▸ *Customers*—All those who interact with customers, but primarily underwriters, direct sales forces, and claims handlers. As such, the allocation might require identification down to the business process level.
▸ *Employees*—Human resources and line management.
▸ *Investors*—The senior management team and often a dedicated investor relations team.
▸ *Regulators*—Those handling compliance, but also senior management who will encounter regulators frequently.
▸ *Rating agencies*—The senior management team.

As with any risk, it is important to recognize that risk ownership does not mean exclusivity, in the sense that all employees in an organization should be aware of their role in the management of risk and their responsibilities. However, we do need to recognize that there are some with a more defined accountability.

Reverse Stress-Tests and Reputation Risk

Reverse stress-tests are a relatively new idea, but they have quickly gained traction with financial services regulators and are now enshrined in local regulation in a number of territories and are also addressed in emerging regulation such as Solvency II.

They are known as reverse stress-tests since, unlike with most stress tests, we start with an outcome and work back, rather than starting with a cause or an event to understand the outcome. With the reverse stress-test, that outcome is failure of the business.

The value of performing a reverse stress-test is in what the process can tell the firm. So, if we consider a firm, failure could arise for a number of reasons, including a loss of capital. This might arise out of a single catastrophic event. It could arise from a liquidity failure. The latter could be caused by a single event, but if we look back at the earlier case study of Northern Rock, we can see that the problem might be exacerbated by reputational issues.

Equally, there might be other losses that are small but which cause key stakeholders to lose confidence, resulting perhaps in loss of capital support, a drop in share price, or loss of business that means that the firm's income is not sufficient to support the business plan.

It is in these latter circumstances that the consideration of reputational risk really comes to the fore. Take a small insurance company which tells its shareholders that it is writing two or three lines of business. For speculative reasons it decides to write a small amount of a fourth line of business because it has been offered what it regards as an attractive opportunity. If there is a loss on this business and the shareholders regard the loss as surprising and unexpected, they might not unreasonably lose confidence on the grounds that they are worried about what else there is in the firm's business activities that they do not know about. It is not inconceivable that in some circumstances this might lead to failure. This is an example of when reputational risk as an outcome (or consequential risk) is actually the most significant element.

A robust reverse stress-testing process that starts with the outcome of failure before examining the scenarios that might cause this and how they manifest themselves will almost certainly include a reputational dimension.

Conclusion

So, what have we learnt? Reputational risk is in fact the flip side of one of the most important commodities in the business world today—brand, and the perception that comes with it. To build a brand can take many years, but it can be lost very quickly as a consequence of mismanaging the reputational elements of an event that might arise out of an operational, liquidity, or other risk.

While most firms will probably have arrived at this conclusion themselves, financial services businesses are also being driven by a regulatory agenda that requires regulators to implement a supervision regime which engenders public confidence in the stability of the financial system itself. This is driving regulation to push firms to implement ways of managing reputational risk.

As such, even though we might regard reputational risk as an outcome of other risks, we should not simply assume that the risk management processes that are in place for those risks are adequate to manage reputational risk also. Firms need to consciously take action to ensure that their risk management processes are adequate for the management of reputational risk.

Summary and Further Steps

▶▶ Review the existing risk taxonomy and risk universe. How is reputational risk defined? Is its relationship with other risks clearly set out? Does this cascade through the organization in all risk management decisions?

▶▶ Review the ownership of reputational risk. Is it clear who is responsible for managing the reputation of the business with key stakeholders?

▶▶ Review the risk management cycle for reputational risk. Are the controls that are in place adequate for the management of the reputational dimension of the risks as well as the financial dimensions? Is there a coordinated communication strategy for the management of reputational risk?

▶▶ Review the existing approach to stress-testing. Are there stress-tests in place, particularly reverse stress-tests that really help the organization to examine the potential reputational downsides, including those that might lead to business failure?

▶▶ Review the existing risk culture in the firm to determine whether it supports the establishment of an effective risk management process for reputational risk.

More Info

Books:

Bruni, Franco, and David T. Llewellyn (eds). *The Failure of Northern Rock: A Multi-Dimensional Case Study*. Vienna: SUERF, 2009. Online at: www.suerf.org/download/studies/study20091.pdf

Articles:

Cummins, J. David, Christopher M. Lewis, and Ran Wei. "The market value impact of operational loss events for US banks and insurers." *Journal of Banking and Finance* 30:10 (October 2006): 2605–2634. Online at: dx.doi.org/10.1016/j.jbankfin.2005.09.015

The Economist. "Lessons of the fall: How a financial darling fell from grace, and why regulators didn't catch it." October 18, 2007. Online at: www.economist.com/node/9988865

Squires, Tris. "Banking on a reputation." *Financial Risks Today* (June 2, 2011). Online at: www.financialriskstoday.com/reputation_june.php

Thirwell, John. "Managing reputation risk—our 'purest' treasure." *Mutally Yours* (May 2011). Online at: tinyurl.com/63d2kaj

Reports:

Kaiser, Thomas. "Nowhere to hide: Reputational risk management." KPMG. Online at: tinyurl.com/5v79m2t

Micocci, Marco, Giovanni Masala, Giuseppina Cannas, and Giovanna Flore. "Reputational effects of operational risk events for financial institutions." Paper presented to the 18th International AFIR Colloquium, Rome, October 2, 2008. Online at: tinyurl.com/3w2y6rx [PDF].

Websites:

European Commission on Solvency II: tinyurl.com/2usz3wb

HSBC on reputational and operational risks: www.hsbc.com/1/2/investor-relations/governance/

Notes

1. For the more "typical" losses, the bank or insurance company had a profit opportunity that justified taking the risk. This is different from reputational risk, where there are no expected revenues/opportunities associated with taking the risk and incurring losses.
2. Boundary events are where an operational failure leads to an increase in an event that primarily arises out of another risk category. For example, a bank customer may default and the loss is made larger because the bank had exceeded its guidelines on lending to that customer.

The Cost of Reputation: The Impact of Events on a Company's Financial Performance

by Daniel Diermeier

Kellogg School of Management, Northwestern University, Evanston, IL, USA

This Chapter Covers

➤ Reputational crises have a significant impact on a company's valuation.
➤ They can be triggered by any business activity and do not necessarily reflect lapses in a company's ethics or integrity.
➤ Both the frequency and the magnitude of such events is increasing.
➤ The underlying factors that drive these developments are likely to increase in importance.
➤ Since reputational risk cannot be hedged or "outsourced," companies need to develop effective reputation management capabilities.
➤ Such capabilities consist of an integrated reputation management system and its core components: (1) mindset, (2) processes, and (3) values and culture.
➤ A reputation management process consists of a decision-making system and an intelligence system.

Introduction

CEOs and board members routinely list reputation as one the company's most valuable assets. Yet every month a new reputational disaster makes the headlines, destroying shareholder value and trust with customers and other stakeholders. During the last year, leading companies such as Toyota, Goldman Sachs, BP, Johnson & Johnson, and HP battled severe reputational crises. In all cases, financial markets punished the companies, leading to a severe and sustained erosion of their market values. In many cases, reputational damage is followed by lawsuits, public hearings, investigations, and regulatory actions.

In contrast to the scandals related to Enron, WorldCom, and Arthur Andersen a decade earlier, these crises are not limited to a specific domain (accounting practices and standards, especially with "new economy" firms) or caused by a dramatic increase in blatantly unethical or illegal activities. Rather, the involved companies were all category leaders, some with iconic status in their respective industries, and the issues involved ranged from quality and safety to disclosure and (alleged) executive misconduct.

The increase in the frequency and impact of reputational issues suggests that more fundamental shifts are occurring in the business environment and that companies are unprepared for dealing with them. What companies lack is an effective reputation management capability in the presence of increasing reputational risk. Too often, reputation management is considered a (sub)function of corporate communication and isolated from business decisions. Rather, companies need to adopt a strategic approach that treats reputational challenges as understandable and even predictable.

As a result, companies should manage their reputation like any other major business challenge: based on principled leadership and supported by sophisticated processes and capabilities that are integrated with the company's business strategy and culture.

Bausch & Lomb

Markets do not always properly adjust to reputational risk. One such example is Bausch & Lomb, a producer of soft contact lenses and lens care products. On April 10, 2006, the US Centers for Disease Control and Prevention linked a surge in potentially blinding fungal infections with Bausch & Lomb's new ReNu contact lens solution. As a result, Bausch & Lomb's stock price dropped from a closing price of US$57.67 on Friday, April 7, to US$45.61 on Wednesday, April 12. The company was heavily criticized for its handling of the crisis and the depressed stock price persisted. Bausch & Lomb subsequently experienced accounting restatements and was acquired by the private equity firm Warburg Pincus.

Remarkably, the link between the infections and ReNu, however, had been uncovered almost two months earlier, on February 22, in a public announcement by Singapore's Ministry of Health. (Bausch & Lomb subsequently withdrew the ReNu solution from its markets in Singapore and Hong Kong). The government announcement had been reported in the region's major newspapers, but had not been covered in the United States. Bausch & Lomb's stock lost a mere 3% from a closing price of US$71.51 on February 21 to US$69.40 on February 23, and quickly recovered. In other words, financial markets ignored the early warning signs.

The Cost of Reputational Crises

Severe erosion of shareholder value is common during reputational crises. During its recent crisis triggered by the sudden acceleration issue, Toyota's stock price dropped by as much as 24%, wiping out about US$33 billion in shareholder value, close to the total market value of Time Warner. In its battle with the US government in the aftermath of the 2008–09 financial crisis, Goldman Sachs lost US$24 billion of its market capitalization, a 26% drop in share price that exceeded the entire value of American Express. During the BP oil spill disaster in the Gulf of Mexico, BP's stock was almost cut in half, the equivalent of about US$90 billion in shareholder value, more than the market value of Procter & Gamble.

In some cases the drop in stock value is temporary, in other cases permanent. Much depends on how the companies handle the aftermath of crisis and commit to fixing the underlying business issue rather than engaging in shallow PR exercises. Toyota, for example, commenced a global quality improvement initiative that involved cultural and process changes at every level of the company.

The Problem of Measurement

In general, the impact of reputational events is difficult to quantify. Many existing studies point to a correlation between superior corporate reputations and financial performance. In most studies, corporate reputation is measured using lists from Fortune's Most Admired Companies[1]. There are various problems with this approach.

First, there is little change in the list membership. This may constitute evidence that reputation is persistent, but may also point to a metric that is too coarse to detect changes in a company's reputation on a smaller timescale, by region or product. Second, both inclusion in the list of most-admired companies and superior financial performance may be consequences of an underlying third characteristic that drives them both, such as "good management.

Studies that show the positive impact of reputation at the more general, macro-level are of limited use to managers as they typically fail to identify underlying factors driving a company's reputation. Given the difficulty with such macro-level studies, a better understanding of the processes that shape perceptions at the micro-level is desirable.

Reputation as a Bank Account

One common view of reputation is that it serves as a "trust bank account" or "buffer." The idea is that, through their actions, companies make "deposits" into a "trust account" that generates goodwill with their various stakeholders and constituencies. In case of a crisis, companies then are able to make a "withdrawal" from this bank account that helps to at least partially isolate them from the impact.

There is some evidence for this claim in the context of corporate social responsibility (CSR). Recent research suggests that in the case of a product recalls, for example, companies with high CSR ratings lose on average US\$600 million less in firm market value than companies with low ratings. However, other evidence suggests that, in a crisis context, previous "good deeds" are swamped by current actions (good or bad). Trust, it seems, can't easily be deposited; it must be earned.

Perception Drivers

To understand these processes in more detail, a rigorous approach using controlled experiments is helpful. The approach is similar to the market research studies that are conducted when companies design or evaluate brands. In such studies, subjects read vignettes of fictitious newspaper articles that describe a crisis. For example, a food manufacturer may be accused of using a potentially harmful food additive in order to increase the shelf life of its products, or the company may be involved in a nasty sexual harassment lawsuit. In addition to this background information, subjects are also provided with the fictitious company's responses, which range from engaged and caring to dismissive.

While a "trust bank account" (here measured by past good deeds) does have some effect, companies' current actions have a greater effect on shaping attitudes toward the company in question, as well as apparently unrelated issues such as the aesthetic evaluation of logos or product design.

Even more strikingly, when subjects were asked to evaluate the taste of a product (e.g. bottled water) from a company with a low "trust bank account," they rated the taste lower and drank less water. Corporate executives are only partially aware of these effects. When asked to predict how public attitudes would be affected by these same scenarios, corporate executives correctly predicted that an engaged response would be viewed more favorably than a defensive response, but they were overly optimistic about the public's ability to refrain from forming opinions when the company offered "no comment."

In sum, corporate reputation strategies have direct and measurable effects on the evaluation of core brand attributes. They can affect overall customer perceptions, evaluation of corporate logos, and even opinions of product taste and levels of consumption. Corporate executives are largely unaware of such effects.

Reputation as a Currency

These findings can be reconciled if we think of reputation less as a bank account and more as a currency. Currencies act as multiplies (not "linearly" as the bank account suggests). That is, if a currency is strong, purchasing power increases for all sorts of goods.

So, what does this mean in the context of reputation? The idea is that the same statement carries more weight and has more impact if it comes from a company with a good reputation. Or alternatively, a company with a strong reputation will need to do less than a company with a weak reputation to achieve the same effect.

Some evidence from the 2011 Edelman Trust Barometer[2] supports this intuition (Table 1).

Table 1. Effect of company trust. (Source: 2011 Edelman Trust Barometer)

Company trust	Will believe negative information if hearing it 1–2 times	Will believe positive information if hearing it 1–2 times
High	25%	51%
Low	57%	15%

In case of "low trust" we find the well-known negativity bias. A negative message has roughly four times as much impact as a positive message. But, strikingly, the situation is reversed in the "high trust" case, where a negative message has only half as much impact as a positive one. So, by moving from a high to a low trust "currency" a company gets an eight-fold increase of positive information impact—not bad.

Still, these results are to be treated with some caution. Ideally, one would want to replicate this behavior in a controlled laboratory setting. Yet this phenomenon would explain the "Teflon" characteristic of some companies, such as Apple, as witnessed in the limited impact of recent issues such as the dropped calls/antenna problem in the iPhone 4 on Apple's reputation. Surveys consistently put the high-tech industry at the top of the list of most-trusted industries.

Reputation Management Capabilities

The difficulty in exactly quantifying the impact of reputational events implies that reputational risk cannot easily be hedged or insured against. It therefore must be managed. This means that companies need to build reputation management capabilities appropriate to their level of risk.

The Impact of Events on a Company's Financial Performance

A company's reputation needs to be managed *actively*. Good business practices and ethical conduct are necessary, but they alone are not sufficient for successful reputation management. That responsibility should lie with business leaders. It should not be delegated to specialists such as lawyers or public relations experts, even though such experts play a valuable role in the reputation management process. Integration with business practices is necessary as reputational challenges arise out of a specific business context. In many cases, the most effective way to manage reputational risk is to improve the capabilities of business leaders (supported by well-designed processes) rather than adding another corporate layer.

Reputational challenges can arise from any area of day-to-day decision making, but executives tend to make decisions without consideration for the reputational impact. The key skill for business leaders is the ability to maintain an external perspective throughout decision-making processes and incorporate this perspective into the design of business decisions, e.g. the launch of a new product and its market-entry strategy. Companies need to understand that their decisions are creating a record today that will serve as the basis for their story tomorrow. Assessing reputational risk requires anticipating what a reputational crisis would look like and then taking proactive steps to prevent and prepare.

During a reputational crisis, the spotlight will not only be on the company's *current* actions, such as how the CEO answers questions and what the company will do to fix the problem, but also on its *past* actions. Reporters will ask when the company first knew about the problem, or why management didn't do more to fix it. The thought process behind each past decision can be brought out into the public arena and questioned. These past actions and decisions are now part of the record and cannot be changed. Even actions that looked reasonable at the time may wither under scrutiny from a hostile audience in a crisis context after any negative consequences come to light.

After the Gulf of Mexico oil spill, every minute decision that BP made concerning its safety processes took on disproportionate significance, leading to severe criticism of the company. And when Toyota had to recall its cars, commentators quickly alleged that its aggressive growth strategy had sacrificed quality and safety.

An easy way to improve decision making is the *Wall Street Journal* test, which suggests that decision makers should ask themselves whether they would be proud if a decision were *accurately* reported on the front page of the *Wall Street Journal*. This test evocatively captures the idea that a decision may look different once it comes under public scrutiny.

Such approaches help to transition from a crisis management mindset to a risk management one. Taking reputational risk seriously does not necessarily mean refraining from giving the green light to decisions that carry some reputational risk. Rather, the goal of proactive reputation management is to identify possible risks and mitigate them through *current* actions to reach an acceptable balance level of risk and control.

Reputation Management Processes

Who should own reputation management? Many executives answer: everyone. That sounds reasonable enough, but it is easy for things that are owned by everybody to actually be owned by nobody. Questions about decision rights, reporting, and accountability still need to be answered.

Many board members agree that the ultimate accountability for reputation management processes needs to be located at a level of the organization whose job description is the long-term viability of the company: the board. One reason why the board is a good choice is that it can keep management's incentives for short-term solutions in check. By setting clear guidelines and emphasizing the need to safeguard reputational equity, the board can help management avoid short-sighted cost-cutting mistakes.

But the board's role is to oversee and supervise; it is not to manage the company. So, where should reputation management reside within a company's decision-making structure? A common response is that it belongs on the agenda of senior management, including the CEO. The reason that reputation management belongs on the CEO's agenda is not only that reputational risk is one of the main risks facing the company, but also that the company's reputation is one of the few sources of sustained competitive advantage. Companies with stellar reputations can charge premiums and are difficult to imitate.

One of the CEO's main tasks is to integrate reputation management into the operational processes of the business. One approach to accomplishing this task has been to create a separate corporate function: a chief reputation officer (CRO) or chief reputational risk officer (CRRO). This approach works only if the position carries weight and if the company can avoid creating yet another corporate officer with little budget and less influence. The danger in this approach is that it could create additional barriers to the integration of reputation management and business strategy, and actually hurt the process rather than help it.

An alternative is the creation of a corporate reputation council (CRC). This is a cross-functional unit composed of senior executives with actual decision-making authority. The actual composition of the council needs to mirror the organizational structure of the company. For example, a matrix organization based on global territory and product lines would have representatives from both the major territories and the business lines. In addition, the main corporate functions (marketing, finance, supply chain, HR, communication, legal, government relations, and so on) need to be represented, as reputational problems are almost always multidimensional. The decision structure must be designed to handle the complexity of such issues.

It is critical that the CRC mirrors the actual operating structure of the business. One of the reasons that Toyota was slow in responding to the 2010 sudden acceleration crisis was the lack of a truly global decision-making structure. While Toyota's economic fortunes were heavily dependent on robust US sales, decision making was largely centered in Japan, with little input from the United States. Similarly, BP lacked a strong presence in the US regulatory and political environment, despite the fact that BP's US oil and gas assets represented more than one-quarter of the group's total annual production.

Good governance and decision-making structures are necessary for effective reputation management, but these alone are not sufficient. Here is why:

▸▸ Reputation consists of the perceptions of customers and other constituencies.

▸▸ In many cases, these perceptions are derived not from actual experience with the company or a deep knowledge of any given issue, but from an ever-changing mixture of opinion and information driven by the media, peer-to-peer websites, and various influencers ranging from experts to advocacy groups.

▸▸ Proactive reputation management requires companies to identify issues early, connect them with business strategy, develop prevention and preparation strategies, and implement possible changes in business practices in advance of an issue's gaining momentum.

This sequence can break down at various points. Executives may not realize the importance of reputation management for business success, governance structures may be lacking, or incentive structures may reward short-term vision. But companies may also fail to adopt effective strategies simply because they are unaware of the imminent danger. In other words, even perfectly designed governance and decision-making structures will be ineffective if they lack critical intelligence: decisions are then made in the dark.

This is the business case for investing in intelligence capabilities. Because reputation is driven by many ever-changing actors, the strategic landscape is frequently diffuse and unclear. Because successful reputational strategies need to be designed before a crisis occurs, simply surveying customers, investors, or other business partners will not do. Once customers or investors start to worry, it is too late—the deck is already stacked against the company. Therefore, in many cases, traditional business research tools such as surveys and focus groups can only measure the damage rather than prevent it in the first place. Proactive reputation management is impossible without good intelligence.

The governance structure needs to be closely connected with the intelligence function. This means that the CRC should provide strategic direction to the intelligence function and receive actionable intelligence that is directly connected to the corporate strategy. The intelligence function provides the core capabilities of issue identification, evaluation, and monitoring. The goal is both to function as an early warning system and to be able to assess the impact of corporate actions through a feedback mechanism. Without an intelligence function, the CRC will be operating in the dark and making decisions based on intuition rather than data. A company's intelligence function may range from informal monitoring of various media sources and proactive stakeholder outreach to the creation of a fully developed internal intelligence capability with its own staff and budget.

Intelligence functions are not only important for management. Given the critical role of the board as guardian of a company's reputation, it is surprising and worrisome that most corporate boards are not supported by a separate intelligence function. Such a function is ideally provided by a third party, not by company staff. Much of the critical reputational intelligence is external to the company, and it may lead board members to ask more probing questions of management.

In summary, a strategic mindset needs to be supported by effective processes. First, companies must develop a proper governance structure that should mirror the company's organizational structure. A cross-functional council is preferable to a separate corporate function unless that function is endowed with sufficient influence and resources. Second, companies need an intelligence capability. In contrast to other corporate capabilities, an intelligence system is not optional; it is essential. Reputational challenges can emerge from anywhere in the company's operations or external business environment. The lack of intelligence capabilities means that the company acts in the dark and loses its ability to manage emerging issues proactively.

The Role of People

Business leaders also need to understand that even the most advanced reputation management system is implemented by people. They need to assess the situation, evaluate risks, and then make appropriate decisions. Getting this right requires not only a strategic mindset but also values and culture in order to provide guidance to individuals. We cannot expect each employee of a company to correctly assess the reputational risk of an issue, but we can expect him or her to raise a red flag when something does not "look right."

Acting as corporate steward does not only mean doing right by customers, employees, and suppliers. It requires the ability to *think strategically*. This implies, on the one hand, viewing reputational decisions not solely as PR issues, but as decisions that are tightly connected to the company's strategy, its core competencies and values, and its distinctive position in the marketplace. On the other hand, it requires the ability to view even a familiar business decision from the point of view of people who are not specialists, but still may have strong opinions on an issue. More often than not, these opinions are not just driven by cool reason, but involve powerful emotions and passionate views of what is right or wrong behavior.

A strategic mindset also requires *situational awareness*. Reputation is essentially public. It is driven by third parties who have their own agenda. Understanding and anticipating the motivations and capabilities of these actors is essential for situational awareness. But reputational challenges are not simply the consequence of wrong decisions, accidents, or bad luck; they are frequently created by activists, interest groups, and public actors, with the goal of forcing changes in business practices through "private politics." Activists are competitors for the company's reputation. They need to be treated as seriously as competitors in the marketplace.

The last component of a strategic mindset is to avoid the *expert trap*. Becoming an expert means learning to see the world in a particular way. A doctor learns to identify symptoms and decide on a diagnosis, a poker player learns to identify "tells" of opponents that provide critical information on the strength of their hand, and a music enthusiast can pick a favorite pianist from dozens of recordings of the same piece. Acquiring and using expertise in a coordinated fashion is, of course, tremendously valuable and is at the root of the efficient organization of business processes. But, in the context of reputational challenges, it can lead us astray.

When a company collapses as a result of an earnings restatement, a trained accountant may focus on the fact that no accounting rules were violated, while everybody else will be affected by images of crying employees leaving their office for the last time. A safety engineer will point to his company's industry-leading safety standards and may be bewildered when the media focuses on one specific victim. A loan officer may view missed mortgage payments as lost revenue, while the borrower may experience them as the fear of losing the family home. The difficulty lies in the public nature of reputational challenges where company actions are evaluated by non-experts through the filter of the media. This requires decision makers to set aside their expertise and see the situation from the point of view of laypeople in a heightened emotional state.

In summary, reputation management is not a corporate function, but a capability. It requires the right mindset integrated with the company's strategy, guided by its culture and values, and supported by carefully designed governance and intelligence processes. Developing this capability is as demanding and as challenging as developing customer focus or the ability to execute. Today's companies need to embrace this challenge.

More Info

Book:

Diermeier, Daniel. *Reputation Rules: Strategies for Building Your Company's Most Valuable Asset.* New York: McGraw-Hill, 2011.

Articles:

Minor, Dylan. "CSR as reputation insurance: Theory and evidence." Working paper. Kellogg School of Management, 2010.

Roberts, Peter W., and Grahame R. Dowling. "Corporate reputation and sustained superior financial performance." *Strategic Management Journal* 23:12 (December 2002): 1077-1093. Online at: dx.doi.org/10.1002/smj.274

Uhlmann, Eric Luis, George E. Newman, Victoria Medvec, Adam Galinsky, and Daniel Diermeier. "The sound of silence: Corporate crisis communication and its effects on consumer attitudes and behavior." Working paper. Kellogg School of Management, 2010. Online at: tinyurl.com/3n89y65 [PDF].

Notes

1. Fortune's Most Admired Companies: money.cnn.com/magazines/fortune/mostadmired
2. 2011 Edelman Trust Barometer: www.edelman.com/trust/2011/

Sustainability and Corporate Reputation: Who Needs Reputation When You've Got Cash Flows?

by William Cox

Management & Excellence, Madrid, Spain, and Sao Paulo, Brazil

This Chapter Covers

- ▸▸ Attempts to link reputation to financials and their weaknesses.
- ▸▸ The illusory links between sustainability, reputation, and financials.
- ▸▸ How individual projects, including sustainability projects, generate financial returns, which renders "reputation" an empty concept.

Introduction: Executives See Link Between Reputation and Sustainability

Of 1,749 corporate executives from various sectors worldwide, 72% see sustainability as very important in managing corporate reputation. In the manufacturing sector, this proportion was as high as 79%—in both cases sustainability's impact on reputation was the number one reason cited for getting involved in sustainability (Bonini, Görner, and Jones, 2010). Although these and similar data suggest that executives believe that sustainability impacts reputation, does it really? And what if we could demonstrate a direct connection between sustainability and revenues, cost savings and free cash flows, among other financial indicators? If sustainability investments were to contribute directly to financials, why worry about the undefined and perhaps undefinable concept of "reputation"?

Attempts to Link Reputation to Financials

Consider typical arguments that suggest a connection between reputation and financials.

The first such attempt claims that companies with good reputations benefit from better equity price development than the average, as suggested by two RepuStars indices. Both are run by the Intangible Asset Finance Society, tracking the equity prices of companies it considers particularly reputable according to data on customers, vendors, investors, and employees. The surveyed behavior and expectations of these groups are said to correlate positively with companies' equity and credit performances (Intangible Asset Finance Society, 2011). The indices admit three companies from each of 19 key sectors.

"Since January 2009, the RepuStars Variety and RepuStars Prime Composite Indices have gained 99.03% and 99.24%, respectively; the S&P 500 Composite Index has gained 38.33%" (Huygens, 2011). What both indices demonstrate is that there is a correlation between equity performance and some characteristics of the companies that comprise the index. These characteristics may or may not have anything to do with "reputation." The outperformance by the stocks in the reputation indices may be related to investor relations efforts, marketing, fundamental financials, governance, investment technicals, or transparency. To invoke the concept of "reputation" adds little explanatory value as to why they are performing better than the S&P benchmark index.

The suggestion among advocates of reputation is that good management produces a residual "asset" which drives revenues even if management and products were to decline in quality. Thus, for reputation to be considered a real asset, it would first have to be highly memorable. Yet if this memory is to be credibly linked to financial results (higher revenues, investor behavior, or a more efficient workforce—i.e. higher productivity), we have little choice but to look at how the remaining useful life (RUL) of individual projects impacts revenues, for example.

A second approach that attempts to link reputation to financials is exemplified in the work of such companies as the Reputation Institute, which simply assigns "factors" to the value of companies' reputations. While these may be useful in helping companies to benchmark themselves against others, they do little to explain the financial value of reputation, nor to justify whether "reputation" is a definable and useful concept. An example is the Reputation Institute's RepTrack System, which it describes as "a proprietary tool that was developed by Reputation Institute to measure corporate reputations. It is grounded on the theory that reputations are emotional attitudes stakeholders have towards companies, and can be measured by assessing their degree of Admiration, Trust, 'Good Feeling,' and 'Overall Esteem' for companies." (see Reputation Institute RepTrack System in More Info).

The Reputation Institute's approach is essentially to survey what people think about certain brands and assign a score to these opinion results. The problem here is that these results are not causally linkable to any substantial financial indicators, such as cash flows or other key financial metric. And, as such, it is still unclear whether "reputation" is related to financial success, and thus to building a company's value.

A third approach is to value brands, which are typically considered integral parts of reputation. BrandZ's study of the values of the top 100 brands considers the brand's contribution to earnings as well as a multiple by which the brand is likely to impact future earnings. One reason this approach is closer to reality is that it focuses on a definable topic—brand—and seeks to determine its contribution to financials. Its weakness is that it presumes the very point it seeks to prove, namely that "reputation" is a reality and somehow produces financial results.

> Attempts to link reputation to financial performance typically are in the form of an index of reputed companies, "factors" based on surveys, and valuations of brands. All attempts use consolidated data without sufficient causal links between reputation and financials. However, the brand valuation effort of BrandZ, a brand equity database, comes closest to actually assigning a serious value to something, in this case brands. Brands are realities, perhaps unlike the concept of "reputation."

The Evidence for a Link between Sustainability and Reputation Is Weak

Thus far we have argued that "reputation" is something of a ghost both because it is ill-defined and because its impact on financials is not substantiated. As such, we will bypass reputation as an intermediary and confront the issue of whether sustainability projects actually contribute to financials, and how they do.

To be sure, we are not implying that advertising, communications, sales approaches, product design, and other investments have no definable effect on financials. On the contrary, they *are* the sources of revenues, cash flows, and enterprise value. Our critique of indices, vague reputational factors, and even brand valuations is that they are too general to isolate the effects on cash flows and building the financial value of companies. This can only be done by analyzing the financial impact of individual projects, yielding their net present values (NPVs) and thus concluding a serious company valuation. And these projects include sustainability investments, such as energy savings, employee training, ethics, governance, transparency, and risk management. All contribute more or less effectively to companies' revenues, cost savings, free cash flows, and PVs of enterprise worth.

Revenues and cost savings are generated at a project level and thus can only be measured at this level. Individual marketing, sales, and related project investments are where revenues come from. The general concept of "reputation" is meaningless if we know the returns generated by these projects.

Sustainability, Reputations, and Financial Returns

Investments in new factories, personnel, and machines are normally subjected to discounted cash flow analysis to determine whether their NPVs are positive and to assess whether the return on average capital employed (ROACE) exceeds the cost of capital, for example. Unfortunately, sustainability investments are rarely properly assessed, even though Dow or Bovespa blue chips invest well over US$100 million annually into social and cultural projects alone. Petrobras, Brazil's largest company in terms of market capitalization (US$230 billion in January 2011), spends roughly US$230 million annually on social and cultural projects for which no returns are known to be calculated. Thus, management shows no returns (and hence no sufficient justification) for the disbursement of US$230 million of shareholders' money. And even for environmentally relevant modernizations that reduce emissions, energy use, and waste, the company does not cite financial benefits even though those environmental projects are the easiest to measure returns on.

Executives appear to view sustainability investments as a free-for-all to which normal practices of financial accountability do not apply. Ironically, they make these investments largely in the name of company reputation and ethics, even though it is hardly ethical to spend shareholders' money without demonstrating financial returns for these investments.

Big corporations spend hundreds of millions annually on social, cultural, and other sustainability projects without knowing whether these are driving revenues or helping to reduce costs. Executives treat sustainability as a *carte blanche* for spending shareholders' money and justify it as "good for reputation."

Investors Believe that Sustainability Positively Impacts Financials

Investors increasingly credit sustainability investments with generating good financials, as data from Sustainable Asset Management (SAM), the researchers for the Dow Jones Sustainability Index (DJSI), argue (see Figure 1). Investments by mutual funds worldwide screened according to sustainable criteria are expected to grow to

US\$25 trillion by 2015 (SAM, 2010), and the top 100 companies (by market capitalization) typically spend US\$100 million to \$200 million per year on so-called triple bottom line ("sustainability") projects, which include social, human resource, sports, cultural, and governance projects (Management & Excellence, 2009; and see Figure 2). As such, sustainability and sustainable investing are entering mainstream finance. Sustainable investments are made in companies that are screened for their strong performances in governance, ethics, environment, financials, transparency, and social engagements, among other related areas.

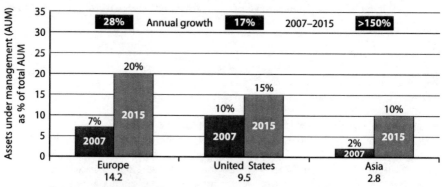

Figure 1. Growth of sustainability investments. (Source: Sustainable Asset Management, 2010)

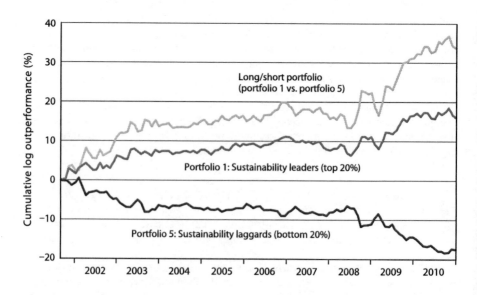

Figure 2. Equity performance of sustainable companies.
(Source: Sustainable Asset Management, 2011)

One likely reason for unchecked spending on sustainability "to manage reputation" is that returns on many sustainability projects are difficult to measure. The central challenge of determining returns from most sustainable investments is that many are processes and programs of a company and are neither traded nor otherwise transacted. As a result, there are no prices for them and their impact on revenues or costs is difficult to isolate. Furthermore, a community education program, a training program for employees, or a governance policy are fairly easy to copy and therefore there is little reason to buy or sell them.

> Investors increasingly believe that sustainability drives good financials and are investing in sustainability to the tune of trillions of dollars annually. This increases the need to know which sustainability projects are delivering positive returns and which waste money. The concept of "reputation" only gets in the way of a serious returns analysis.

Return on Sustainability: Determining Financial Returns from Sustainability

A new approach to measuring the financial impacts of individual sustainability projects is "return on sustainability," or ROS. ROS determines the contributions of sustainability projects to companies' current revenues, cost savings, earnings before interest, taxes, depreciation, and amortization (EBITDA), free cash flows, and the PV of companies' values.

The ROS process begins by looking at what could drive the returns of sustainability projects, which are summarized in Table 1.

Table 1. The four reputation strategies

Project area	Project	Facilitators (intermediate impacts), independent variables	Dependent variables	Impacts	Methods to measure impacts	Buyers, sellers, regulation, separable	Final return
Corporate social responsibility	Community education program	Brand, affinity	New client business, more business/ clients, more loyal clients	Sales, revenues	Survey, pre/post revenue analysis	None	Free cash flow (FCF), limited remaining useful life
Cultural	Arts center	Brand, affinity, loyalty	Exposure, confidence in brand	Revenues	Survey	None	FCF
Environmental	Installing energy-efficient lightbulbs	Environmentally relevant changes, modernizations	Saving resources, reducing inefficiencies	Operating expenses, capital expenditure	Pre/ post cost analysis	Regulation	FCF to perpetuity
Human resources	Training in ethical behavior	Reduction in ethical problem cases	Improved efficiency	Operating expenses	Survey, pre/post cost accounting	None	FCF for several years

(continued overleaf)

Table 1. *(continued)*

Project area	Project	Facilitators (intermediate impacts), independent variables	Dependent variables	Impacts	Methods to measure impacts	Buyers, sellers, regulation, separable	Final return
Innovation	Innovation incentive program	New ideas, processes, technological improvements	Results of each innovation project implemented	Revenues, operating expenses, capital expenditure	Various data	If technical innovations: buyers, sellers, regulations/ contracts	FCF depending on innovations implemented
Governance	Allowing shareholders to vote on executive remuneration package	Greater demand for stock	Upward stock price pressure driven by confident investors	Higher stock prices	Pre/post analysis of stock sales volumes	Regulation	Higher market capitalization
Investor relations	Road shows	Investor affinity, confidence	Stock demand, stock sales	Market capitalization (stock price)	Surveys, pre/post stock price development	None	Perpetual cash flows discounted back to cash flow in year 1
Sustainable management	Improved risk management	Fewer occurrences (e.g. client defaults)	Cost savings, greater efficiency	Lower operating expenses, loss provisions, and discount rate	Pre/post project relative to industry benchmark	Regulation	FCF

The ROS process has been implemented for a wide variety of different sustainability projects, typically yielding the project ROS margins over three-year periods shown in Table 2. The table shows the present values of project EBITDAs over a three-year period. The projects are based on actual client projects carried out in the financial services sector.

Table 2. Typical returns of sustainability projects by type. (Source: Management & Excellence, 2011)

Sustainability project	ROS margin PV 2009–12 (%)	NPV 2009–12 (US$000)
Soccer team	78.3	38,093
Community project	42.4	2,420
Internal training	254	8,354
Governance project	69.3	2,677
Environmental project	82.4	4,580
Ethics project	540	3,450

A ROS assessment consists of isolating, testing, and calculating the financial values of variables that will measurably drive such factors as revenues, cost savings, and productivity (see Table 1 on "drivers"). Working the resulting project EBITDAs into a company's financial statements yields the free cash flows generated by each sustainability or intangible project.

The final ROS step is to determine a project discount rate that will accurately reflect the risks of the market, sector, company, and project. Usually, the corporate weighted average cost of capital (WACC) is simply applied to all the company's projects. Yet this yields a distorted picture of a project's NPV because the risk profile of a project is likely to be different (normally 200–300 bps lower) from that of the company. In the case of large investments in sustainability, using the wrong discount rate will generate an undervaluation of the company as a whole because the PVs of the project cash flows are undervalued. Even if the discount rate of a project is only marginally lower than that of its host company, the difference in the perpetual value of cash flows from the properly valued project is significant. Table 3 illustrates this with an actual example from a large bank.

Table 3. Cash flows from sustainability projects using company and ROS-adjusted project discount rates

Unit	Discount rate	Funds flow in year 1 (US$ million)	Perpetuity value (US$ million)	Factor
Company	0.12	32.1	267.5	8.3 times
Project with company discount rate	0.12	0.775	6.46	8.3 times
Project with ROS project discount rate	0.09	0.775	8.611	11.1 times

Thus, to know which projects produce the most return and therefore the greatest impact on value, there is no way but to analyze each project separately and add these sums up to arrive at a "total value of sustainability"—and, ultimately, a total company value. If the total perpetual value of all projects exceeds the enterprise value, the stock of the company is likely to be undervalued because its cash flows from sustainability projects are not being fully appreciated by the market.

> Sustainability projects generate positive or negative returns like any other project. But normally these projects are less risky than the company business as a whole and therefore need to be discounted by an adjusted WACC, not the company WACC. Applying the wrong discount rate to sustainability projects could undervalue a company.

Realizing the Full Potential of Sustainability Returns

Although sustainability projects such as those cited above may yield impressive returns, how do we know that these returns are the highest possible for each project? ROS uses survey and consulting methods to test for unrealized return potential of sustainability projects.

Often projects are simply not optimally implemented, such as launching a new ethics program just before Christmas when everyone is only looking forward to the holidays, or implementing education programs in areas where the company's products are not sold.

Table 4 lists the sustainability projects of a Bovespa (Bolsa de Valores do Estado de São Paulo) Index-listed company and shows the ROS measurement of the "operational effectiveness" of sustainability projects. The score shows how effectively (per cent of effectiveness) projects were implemented. The difference between this score and 100% is its estimated quantified potential. The last column shows the present value of these projects if they were optimally implemented. The benefit of this approach is to get higher returns out of every invested dollar, which can lead to a higher expected company value.

Table 4. Cash flows and values (in Brazilian real, R$) of sustainability projects according to their operational effectiveness

Sustainability project for external stakeholders that impacts reputation	Size of investment	ROS in %	One year PV of all cash flows: contribution to enterprise value*	Operational effectiveness score of these values	One year PV of all cash flows: contribution to enterprise value* at 100% operational effectiveness
Community welfare	R$25 million	60%	R$571 million	70%	R$815 million
Education for children	R$10 million	10%	R$157 million	30%	R$524 million
Cultural support	R$31 million	12%	R$496 million	25%	R$1,984 million
Environmental credit cards	R$0.5 million	1,800%	R$841 million	80%	R$1,051 million
Sports sponsorship	R$60 million	300%	R$2,571 million	95%	R$2,706 million
Sustainability advertising	R$15 million	25%	R$267.8 million	100%	R$267.8 million
Investor relations (sustainability related only, e.g. sustainability report)	R$1 million	1,100%	R$157 million	90%	R$174 million
All other projects	R$420 million	30%	R$7,800 million	42%	R$18,571 million
Total PV of value of sustainability projects			R$12,861 million		R$26,092 million

* Discounted by corporate WACC (0.10) minus constant growth rate (0.03).

Using ROS or a similar return on investment (ROI) instrument to determine returns on a sustainability project yields four key benefits:

➤ it determines project returns;
➤ it allows you to improve project operations and raise returns;
➤ potentially it raises cash flows and estimates of company value by applying more accurate project discount rates;
➤ it helps to realize the project's full returns potential.

Summary and Further Steps

▸▸ Although executives like to justify expenditure on sustainability projects by invoking its impact on reputation, the concept of "reputation" is too vague to be linked to financial outcomes in any specific and serious manner.

▸▸ Nevertheless, well-managed and communicated sustainability projects contribute substantially to companies' revenues and cost reductions, thus yielding returns that are typically greater than their costs of capital.

▸▸ Thus, given that individual sustainability projects generate measurable financial results—whereas the "ghost" of reputation does not—reputation becomes a moot concept which does not help us to assess risk or return. The risks and returns of sustainability can only credibly be assessed at a project level where actual cash flows can be determined.

▸▸ Companies investing in intangibles should use ROS or another ROI instrument to assess the cash flows from project investments instead of blindly justifying them as "contributing to reputation."

More Info

Books:

Anson, Weston. "Alternative valuation methodologies." In *The Intangible Assets Handbook: Maximizing Value from Intangible Assets.* Chicago, IL: American Bar Association, 2007.

Articles:

Banick, Sarah. "ZIBS Forum: Roger Sinclair on 'viewing brands as assets.' Goizueta Business School, Emory University, 2010. Online at: www.zibs.com/sinclair.shtml

Bonini, Sheila, Stephan Görner, and Alissa Jones. "How companies manage sustainability: McKinsey Global Survey results." *McKinsey Quarterly* (March 2010). Online at: tinyurl.com/y68eymb

BrandZ. "BrandZ top 100 most valuable brands 2009." Online at: www.wpp.com/wpp/companies

Cox, William H. "Sustentabilidade deve dar lucro." *Harvard Business Review Brasil* (September 2010): 60–62. Online at: www.hbrbr.com.br/index.php?codid=300

Cropper, Maureen L., and Wallace E. Oates. "Environmental economics: A survey." *Journal of Economic Literature* 30:2 (June 1992): 675–740. Online at: www.jstor.org/stable/2727701

Flatt, S. J., and S. J. Kowalczyk. "Creating competitive advantage through intangible assets: The direct and indirect effects of corporate culture and reputation." *Advances in Competitiveness Research* 16:1/2 (2008).

Huygens, C. "RepuStars 2011 June 13." *Mission: Intangible* (Intangible Asset Finance Society blog) (June 13, 2011). Online at: tinyurl.com/6ld5ruy

More Info

Reports:

Dearden, Lorraine, Howard Reed, and John Van Reenen. "The impact of training on productivity and wages: Evidence from British panel data." CEP Discussion Paper 674. London School of Economics and Political Science, February 2005. Online at: eprints.lse.ac.uk/779/

Nucleus Research. "ROI case study: SumTotal anonymous bank." Research note D58. December 2004. Online at: www.sumtotal.com.au/assets/casestudies/large_usbank.pdf

SAM and PricewaterhouseCoopers. "The sustainability yearbook 2010: Sustainability investing: The paradigm for institutional investors." 2010. Online at: tinyurl.com/4y3pqez

SAM Research and Robeco Quantitative Strategies. "Alpha from sustainability." White paper. 2011. Online at: tinyurl.com/5ufy6nb [PDF].

Ulrich, Dave, and Norm Smallwood. "HR's new ROI: Return on intangibles." *Human Resource Management* 44:2 (Summer 2005): 137–142. Online at: dx.doi.org/10.1002/hrm.20055

Websites:

BrandZ: www.brandz.com

Dow Jones Sustainability Indexes: www.sustainability-index.com

Intangible Asset Finance Society (IAFS): www.iafinance.org

Management & Excellence: www.management-rating.com

Management & Excellence—Return on Sustainability (ROS®): www.management-rating.com/index.php?lng=en&cmd=110

Reputation Institute RepTrak System: www.reputationinstitute.com/advisory-services/reptrak

Measuring Brand Reputation

by Andrew Tucker

Mettle Consulting, London, and Brunel University, Uxbridge, UK

This Chapter Covers

- What brand reputation is.
- How value is achieved through brand reputation.
- Why existing approaches to brand reputation miss the target.
- Measuring brand reputation.
- Brand reputation in the UK energy sector.
- Brand reputation of Toyota.

Introduction: What Is Brand Reputation?

Brand, reputation, and strategy are like a three-legged stool—remove one leg and the stool topples. Whole disciplines have grown up around each leg of the stool, but companies only achieve sustained commercial success when all three are well manufactured, balance each other, and can take the weight of expectations. Of course, building sustained commercial success is more complicated than building stools! Amid the mountains of academic research and practitioner advice on strategic brand and reputation management, there is a gap in how brand and reputation can be manufactured to balance each other and take the weight of expectations. First, let us clarify the core concepts that are in play. *Brand* is the expectation of what a product or service delivers. Simply put, brand is what a company says about itself. *Reputation* is the collective perception of a company's stakeholders, based on whether the brand matches the company's performance and behaviors. In other words, reputation is what others think about your company. *Brand reputation*, then, is the management of the dynamic interaction between brand and reputation; it is how you evaluate whether what you say about yourself and what others think about you are sufficiently aligned to achieve sustained commercial success.

There is a straightforward business case for building and maintaining a strong brand reputation. 91% of customers choose to buy products or services from a reputable company, but 77% of customers would actively boycott the products or services of a disreputable company.[1] For listed companies with well-known brands, a 5% change in reputation corresponds to a 3% change in market value.[2] Of course, many leading companies already proactively manage their corporate reputations to realize bottom-line results. For example, Shell invested US$6 million in gaining community consent in the two years prior to its 1998 Malampaya deepwater gas-to-power project in the Philippines. Going beyond the local environmental impact assessment laws, Shell engaged with the communities to be impacted by the US$4.5 billion project through a series of community outreach meetings, information dissemination, participatory workshops, and dialogs with regulators. As a result, the company estimates it saved up to US$72 million in completing construction ahead of schedule, avoiding contractual penalties, and being able to lay pipelines without local protests.[3]

However, too many supposedly sophisticated companies manage their brand reputations poorly. Recently, News International's disastrous reputation management of its News of the World brand led to the forced abandonment of its 2011 bid for BSkyB; BP's corporate reputation for incompetence and poor safety culture has materially diminished its brand value in the United States after the 2010 Gulf of Mexico incident; and the Royal Bank of Scotland is struggling to escape the massive damage to its various brands caused by its corporate reputation for arrogance and mismanagement exposed by the global credit crunch in 2008.

But for every newsworthy brand reputation failure, there are many other companies reaping real benefits from managing their reputations well. For example, Apple's reputation for design and innovation allows it seemingly easy access to already crowded product markets. Tesco's 20-year reinvention from discount retailer in the early 1990s to today's high-street behemoth has reaped market-beating shareholder returns. Virgin Group's reputation as a trendy upstart has shielded it from its patchy customer service levels. This chapter briefly sets out to address the gap in both the academic and business practice literature around brand reputation. It looks at the value that can be achieved by balancing brand and reputation through proactive management. It briefly examines why measuring brand reputation has proved so difficult to date. An innovative approach to brand reputation is presented, using data collected on the UK energy market in June 2011 and on Toyota in May 2010. It offers a case study of a well-known company that is currently engaged in brand reputation management. Last, it offers a summary for your company to balance its brand and reputation management to achieve sustained commercial success.

What is Brand Reputation?

Brand is what a company says about itself. Reputation is what others think about your company. Brand reputation is how you evaluate whether what you say about yourself and what others think about you are sufficiently aligned to achieve sustained commercial success.

Achieving Value Through Brand Reputation

A large academic and practitioner literature has built up over the last decade on the benefits of enhancing an organization's reputation. When this literature is cross-referenced with the literature on the benefits of actively managing brand, a clear set of shareholder-value drivers emerges. Successfully managing brand reputation brings increased shareholder value in two ways. Internally, enhanced brand reputation helps to recruit and retain talent, improves productivity and innovation, and increases investment potential. Externally, it allows companies to charge a premium price and drives acceptance of new product development.[4] However, the opposite is also true. A diminished brand reputation destroys shareholder value in two ways. Internally, diminished brand reputation undermines investor support and makes supply chain management harder. Externally, it makes it harder to attract and retain customers, undermines regulatory relations, and drives up the cost of winning new business.[5]

The UK grocery supermarket chain Tesco is an example of a company that has managed its brand reputation consistently well over a 20-year period. In the early 1990s, Tesco's brand was viewed as a large-scale discount retailer, much like Aldi today. Its reputation was viewed as "pile it high, sell it cheap," similar to how large mid-market bookstores are seen today. It endured high customer turnover and low staff morale, had few premium product lines and an erratic supply chain, and generated few business innovations. As a consequence, Tesco trailed a distant third behind its competitors, Marks & Spencer and Sainsbury's. Its stock traded at a discount due to its weak brand and poor reputation.

Following intensive stakeholder research, Tesco embarked on a number of brand reputation initiatives that have collectively transformed the brand in 15 years to what it is today. Table 1 shows the most significant initiatives that the company has undertaken during this period. It first established an ongoing customer insight data source through the Tesco Clubcard loyalty scheme in 1995. It made a break with its past customer experience by opening Tesco Express stores in the United Kingdom and abroad from 1996, and it promoted Terry Leahy—a key director in launching the brand reputation initiatives—to CEO in 1997.[6] In 2000, Tesco launched its online service. Although this was several years after competitor first movers, Tesco benefited by learning from their mistakes so as not to damage its brand with poor delivery. Since then, Tesco has extended its brand into mobile telephony, banking, electrical goods, and furniture. Across the period, the advertising campaigns followed the initiatives rather than the other way round. Also, Tesco maintained its research program (embedded in its clubcard loyalty scheme) to ensure that the initiatives were adding the expected sustained value. The subsequent value creation is shown in Figure 1.

Table 1. Tesco's reputation initiatives 1992–2004

Year	Initiative
1992	"Every little helps" slogan
1993	Tesco's economy own brand launched
1995	Introduction of Clubcard, a customer loyalty card
1996	First Tesco Express stores, high street grocery retailing outlets that are smaller than the company's large supermarket centers
1997	Terry Leahy appointed CEO
2000	Introduction of online ordering service
2004	Tesco Mobile phone deals for customers

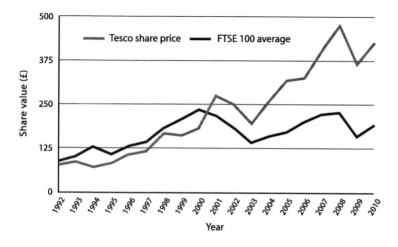

Figure 1. Tesco derives value from managing brand reputation

Missing the Target—Existing Approaches to Brand Reputation

The key reason that managers have struggled to deal in any systematic way with the dynamic interaction between brand and reputation is that, until recently, it has been impossible to measure brand reputation accurately, consistently, and comparatively. As a result, the old business school adage that "what gets measured gets managed" has been upheld. In large part, managers have been hamstrung by a bifurcation in the research field.

On one side of the field, brand valuation companies like Interbrand and Millward Brown have adopted econometric models that estimate the economic value of a brand in its current use to its current owner, using discounted future net earnings attributable to the brand. While econometric models are valuable in their production of notional brand values, they are less useful as management tools for three reasons.

▸ First, they focus on historical customer purchase behavior. This means that other stakeholders important to the business—employees, regulators, media, and supply chain—are excluded. It also means that historic behavior is treated as the sole indicator of future behavior, thus making the model artificially static and impervious to externalities.

▸ Second, the determination of the weighting factor applied to the basic financial analysis is subjective and proprietary.[7] This means that brands are compared with each other based on nontransparent criteria. While a company might accept this weighting for itself, its comparative use is impossible to accept with confidence, so making competitive strategizing inherently less certain.

▸ Third, the nature of the analysis is generic in assuming that all brands operate alike. So, Proctor & Gamble and Unilever brands receive no reputation halo effect from their parent companies, an effect that is clearly visible in financial analysts' calculations of brand value.

On the other side of the field, corporate reputation indices like those produced by Fortune magazine, Management Today, and the Reputation Institute are underpinned by models that incorporate only a single stakeholder group's attitudes toward companies. Although attitudinal models are useful in their production of a global ranking of well-known companies, these indices are less useful as management tools for three reasons. First, brand is only indirectly alluded to in the research methodology, despite the initial market segmentation being heavily influenced by stakeholders' awareness of large brands. Both Fortune and Management Today populate their rankings with investors' and managers' awareness of branded companies, while the Reputation Institute populates its rankings with general population awareness of branded B2C companies.[8] Therefore, these indices produce no clear management advice on dealing with the dynamic interaction between brand and reputation. Second, because these indices are historic assessments by single stakeholder groups, the analysis produced suffers from a lack of input from other important stakeholders in the business—employees, regulators, media, and supply chain. Third, the indices are constrained only to those criteria which were established in the original survey design. This means that the resulting analysis cannot be tailored to individual companies.

Measuring Brand Reputation

Several lessons, then, can be learned from the highlighted difficulties in the research field.

▸ Brand reputation requires management according to the various relevant stakeholder audiences, like customers, prospects, employees, senior management, shareholders, media, regulators, and supply chain. The reputation expectations of customers and shareholders are not necessarily the same, and they need to be addressed differently.

▸ Although the brand is the same, that different reputation profiles should exist at the same time is not surprising. Businesses need to optimize the reputation profile for each audience rather than to try and be the same thing to everyone. Being consistent with brand messaging for each reputation audience is key.

▸ Managing multiple, conflicting brand reputation metrics is unrealistic. It is a superhuman task to amalgamate and make sense of customer insight interviews, investor relations surveys, employee engagement feedback, prospecting data, media relations efforts, and public affairs campaigns. Managers require a single framework within which to measure and calibrate brand communications and reputation initiatives.

What is required, then, is a robust framework for measuring the extent to which a company's brand messaging impacts multiple stakeholders' perceptions of reputation and, hence, future actions. In other words, we need a single way of understanding, measuring, and managing whether what a company says about itself indicates its stakeholders' future behavior toward the company. The link between brand and reputation is a matter of trust. Trust, as it occurs in managing brand and reputation, involves stakeholders granting companies enough room to operate, while recognizing that this judgment comes at some risk to the stakeholder. That is, trust facilitates resolution of the inevitably conflicting interests between a company and its stakeholders. At the same time, the extension of trust between companies and stakeholders enables coordination and cooperation, so opening up more potential solutions than if trust were not extended, and expanding the company's operating space.

Different stakeholders have varying kinds of trust relationships with the same company. For example, customers' trust might be driven largely by cost, quality, and efficacy of product, whereas stockholders' trust might be driven by quality of management, consistency of returns, and strength of corporate governance. In both cases, the stakeholder is taking a risk that the company's products or returns will be as that stakeholder expects. That is, the stakeholder is trusting the company according to different criteria.

The challenge, then, is to model the different types of trust in the relationship between company and stakeholders, to assess the relevant levels of these trust types per stakeholder, and to measure trust levels across all relevant stakeholders, as a way of reporting on stakeholders' future behavior toward the company. Recently published academic research has shown that a three-part trust typology is robust and operationally productive.[9] From this research, we can see that stakeholders trust companies in the following three ways.

▸ *Alignment trust* measures the depth of trust that stakeholders have in what your business promises to deliver. This dimension reflects issues connected with business competence and fit with what stakeholders want.

▸ *Process trust* explores the fairness in the way in which you do business. This dimension covers those elements by which people judge whether your business deals fairly, transparently, and decisively with issues.

▸ *Values trust* measures the extent to which your stakeholders believe you reflect their ethics and aspirations. This dimension captures the trust that people have in your business, based on its values and empathy with them.

Different stakeholders will have different levels of these three types of trust, but all stakeholders can be assessed against these three dimensions. When measuring brand reputation, then, one is measuring stakeholders' trust profiles—the relative levels of the trust types—and assessing whether these levels are currently sufficient to deliver competitive advantage and corporate strategy. What is not being assessed is distance from an absolute level of trust. The goal is to have the right amounts of trust to meet your commercial goals, not ever higher trust levels for no commercial reason.

Overall, there are around 25–30 individual trust-related questions, spread across the three dimensions that define a company's trust profile. The precise number varies slightly according to the tailored needs of the company in question and its sector.

Why Trust Drives Brand Reputation

Trust involves stakeholders granting companies enough room to operate, while recognizing that this judgment comes at some risk to the stakeholder. That is, trust facilitates resolution of the inevitably conflicting interests between a company and its stakeholders. At the same time, the extension of trust between companies and stakeholders enables coordination and cooperation, so opening up more potential solutions than if trust were not extended, and expanding the company's room to operate. But, companies do not need absolute levels of trust—they need levels that are sufficient to gain competitive advantage. Anything else is a waste of effort and resource.

Brand Reputation in the UK Energy Sector

As an example of this brand reputation methodology, we recently collected data on the UK energy sector. The sector has recently been tarnished by increasing gas prices and the fallout from BP's Gulf of Mexico incident in 2010. Working with one of the companies in the sample, it was decided that the two priority stakeholders for measurement were customers and investors.

In June 2010, qualitative research was conducted to understand the relevant importance of reputation drivers for customers and for investors. Quantitative research was conducted with 750 UK gas customers who also drive cars (and so buy gasoline). Using the three trust types outlined above, brand reputation in the UK energy market with customers can be illustrated as in Figure 2.

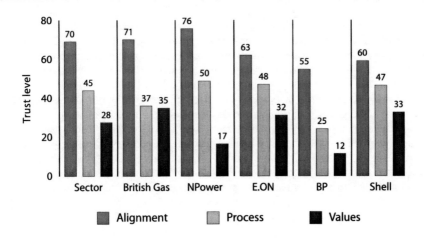

Figure 2. Brand reputations with customers in the UK energy market

British Gas just outperforms the sector on values trust, but this is only due to a favorable weighting related to customer insight around corporate social responsibility and environmentalism. Overall, British Gas is performing satisfactorily on its product and service delivery, but could gain competitive advantage by addressing weaknesses in its customer service levels in particular. NPower outperforms the sector on alignment trust due to its superior capacity to deliver on its brand promise. Overall, NPower has the most extreme trust profile, heavily weighted toward customer brand expectations but gaining no benefit from an empathy with its customers. E.ON outperforms the sector on process trust due to its superior customer service standards. Overall, E.ON has the most balanced trust profile, which gives it stability in a turbulent market although offering little in the way of competitive advantage.

BP and Shell are included in the sample as comparator energy suppliers. They are significant for their relatively strong showing on alignment trust considering that customers do not actually ever see their product. More than a year after the Gulf of Mexico incident, all three of BP's trust indicators remain significantly below Shell's, especially on process and values trust. While alignment trust—the ability of BP to deliver its product efficiently and competently—has nearly recovered to comparable levels, large gaps remain around process and values trust relative to its nearest competitor. BP's brand is seen by UK customers to be tarnished by its corporate reputation. That is, UK customers believe that BP is not "fair dealing" with them in its iterative transactions, nor are BP's corporate values in tune with those customers. This situation suggests that customer confidence in the BP brand, as opposed to the Shell brand, is weak and fragile, and that it could be easily undermined by further incidents.

We collected data on investors using the same methodology. The results are shown in Figure 3. Comparing the pre- and post-Gulf of Mexico data, the real impact on investor sentiment is apparent. In 2008, investors saw little difference in the three trust types between BP and Shell. Both companies were perceived to deliver against their brand promise (relative to their sector rather than other noncomparable brands), have reasonable iterative relationships with their shareholders (based on consistent dividends, use of corporate assets, and financial soundness), and have similar levels of shared values with investors (sufficient environmental credentials to withstand regulatory scrutiny, a willingness to innovate, and the ability to attract talent).

Post-incident, at end 2010, BP's reputation had suffered considerable falls in all three trust types. The greatest gap appeared in alignment trust, as shareholders lost their previously regular dividend payments, and estimates of the legal costs of settling the incident spiraled beyond the actual cleanup costs. However, of equal significance for BP managers is the gap with Shell around process trust. This suggests that Shell, in a complete reversal from the 2004 reserves scandal, has established a shared value premium due to its perceived superior financial soundness and use of corporate assets.

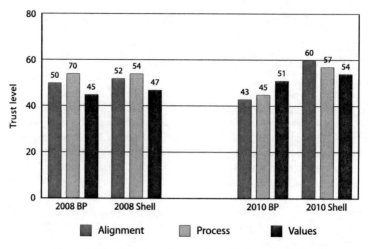

Figure 3. BP vs Shell brand reputation with investors 2008–10

How to Measure Trust

The question asked by senior leadership's is usually: "How do I restore/regain/maintain trust with my stakeholders?" It is not "Is trust a useful thing?" So the answer must be something more practical, operational, and implementable. To achieve that, it is necessary to model trust between a company and its stakeholders. Customers trust companies for different reasons than investors, employees, the media, or regulators. Recent academic research models three types of trust. Although the terminology varies, the main criteria are delivery and competence, fairness and transparency, and vision and empathy. These criteria can be measured using survey questions and careful sampling. This data can be used to answer senior leadership's question about trust.

Brand Reputation of Toyota

As another example of this brand reputation methodology, we collected data on Toyota directly following its 2010 recalls due to faulty accelerator pedals (Figure 4).

The marque's recalls in the first and second quarters of 2010 impacted on brand engagement by customers, investors, and employees, but not with regulators and trade associations. The reason for the different reactions to the recalls may be because the last two stakeholder groups are less prone to influence by the sensationalist and widespread media coverage in the United Kingdom and globally. In terms of brand reputation management, the data suggest that effort and resources should be targeted at the three identified problem stakeholder groups, while a watching brief can be maintained on the two satisfactory stakeholder groups.

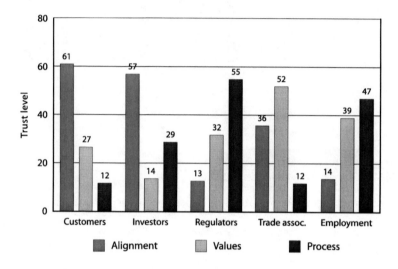

Figure 4. Toyota's trust profile in the United Kingdom, May 2010

Having highlighted investors, customers, and employees for extra effort and resources, qualitative research was used to set targets for improvement. In order to rebuild a strong reputation, management recognized the need to change the trust profiles of investors and employees and to regain the trust profile of customers. To do this, the options for management included:

▶ restoring trust with customers by highlighting the alignment dimension in advertising campaigns (the values dimension weathered the reputation crisis well);

▶ rebuilding trust with investors by focusing on the values dimension in investor relations efforts (the alignment dimension is already rebounding);

▶ regaining trust with employees through internal communications programmed to stress the process dimension—for example, by clearly stating rewards for loyalty, willingness to listen to employees, and flexibility in dealing with revised work patterns.

Figure 5 shows the specific areas of management intervention required to rebuild Toyota's brand reputation in the wake of the 2010 faulty accelerator pedal recall.

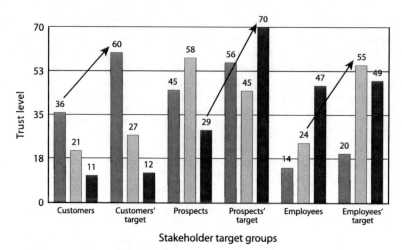

Figure 5. Toyota's brand reputation rebuilding targets 2010-11

Case Study

Measuring Brand Reputation as Basis for Brand Relaunch

A well-known and well-established British B2C and B2B company with a global presence recognized that its reputation was misaligned with its strategy following rapid board turnover, customer dissatisfaction, adverse media and regulator reaction, and falling employee retention. Despite this, profits remained solid, and analysts were predicting a rosy future. However, senior management and the board acted to ensure the long-term success of the business.

To manage its brand reputation, the company set four objectives:

▶▶ to gain independent insight into its current reputation, benchmarked against its competitor set;
▶▶ to develop a balanced scorecard against the three trust types;
▶▶ to input the scorecard into the group risk assessment matrix;
▶▶ to create a meaningful and relevant engagement and communication program to act on the insight in order to meet business priorities.

The eight-week process involved:

▶▶ agreeing which stakeholders needed to be included in the balanced scorecard (those chosen were: customers, employees, senior management, suppliers, trade bodies, investors, media, politicians, and pressure groups);
▶▶ holding in-depth interviews with a representative sample of stakeholders to calibrate trust types;
▶▶ doing an online quantitative survey of all stakeholder groups using questions that probed the three trust types.

The outputs were:

▶▶ empirical benchmark and scorecard calibration of where the company currently stood;

▶▶ analysis and debrief of areas where attention to reputation should be focused;

▶▶ an external vision of where the company currently sat as against the internal position (gap analysis);

▶▶ data to inform ways of changing the current brand reputation profile; the analysis focused on a customer retention initiative, product portfolio change, employee engagement, and a regulatory change campaign.

Using these data as a "line in the sand," the company embarked on a five-stage journey to reposition its brand reputation. This involved:

▶▶ redefining what the brand's reputation should be in the future;

▶▶ evaluating whether the current corporate identity was still fit for purpose;

▶▶ embedding the new brand story with internal audiences because these (rather than senior management) are the key reputation agents;

▶▶ unveiling the new brand story to selected external audiences in order to establish the brand's new reputation;

▶▶ annual measurement of progress against a balanced scorecard.

Summary and Further Steps

▶▶ Brand reputation can and should be managed strategically. Failure to do so will cost you a valuable asset and severely impair your ability to deliver your corporate strategy.

▶▶ Don't guess—measure. Using robust research methodologies, large strategic issues can be addressed with data rather than by using intuition and unstructured insights.

▶▶ Don't drown in data—bringing together your brand and reputation research under one conceptual framework allows the whole company to pull together on your key intangible asset.

▶▶ An individual's professional reputation can be enhanced or destroyed by his or her employer's reputation. A strong organizational reputation produces tangible benefits for you and the organization.

More Info

Books:

Carpenter, Daniel. *Organizational Image and Pharmaceutical Regulation at the FDA*. Princeton, NJ: Princeton University Press, 2010.

Fombrun, Charles. *Reputation. Realizing Value from the Corporate Image*. Cambridge, MA: Harvard Business School Press, 2008.

More Info

Articles:

Aron, Debra J. "Worker reputation and productivity incentives." *Journal of Labor Economics* 5:4, Part 2 (October 1987): S87–S106. Online at: www.jstor.org/stable/2534912

Bhattacharya, Rajeev, Timothy M. Devinney, and Madan M. Pillutla. "A formal model of trust based on outcomes." *Academy of Management Review* 23:3 (July 1998): 459–472. Online at: www.jstor.org/stable/259289

Fisher, Justin, Jennifer van Heerde, and Andrew Tucker. "Does one trust judgement fit all? Linking theory and empirics." *British Journal of Politics & International Relations* 12:2 (May 2010): 161–188. Online at: dx.doi.org/10.1111/j.1467-856X.2009.00401.x

Herbig, Paul, and John Milewicz. "The relationship of reputation and credibility to brand success." *Journal of Consumer Marketing* 10:3 (1993): 18–24. Online at: dx.doi.org/10.1108/EUM0000000002601

Kwon, Ik-Whan G., and Taewon Suh. "Factors affecting the level of trust and commitment in supply chain relationships." *Journal of Supply Chain Management* 40:2 (March 2004): 4–14. Online at: dx.doi.org/10.1111/j.1745-493X.2004.tb00165.x

Lewellen, Katharina. "Risk, reputation, and IPO price support." *Journal of Finance* 61:2 (April 2006): 613–653. Online at: dx.doi.org/10.1111/j.1540-6261.2006.00850.x

Pharaoh, Andrew. "Corporate reputation: The boardroom challenge." *Corporate Governance* 3:4 (2003): 46–51. Online at: dx.doi.org/10.1108/14720700310497113

Prahalad, C. K., and G. Hamel. "The core competence of the corporation." *Harvard Business Review* (May–June 1990).

Rindova, Violina P., Ian O. Williamson, Antoaneta P. Petkova, and Joy Marie Sever. "Being good or being known: An empirical examination of the dimensions, antecedents, and consequences of organizational reputation." *Academy of Management Journal* 48:6 (December 2005): 1033–1049. Online at: www.jstor.org/stable/20159728

Roberts, Peter W., and Grahame R. Dowling. "Corporate reputation and sustained superior financial performance." *Strategic Management Journal* 23:12 (December 2002): 1077–1093. Online at: dx.doi.org/10.1002/smj.274

Website:

Online Reputation Management Association: www.orm-association.org

Notes

1. Edelman Trust Barometer 2009.
2. Black, E. L., T. A. Carnes, and V. J. Richardson. "The market valuation of corporate reputation." *Corporate Reputation Review* 3:1 (January 2000): 31–42. Online at: dx.doi.org/10.1057/palgrave.crr.1540097
3. Sohn, Jonathan (ed). *Development Without Conflict: The Business Case for Community Consent.* Washington, DC: World Resources Institute, 2007. Online at: www.wri.org/publication/development-without-conflict
4. See More Info section for further information.
5. See More Info section for further information.
6. Since 1996 Tesco has consistently topped *UK Management Today's* "Most admired companies," with its CEO, Sir Terry Leahy, being named "Most admired leader" eight times.
7. See Interbrand's "Role of brand index" and "Brand strength score," Millward Brown's "BrandDynamics" and "Brand momentum."
8. For the relevant methodologies, see money.cnn.com/magazines/fortune/mostadmired/2011/faq/; www.bmac.managementtoday.com/BMAC_HowItWorks.htm; and www.reputationinstitute.com/advisory-services/reptrak.php
9. Fisher *et al.* (2010).

Measuring Corporate Reputation: Methodology, Findings, and Practical Implications of the BMAC Surveys

by Michael Brown and Paul Turner

Birmingham City Business School, UK

This Chapter Covers

- Key findings about the measurement of corporate reputation, drawn from the data of the Britain's Most Admired Company (BMAC) surveys, and how these findings may be applied in practice.
- An overview of the survey's methodology and how data are collected, codified, classified, and collated.
- A longitudinal review of the 10 companies that have been identified as Britain's most admired since 1990.
- A longitudinal review of the nine constituents that make up reputation and their changing interrelationships.
- A selection of mini case examples illustrating BMAC results as an alternative measure of performance.
- Consideration of the practical contributions and implications that the BMAC research has for strategic thinking, reputation, policymaking, and practitioners.

Introduction

The growing interest in the resource-based view of strategy and performance in business (Figure 1) brings with it an increasing emphasis on intangibles, such as knowledge, information, and corporate reputation, and on how to articulate their value and ongoing performance.

Twenty years ago a team set out to measure the corporate reputation of British companies.[1] The result was an annual Britain's Most Admired Company (BMAC) survey, which has gathered executives' and expert sector analysts' perceptions—i.e. their tacit knowledge—using characteristics that contribute toward a measure of corporate reputation. The results of the first surveys were published in *The Economist*, but since 1994 they have appeared in *Management Today*.[2]

Each year[3] the survey builds on this growing wealth of data. On its 20th anniversary the survey continues to capture approximately 90 data points for each individual sector; that is, 2,070 data points for each survey, which equates to 39,300 data points between 1990 and 2009, and an equivalent of 4,370 company years. The longitudinal insight offered by the continuity of data enables companies' reputational performance to be charted over the period. As a result, specific trends relating to corporate reputation can be identified and assessed. In addition, trends relating to the individual characteristics that form the basis of reputation measurement can be considered. Correlations between these characteristics can be analyzed, as can patterns in each of the characteristics that might add value to the understanding of this subject.

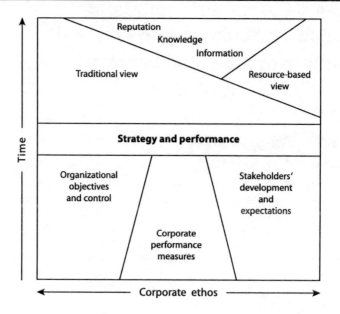

Figure 1. The growing interest in the resource-based view of strategy

This chapter will present some key findings, drawn from the data of the BMAC surveys, about the measurement of corporate reputation and how these may be applied in practice.

BMAC: Methodology and Modifications

Brown and Turner (2008) define corporate reputation as the contribution of a multitude of stakeholders who, by how they think and feel about a company, determine how it is seen by itself and by others. The BMAC survey is a peer perception survey based on the views of the senior executives of UK companies and sector investment analysts about a series of characteristics that contribute to a measure of corporate reputation. The methodology of the survey has remained largely unchanged over the period. Some modifications, however, have been introduced into the codification, classification, and compilation of the BMAC data to complement the durability of the survey and its potential longitudinal value.

In terms of the codification, each year the top 10 companies in each sector are identified by their market capitalization value. Senior executives of each company and analysts are invited to provide their perceptions for each of the other nine companies (i.e. other than their own) across each of the nine characteristics (classifications or constituents). The characteristics are:

» quality of management (QM);
» financial soundness (FS);
» quality of products (QP);
» ability to attract, retain, and develop top talent (AAT);
» value as a long-term investment (VLTI);

▸▸ capacity to innovate (CI);
▸▸ quality of marketing (QMar);
▸▸ community and environmental responsibility (CER);
▸▸ use of corporate assets (UCA).

The last characteristic, use of corporate assets (UCA), was added in 1994.

The coding system that accompanies the survey is as follows:

0	1
Sector	

0	1
Company	

0	2
Target respondent	

Here is an example:

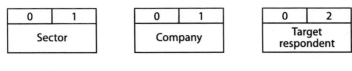

0	7
Sector	

0	1
Admiral plc	

0	2
Chief executive	

The sectors are derived by integrating a number of sources, which included the London Stock Exchange listings of companies, and industrial and media classifications. The validity of the sector groupings is confirmed by business analysts, editors of business journals, and the Institute of Actuaries. Once the sectors are agreed, the top 10 companies in terms of their market capitalization at a specific time are identified. Sector classifications are dynamic and are subject to change. Some sectors have disappeared, such as textiles; others have merged, such as electricity and water, which have become "utilities"; while other sectors have diversified. For example, as the construction sector grew it was split into "home construction" and "heavy construction." Throughout the duration of the survey, however, many sectors have remained broadly similar, thereby allowing valuable longitudinal studies of companies.

The general criteria for inclusion in the survey are as follows.

▸▸ The company should be a publicly owned (British) company. In the event of split nationality, the significant part should be British; examples of such companies are Unilever and Shell.
▸▸ The company should be quoted on the London Stock Exchange.
▸▸ The company should produce an annual report and accounts.
▸▸ The company should have a market capitalization value published by the London Stock Exchange and reported in the news media.

Adopting these criteria has helped to maintain a degree of continuity in the survey. The result is that almost all the top 100 FTSE companies and approximately 90% of the top 200 UK companies are included.

Companies' scores against the characteristics are obtained by a Likert-based scale of 0 to 10, where 0 = poor, 5 = average, and 10 = excellent. Bipolar scales in the form of opposite adjectives, poor to excellent, are designed to capture the respondents' attitudes toward each company within the industry, for each of the characteristics. The means of collecting these data has evolved with the availability of new technologies. While a first and second-wave written communication remains an important approach, a third, fourth, and fifth approach have been adopted as this unique database has been developed. Stage 3 now incorporates specific electronic communication with executives and analysts who have contributed in the past and provided their personal contact details. Stage 4 is a specific electronic communication with senior executives, and stage 5 includes telephone interviews. Following the collation of the data, the most admired companies for each *characteristic*, as well as the most admired company in each *sector*, are identified, and this is extended to an overall *British* most admired company.

Individual Company Performance in BMAC 1990–2009

It is possible to take a longitudinal view of the reputational performance of British companies using the BMAC surveys from 1990 to 2009. Table 1 shows that during this period just 10 companies have been overall BMAC winners. These are Royal Dutch Shell, Marks & Spencer, GlaxoSmithKline, Rentokil, Cadbury, Tesco, Reuters, BP, Diageo and BSkyB. Nine of the winning companies were still quoted on the London Stock Exchange in 2010. The exception is Cadbury, which was taken over by the American company Kraft.

Table 2 provides a more detailed breakdown of the most admired companies and the number of times and specific dates that they have been identified as most admired. The most prolific winner of the overall most admired company—and also for the characteristics of quality of management and its ability to attract, develop, and retain top talent—is Tesco. As well as being the most admired company overall on six separate occasions, it has also been the most admired company on six occasions in terms of its quality of management. In terms of its capacity to attract, develop, and retain top talent, Tesco has been most admired for this characteristic on five occasions.

If we look at the other characteristics, other familiar names are identified. For example, for their financial soundness, two companies have won on four occasions: Shell and Land Securities. In regard to the quality of its products, one company, Cadbury, has been most admired on four occasions. BSkyB, the most recent overall winner, has been identified as most admired for its capacity to innovate, winning on seven occasions out of the past 12 years. In addition, it has also been most admired for the quality of its marketing on four occasions—more than any other company. Body Shop (now owned by L'Oréal) won the community and environmental responsibility characteristic on four occasions in the 1990s. Finally, BP was most admired on four occasions over the last 10 years for how effectively and efficiently it used its corporate assets. What this demonstrates is that perceptions of each company are not homogeneous across each of the characteristics.

Table 1. Britain's most admired companies 1990–2009

Year	Overall most admired company	Quality of management (QM)	Financial soundness (FS)	Quality of products (QP)	Attracting, retaining top talent (AAT)	Value as long-term investment (VLTI)	Capacity to innovate (CI)	Quality of marketing (QMar)	Community and environmental responsibility (CER)	Use of corporate assets (UCA)
1990	Shell Transport & Trading	BTR	Shell	Pearson	ICI	Land Securities	Carlton Communications	Amstrad	Marks & Spencer	–
1991	Marks & Spencer	Shell	Land Securities	Rolls-Royce	Marks & Spencer	Marks & Spencer	Rolls-Royce	Amstrad	Marks & Spencer	–
1992	Glaxo	Rentokil	Central TV	Glaxo	Unilever	Glaxo	Glaxo	Unilever	Body Shop	Hanson
1994	Rentokil	Vodafone	GEC	Glaxo Holdings	Glaxo Holdings	Rentokil	Glaxo Holdings	British Airways	Rentokil	Rentokil
1995	Cadbury Schweppes	Cadbury Schweppes	Land Securities	Whitbread	Vodafone	Unilever	British Land Company	Cadbury Schweppes	British Telecommunications	Smiths Industries
1996	Tesco	Tesco	Marks & Spencer	Tesco	Mercury Asset Management	Smiths Industries	Burford	Cadbury Schweppes	Argyll Group	Burford
1997	Reuters Holdings	Smiths Industries	Shell Transport & Trading	Reuters Holdings	Tesco	Reuters Holdings	Burford	Cadbury Schweppes	Body Shop	Lloyds TSB
1998	Tesco	Schroders	Shell Transport & Trading	Cadbury Schweppes	Tesco	Cadbury Schweppes	Tesco	Tesco	Body Shop	Tesco
1999	Tesco	Tesco	Land Securities	Daily Mail & General Trust	Tesco	SmithKline Beecham	BSkyB	SmithKline Beecham	Body Shop	BP Amoco
2000	GlaxoSmithKline	BP Amoco	Land Securities	Cadbury Schweppes	GlaxoSmithKline	GlaxoSmithKline	BSkyB	GlaxoSmithKline	Iceland	BP Amoco
2001	Shell Transport & Trading	AstraZeneca	Shell Transport & Trading	AstraZeneca	BP	Shell Transport & Trading	BSkyB	BSkyB	Shell Transport & Trading	BP
2002	BP	Tesco	Shell Transport & Trading	Cadbury Schweppes	BP	BAA	Tesco	GlaxoSmithKline	Cadbury Schweppes	Rentokil Initial
2003	Tesco	Tesco	Morrison (Wm)	Tesco	Tesco	Tesco	BSkyB	Tesco	BOC	Tesco
2004	Cadbury Schweppes	Royal Bank of Scotland	HSBC	Cadbury Schweppes	Vodafone	Wolseley	Man	BSkyB	Unilever	Enterprise Inns
2005	Tesco	Cadbury Schweppes	HSBC	Diageo	Unilever	Wolseley	Tesco	BSkyB	BT Group	Tesco
2006	Tesco	Tesco	Tesco	GlaxoSmithKline	Virgin Mobile	Tesco	ARM Holdings	Cadbury Schweppes	BT Group	Barratt Developments
2007	Marks & Spencer	Persimmon	Tesco	Marks & Spencer	Marks & Spencer	Marks & Spencer	BSkyB	Marks & Spencer	BSkyB	Marks & Spencer
2008	Diageo	Berkeley Group	Associated British Foods	Diageo	Diageo and Tesco	Johnson Matthey	BSkyB	Diageo	Unilever	Unilever
2009	BSkyB	Tesco	GlaxoSmithKline	BSkyB	GlaxoSmithKline	Tesco	BSkyB	BSkyB	Cadbury	BP

189

Table 2. Most admired companies 1990–2009 (excluding 1993)

Company	Britain's most admired company	Quality of management	Financial soundness	Quality of goods or services	Ability to attract, develop, retain top talent	Value as a long-term investment	Capacity to innovate	Quality of marketing	Community and environmental responsibility	Use of corporate assets	Total of MAC wins
Tesco	2006, 2005, 2003, 1999, 1998, 1996	2009, 2006, 2003, 2002, 1999, 1996	2007, 2006	1996	2008, 2003, 1999, 1998, 1997	2009, 2006, 2003	2005, 2002, 1998	2003, 1997		2005, 2003, 1998	31
Glaxo-SmithKline	2000, 1992		2009	2006, 1994, 1992	2009, 2000, 1994	2000, 1999, 1992	1994, 1992	2002, 2000, 1999			17
BSkyB	2009			2009, 2003			2009, 2008, 2007, 2003, 2001, 2000, 1999	2009, 2005, 2004, 2001	2007		15
Cadbury	2004, 1995	2005, 1995		2004, 2002, 2000, 1998		1998		2006, 1996, 1995	2009, 2002		14
Marks & Spencer	2007, 1991	1991, 1990	1996	2007	1991	2007, 1991		2007	1991, 1990	2007	11
Shell	2001, 1990	1991, 1990	2002, 2001, 1998, 1997			2001			2001		10
BP	2002	2000			2002, 2001					2009, 2001, 2000, 1999	8
Unilever					2005, 1992	1995		1992	2008, 2004	2008	7
Rentokil	1994	1992				1994			1994	2002, 1994	6
Diageo	2008			2008, 2005	2008			2008			5
Land Securities			2000, 1999, 1995, 1991			1990					5
Body Shop									1999, 1998, 1997, 1992		4

Other most admired companies winners include: Total of three MAC: Burford, BT, Reuters, Smiths Industries, Vodafone; Total of two MAC: Amstrad, AstraZeneca, HSBC, Rolls-Royce, Wolseley; Total of one MAC: Associated British Foods, Argyll Group, ARM, BAA, Barrett Developments, Berkeley Group, BOC, British Land, BTR, Carlton Communications, Central TV, Daily Mail and General Trust, Enterprise Inns, GEC, Hanson, Iceland, Johnson Matthey, Lloyds TSB, Man, Mercury Asset Management, Morrison (Wm), Orange, Pearson, Persimmon, RBS, Schroders, Virgin, Whitbread.

Figure 2 shows the longitudinal reputation performance of Tesco, Shell, Marks & Spencer, BSkyB, and Rentokil. Few companies have offered such consistent evidence of superior corporate reputation over the last two decades as Tesco. Under the leadership of Sir Ian MacLaurin and Sir Terry Leahy, the company has been Britain's most admired company on six separate occasions. In terms of all the possible top positions it could occupy since 1990, Tesco has occupied as many as 23%. In contrast, the graph traces the reputational journey of Marks & Spencer from its position of being the most admired company in 1991, to its near collapse in 2001, and its subsequent revival to become Britain's most admired company once again in 2007. The graph also shows BSkyB's growth and reputational development since it was first included in the survey in 1997.

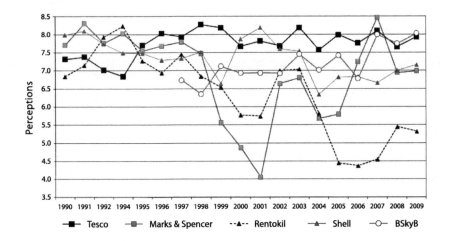

Figure 2. A sample selection of Britain's most admired companies 1990–2009
(except 1993, when survey was not conducted)

The results show that corporate reputation is an extremely dynamic entity and requires a proactive approach to its management.

The Changing Nature of the BMAC Characteristics 1990–2009

In addition to providing longitudinal data on the reputational performance of leading companies, the BMAC survey also provides a view on the relationship between the various characteristics that make up corporate reputation and how the perceptions of the importance of individual constituents have changed. Table 3 gives the correlation coefficients of the BMAC characteristics published in the *British Journal of Management* in 1992[4] and compares these with the correlation coefficients of the survey characteristics in 2009. Most noticeable is the low correlation associated with the community and environmental responsibility characteristic.

Table 3. Correlation coefficients in 1992 and 2009

				1992				
	QM	FS	QP	AAT	VLTI	CI	QMar	CER
QM								
FS	0.75							
QP	0.64	0.58						
AAT	0.83	0.71	0.70					
VLTI	0.80	0.89	0.63	0.76				
CI	0.58	0.40	0.64	0.71	0.46			
QMar	0.61	0.41	0.69	0.69	0.48	0.75		
CER	0.41	0.45	0.61	0.45	0.52	0.35	0.40	
UCA	0.85	0.73	0.57	0.77	0.79	0.52	0.55	0.45

				2009				
	QM	FS	QP	AAT	VLTI	CI	QMar	CER
QM								
FS	0.77							
QP	0.72	0.67						
AAT	0.83	0.80	0.81					
VLTI	0.79	0.83	0.76	0.86				
CI	0.74	0.65	0.80	0.80	0.75			
QMar	0.68	0.61	0.73	0.77	0.66	0.79		
CER	0.50	0.54	0.57	0.65	0.59	0.60	0.66	
UCA	0.79	0.77	0.72	0.79	0.79	0.73	0.67	0.62

QM = Quality of management; FS = Financial soundness; QP = Quality of goods and services; AAT = Ability to attract, develop, and retain top talent; VLTI = Value as long-term investment; CI = Capacity to innovate; QMar = Quality of marketing; CER = Community and environmental responsibility; UCA = Use of corporate assets.

The quality of management characteristic, QM, is the strongest determinant of reputational performance. Figure 3 illustrates the longitudinal correlation coefficients of the quality of management with each of the other characteristics between 1994 and 2009.

▸ For all but one characteristic (CER), the correlation coefficient lies between 0.6 and 0.9. This indicates a strong positive relationship between quality of management and each of these characteristics.

▸ The correlation coefficients between quality of management (QM), use of corporate assets (UCA), and ability to attract, develop, and retain top people (AAT) are consistently the highest.

▸ The correlation between quality of management (QM) and community and environmental responsibility (CER) is the lowest between any two characteristics over the whole duration of the survey.

▸▸ The fastest-growing correlation with quality of management (QM) between 1994 and 2007 was community and environmental responsibility (CER).

▸▸ With the onset of the economic and financial recession, the correlation of quality of management with community and environmental responsibility dropped the most between 2007 and 2009 to a level it was at 10 years ago.

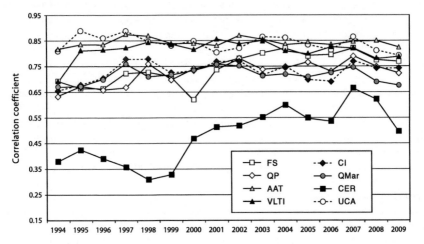

Figure 3. Longitudinal correlation coefficients of quality of management (QM) characteristic with each of the other reputational characteristics, 1994–2009

Implications and Uses of BMAC Research

It is possible to look at corporate reputation in three ways.

▸▸ *Reputation is a measure.* It is a measure of the esteem or admiration attached to a company by the BMAC survey, incorporating peer perceptions from Britain's leading executives and analysts.

▸▸ *Reputation is an intangible asset.* It is also an intangible asset that is owned by companies, though not recorded in their annual report and accounts.

▸▸ *Reputation is a process.* Reputation is the internal identity of the company and incorporates objectives and methods to raise and enhance the reputation of the company from the inside. Reputation is also the external image of the company as witnessed by external stakeholders.

Reputation is an internally owned, corporately managed, externally evaluated, intangible asset that is outside the immediate control of its owners. The idea that there is an internal and external element to reputation is accepted; indeed, the internal identity and the external image are powerful discerning factors in the literature. In terms of Jay B. Barney's VRIN (valuable, rare, imperfectly imitable, nonsubstitutable) framework,[5] reputation is a heterogeneous competence possessed by companies that have varying degrees of value. Charles Fombrun[6] identifies this as reputational capital. A company's reputational capital is the excess market value of its shares, i.e. the amount by which the company's market value exceeds the book value of its assets. A unique reputation is a rare competence or capability that, according to Kay (1993), derives from the company's history, location, and culture, or from distinctive capabilities that already exist elsewhere.

Reputation, therefore, is not a competence or capability that can be copied easily. It is unique in the sense that, just as no two people possess the same personality or reputation, no two companies can possess the same personality or reputation. In fact, when a competence represents the subjective opinions of cognitive knowledge given by informed individuals, the likelihood of imitating a corporate reputation is further reduced.

Finally, Barney asks if the company is organized to exploit the full competitive potential of its resources and capabilities. It is here that Kay's consideration of internal and external network relationships provides companies with the greatest opportunity to exploit their reputation. The corporate management of this, however, is perhaps one of the most difficult tasks facing a company, as it incorporates appropriate systems for signaling the corporate image to stakeholders and retrieving from stakeholders their performance expectations (Grant, 2002). It is no accident that over the last 20 years one of the newest directorial positions has been that of communications director.

BMAC and Strategic Thinking

Core competencies, and distinctive and dynamic capabilities, are concepts that have evolved out of the resource-based view of strategy.[7] Core competencies are more than a "bundle of skills and techniques" that enable a company to provide a particular benefit to customers, as Hamel and Prahalad (1994) suggest. Teece, Pisano, and Sheun (1997) argue that they are:

"A set of differentiated skills, complementary assets and routines that provide the basis for a firm's competitive capabilities and sustainable advantage in a particular business … Such competencies have an important tacit dimension."

Corporate reputation comes about from the contribution of both tangible and intangible assets. It incorporates how the company's performance is perceived and translated by internal and external constituents. It is a unique resource. It is an internally owned intangible asset, externally evaluated by a growing number of external stakeholder groups. Perhaps the most suitable interpretation of corporate reputation is in Richard P. Rumelt's foreword to the Hamel and Heene conference, 1994 (quoted in Davis, 2004), which identifies reputation as:

>> a unique core competence that spans businesses, products, and borders of a corporation;

>> a core competence that evolves more slowly than products and is more damageable;

>> a competence that is gained and enhanced by work; it is the collective learning of the organization.

An Empirical Approach to BMAC: Accumulation, Articulation, and Codification of Tacit Knowledge

BMAC is a methodology that measures corporate reputation from the tacit knowledge of specialists, including corporate senior executives and industry sector analysts. It is a forum where a form of collective learning occurs. Here, important tacit knowledge is accumulated when individuals express their opinions and beliefs. The BMAC survey provides a means by which senior executives and analysts within specific industries are invited to offer their opinions, views, beliefs, thoughts, and perceptions—collectively referred to as "tacit knowledge"—without having to explain themselves.

The BMAC methodology allows for the experts' views to be articulated in such a way that their perceptions on each of the nine characteristics within each industry sector can be considered against each company within that industry sector. In addition, their perceptions can be summed together to provide a total for each company within the industry.

Codification, the step that follows articulation, incorporates the process of arranging, developing, digesting, or systematizing the tacit knowledge. This allows empirical tests to be conducted on a variety of propositions, ranging from the impact of individual characteristics to that of all the characteristics.

The Use of BMAC Information in a Policy Setting

The BMAC survey offers information that can be applied to policy decisions as a counter both to what Lovallo and Kahneman (2003) called the "planning fallacy," caused by overoptimism, and even to managerial hubris. BMAC data and analysis allow alternative perspectives to evolve and develop. This is what Lovallo and Kahneman call "the outside view." They argue that companies need to introduce into their mindsets an objective forecasting method that counteracts their own personal and organizational sources of optimism. Through the BMAC survey, peer perceptions offer a source of information to help decision-making. As we have demonstrated, the outside view of a company offered by peers will be a source of external information contributing to a realistic, nonfinancial assessment of company performance and hence will balance any possible hubristic views held by executives on the basis of their own cognitive perceptions.

The BMAC data and information, and their application to knowledge, have relevance to several important business decision and policy-related areas. They provide an additional source of information that complements the economic and financial basis of decisions—which itself may be distorted because of the inefficient allocation of capital to key projects. The BMAC results are used by companies that are keen to show their reputational performance, and BMAC data have the potential to be used in a complementary way to financial analysis by a variety of business professionals.

- ▸ The *nonexecutive director* may exert reputation information to shape policy as a "tacit knowledge specialist," bringing to the company perceptions of the expectations of multiple external stakeholders.
- ▸ *Business analysts* may use BMAC sector summaries to complement their wide range of information sources.
- ▸ *Investors* utilize the information contained in BMAC surveys to supplement other market reports.
- ▸ *Corporate communications* specialists may use BMAC data as an external diagnostic tool for the reputational health of their organization. BMAC offers a series of dimensions on which companies might be expected to

make comparisons with their own organization. These findings can then be effectively compared with others and would complement other financial and marketing comparisons, such as those embodied in the economic value added (EVA) and market value added (MVA) analysis.

▸▸ *Researchers*, such as degree, masters, and PhD students, continue to test BMAC data against a series of propositions, whether it be studying one of the characteristics, or looking across industry sectors.

▸▸ *Consultants*. Measuring corporate reputation has led to an increasing demand to share the survey findings with consultants and some of their clients.

▸▸ *Accounting standard bodies*. International accounting standard bodies are giving increasing attention to the accounting treatment of intangibles. These include how to value acquired intangibles, such as research and development in progress, and how to value internally developed intangibles, such as software development costs. The greater the proportion of intangible to tangible assets, the greater the pressure on accounting bodies to attempt to measure intangibles. International Accounting Standard (IAS) 38, on intangible assets, calls for the capitalization of internally developed intangibles with identifiable benefits. BMAC has demonstrated that there are possible financial benefits to be achieved from being identified as having a superior reputation.

"By supplementing traditional forecasting processes, which tend to focus on a company's own capabilities, experiences and expectations…executives can gain a much more accurate understanding of likely outcomes. Such an outside view provides a reality check on the more intuitive inside view." (Lovallo and Kahneman, 2003: 56)

The Implications of BMAC Information for Practitioners

An important objective of measuring corporate reputation has been to inform practicing managers. This is in line with the views of Tranfield and Starkey (1998), who argue that the fundamental objective of management research should be to improve the relationship between theory and practice. It is important and appropriate that the research findings should be considered in the context of practicing managers. This section demonstrates what Tranfield and Starkey (1998) claim to be the distinguishing competence of structured research by demonstrating an ability to develop ideas and relate them to industry and managerial practice.

The reputation survey has accumulated a stock of information, gained exclusively from practitioners themselves. This information has been deconstructed, analyzed, and tested by academic and nonacademic publics. From this stock of information, practitioners are able to enhance their knowledge and, ultimately, their business decision-making capabilities. It shows them that perception of companies' reputation, admiration, or esteem is an important contributor to organizational information and more effective decision-making. It is also a complementary (nonfinancial) driver of a more sustainable competitive advantage.

▸▸ Reputation can be measured, and has proved to be an innovative means of indicating a company's performance beyond the traditional accounting and financial methods.

▶▶ Reputation is one of a company's most influential intangible assets, with the potential to enhance the capitalization value of admired companies such as Tesco and to fuel the destiny of less admired companies like Woolworths. However, with the rise in external stakeholders, it is increasingly being assessed by constituents such as the media, who, though they have little control over the company, are increasingly exercising their power.

▶▶ The existence of managerial hubris cannot be ignored, as this can lead to stakeholders being given a misleading picture of the company.

▶▶ The greater the degree of managerial overconfidence, the more likely companies are to experience inferior share prices and returns.

▶▶ The greater the degree of managerial overconfidence compared with other companies with better performance information, the more likely the company is to fail.

▶▶ Peer perceptions, expressed by senior executives and sector analysts, result in above average returns for investors who incorporate this tacit knowledge into the management of their investment portfolios.

Case Study

Marks & Spencer's Reputation Roller Coaster 1991, 2001, and 2007

Marks & Spencer has had a mixed reputational performance and provides a good example of how a company can lose and then regain its reputational standing. In 1991 the company was the overall most admired, but in 2001 it fell to 233rd place out of 239 UK companies, before becoming Britain's Most Admired Company again in 2007. Figure 4 illustrates Marks & Spencer's performance against each of the characteristics measured by the BMAC survey for 1991, 2001, and 2007.

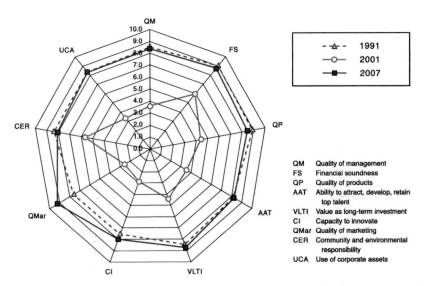

Figure 4. Spidergram illustrating fall in Marks & Spencer's reputation from 1991 and its rise after 2001

In 1991 Marks & Spencer had high scores in several of the characteristics measured, including quality of management, attraction and retention of talent, quality of products, financial soundness, and community and environmental responsibility. High ratings appeared to be an integral part of a successful culture that was reflected in the company's actual business performance. Two characteristics were below average at this time: innovation and marketing, and the perceived poor performance in both areas was borne out by the reality, which included a fall in both profits and share price in the late 1990s.

To address these problems, a combination of new management, new products, and innovative marketing, epitomized by chairman Stuart Rose's "Plan A," returned the company to high profitability and, in 2007, to the leading BMAC position (Brown and Turner, 2008: 29–31; and Bevan, 2007).

How Can the BMAC Survey Aid Managers?

Rather than managers basing their performance reviews on pure accounting measures, the reputation survey indicates perceptions of a company's performance across nine important characteristics. These measures are an indication of external stakeholders' assessments and are therefore a valuable source of additional information. The survey can also be incorporated as an innovative corporate and strategic business unit benchmarking source. A number of different benchmarking opportunities exist:

>> benchmarking against another company in the same industry sector;
>> benchmarking against better-performing companies in its industry sector for each of the nine characteristics;
>> benchmarking against better-performing companies outside one's own industry, across multiple industrial sectors, that are champions of each of the nine characteristics.

In addition, the survey provides a corporate health check for companies. A company is able to identify and measure peer perceptions for each of the nine characteristics, identifying which are more admired than others and those whose reputation is inferior. As the number of annual surveys grow, additional opportunities for self-examination develop. For example, a company is able to compare its performance across each of the characteristics and consider how these are changing over time. Managers are also able to observe perceptions in their own company, identifying perhaps where asymmetry exists across different management levels (senior, middle, and junior managers). The result is that the BMAC survey is a valuable assessment mechanism which, if well applied, encourages a more responsive and effective decision-making culture.

Summary and Further Steps

>> This chapter has offered an insight into Britain's Most Admired Companies research into measuring corporate reputation. The survey provides an independent, nonfinancial research method to gather peer perceptions of corporate reputation that have implications for policy-making and management practice. These perceptions are obtained from a well-informed and powerful

group of executives and analysts. It is they who are best positioned to appraise the expectations of external stakeholders and also to consider how other companies in the same industry are meeting those expectations.

▶▶ The book values of companies can account for as little as 20% of their total value. The foundations of such companies would seem to be dangerously fragile to bear such a weight unless they have something else. Intangibles are that something else, and many of them—such as culture, networks, and employee knowledge—are assets that the company can manage internally.

▶▶ Reputation is a unique resource: it is an internally owned intangible asset that is externally evaluated by a growing number of external stakeholder groups. It is a core competence and a distinctive capability, and it adheres well to Barney's (1991, 1996) VRIN characteristics. Its financial value is not recorded or presented in a company's annual report and accounts. Therefore, in this context, it correlates with much of the resource-based view (RBV) literature, although it also has external ties to the traditional strategic view literature. The traditional argument—that strategic decision-making incorporates an expectation and understanding of the competitive, external, exogenous environment—applies equally well to the view that reputation is seen externally. Reputation therefore occupies a hybrid and unique position between the RBV and the traditional approach to strategy.

▶▶ Research has demonstrated that there is a strong asymmetry between what is known inside the company and what is known externally. What it does not do, however, is to question the assumption that the knowledge possessed by company executives is always correct. The annual BMAC survey studies have provided, and continue to provide, a useful counterbalance to such information. This position is summarized effectively by Teece, Pisano, and Shuen (1997): "Reputation's main value is external, since it is a kind of summary statistic about the firm's current assets and position, and its likely future behaviour."

▶▶ Ultimately it is a company's executives who are responsible for being aware of the company's internal identity and of its public's external expectations. Since 1990 the BMAC survey has sought to gather expert perceptions formed both internally and externally and to share the findings with practitioners.

More Info

Books:

Barney, Jay B. *Gaining and Sustaining Competitive Advantage*. Reading, MA: Addison Wesley, 1996.

Bevan, Judy. *The Rise & Fall of Marks & Spencer ... And How It Rose Again*. Revised and updated ed. London, UK: Profile Books, 2007.

Brown, Michael, and Paul Turner. *The Admirable Company*. London, UK: Profile Books, 2008.

Fombrun, Charles J. *Reputation: Realizing Value from the Corporate Image*. Boston, MA: Harvard Business School, 1996.

Fombrun, Charles J., and Cees B. M. Van Riel. *Fame and Fortune: How Successful Companies Build Winning Reputations*. New York: FT Prentice Hall, 2004.

Grant, Robert M. *Contemporary Strategy Analysis: Concepts, Techniques, Applications*. Oxford, UK: Blackwell, 2002.

Hamel, Gary, and C. K. Prahalad. *Competing for the Future*. Boston, MA: Harvard Business School Press, 1994.

Kay, John. *Foundations of Corporate Success*. Oxford, UK: Oxford University Press, 1993.

Articles:

Barney, Jay. "Firm resources and sustained competitive advantage." *Journal of Management* 17:1 (March 1991): 99–120. Online at: dx.doi.org/10.1177/014920639101700108

Bowman, Cliff, and Veronique Ambrosini. "How the resource based and the dynamic capabilities views of the firm inform corporate-level strategy." *British Journal of Management* 14:4 (December 2003): 289–303.
Online at: dx.doi.org/10.1111/j.1467-8551.2003.00380.x

Connor, Tom. "The resource based view of strategy and its value to practicing managers." *Strategic Change* 11:6 (September/October 2002): 307–316.
Online at: dx.doi.org/10.1002/jsc.593

Davis, Jeremy G. "Capabilities: A different perspective." *Australian Journal of Management* 29:1 (June 2004): 39–43. Online at: dx.doi.org/10.1177/031289620402900108

Fombrun, Charles, and Mark Shanley. "What's in a name? Reputation building and corporate strategy." *Academy of Management Journal* 33:2 (June 1990): 233–258.
Online at: www.jstor.org/stable/256324

Lovallo, Dan, and Daniel Kahneman. "Delusions of success: How optimism undermines executive decisions." *Harvard Business Review* 81 (July 2003): 57–63.
Online at: tinyurl.com/67rqrkm

Saunders, John, Michael Brown, and Stuart Laverick. "Research notes on the best British companies: A peer evaluation of Britain's leading firms." *British Journal of Management* 3:4 (December 1992): 181–193.
Online at: dx.doi.org/10.1111/j.1467-8551.1992.tb00044.x

Teece, David J., Gary Pisano, and Amy Shuen. "Dynamic capabilities and strategic management." *Strategic Management Journal* 18:7 (August 1997): 509–533.
Online at: tinyurl.com/43efkon

Tranfield, David, and Ken Starkey. "The nature, social organisation and promotion of management research: Towards policy." *British Journal of Management* 9:4 (December 1998): 341–353. Online at: dx.doi.org/10.1111/1467-8551.00103

Wernerfelt, Birger. "A resource based view of the firm." *Strategic Management Journal* 5:2 (April/June 1994): 171–180. Online at: dx.doi.org/10.1002/smj.4250050207

Notes

1. This survey was initially conduced with Loughborough University and published in *The Economist*, then for 16 years with, respectively, Nottingham Business School and *Management Today*, and currently with Birmingham City Business School and *Management Today*.

2. *Management Today* is a Haymarket publication. The findings of the Britain's Most Admired Companies survey are published in the December issue.

3. The 1993 survey was conducted during a period of transition between *The Economist* and *Management Today* and as a result was not published.

4. Saunders *et al.* (1992).

5. Barney writes about intangible assets and incorporates the notion of VRIN, reflecting the assumption that competitive advantage may be achieved if a company's intangible assets are valuable, rare, imperfectly imitable, and nontransferable. Two key references are his book *Gaining and Sustaining Competitive Advantage* (Barney, 1996) and his article "Firm resources and sustained competitive advantage" (Barney, 1991).

6. Charles Fombrun is a key and influential writer on corporate reputation. He is coauthor of the seminal article "What's in a name? Reputation building and corporate strategy" (Fombrun and Shanley, 1990), sole author of the book *Reputation: Realizing Value from the Corporate Image* (Fombrun, 1996), and coauthor of the book *Fame and Fortune* (Fombrun and Van Riel, 2004).

7. The resource-based view (RBV) of strategy is a more recent alternative view of strategy. Rather than focus all of a company's attention on understanding the external environment, the RBV considers those resource assets which the company has that might be strong enough to lead its strategy. For an insight into this, see Bowman and Ambrosini (2003), Connor (2002), and Wernerfelt (1994).

Reputation and Strategic Issue Management
by John Dalton

London School of Public Relations, UK

This Chapter Covers

▸ An overview of the relationship between reputation and issue management.
▸ The importance and context of issue management as a tool of reputation management and strategic business planning.
▸ The impact of social media in managing issues.
▸ The value of issue analysis to decision making and business insights.
▸ The structure and process of issue management.
▸ The interconnection between issue management, risk, and crisis management.

Introduction

What is the purpose of a business? According to Peter Drucker, "the purpose of a business is to create a customer." Such a statement makes good sense, as without customers there can be no functional business. Essentially, if the purpose of any business is to fulfill some human need within society, then that business, whatever its nature, should take an active interest in its own reputation as a way of securing its future prospects. Central to building and defending a sound organizational reputation is the capability to be proactive and to recognize and evaluate potential and ongoing risks (issues). Legitimacy and transparency are at the heart of issue management, and whether the messages developed and delivered through corporate communications are credible to stakeholders. If reputation can be viewed as a form of assessment of a corporation's behavior and performance, then understanding and identifying risks and issues—that may at a later stage damage this valuable asset—must be an active part of any reputation management structure and process.

Most organizations recognize the importance of reputation to their organizations, yet few have dedicated structures and people in place to oversee the critical function. In the author's opinion, we are witnessing the era of a *reputation economy*, whereby economic sustainability is based less on what you *claim* (typically through a mixture of mass media and social media) and more on what you actually *do*, i.e. your accountability and consistent delivery of brand values. Concurrent with this is a shift in values and public attitudes towards corporations and an increasing ethical overlap between business and personal morality.

Consumers now expect organizations to act in a fair and reasonable manner, and not only to make a brand/organizational promise, but to deliver it. Faced with increasing market volatility and complexity, corporations are realizing the need to have structures and processes in place to ensure that risk issues do not evolve into nasty reputational surprises, damaging brand equity, which can quickly result in loss of shareholder confidence and, in the long term, profitability. The hasty demise in July 2011 of the British newspaper, the *News of the World*, is a good example of an issue that rapidly became a crisis, with devastating consequences.

Risk and issue management are by their nature proactive so, in order to build, defend, and maintain a good reputation, corporations need a series of key interdependent competencies to manage reputation risks:

▸ Strategic risk and issue management.
▸ Effective brand/marketing communications and message development.
▸ Corporate identity and image development.
▸ Crisis management planning.
▸ Innovation and communication of change.
▸ Sustainability and corporate social responsibility.
▸ Ethics and regulatory/compliance.

Is the Management of Issues Important?

Issues and their management are similar to the way in which we perceive our health. Most of us care about our health and fear long-term diseases such as cancer, yet many of us indulge in lifestyles that can increase the risk of exposure to serious illness. Interestingly, a simple search on the internet quickly reveals the importance of crisis management in the business lexicon. Type in "issue analysis" or "issue management" and there is significantly little presence on the web. Why? Because most people in business habitually use the terms "issue" and "issue management," yet there is poor understanding of how issues can be properly managed.

Conversely, the term "crisis" is more popular in terms of awareness, training, and consequences. A crisis evokes fear and potentially threatens the very existence of a business. The simple explanation is that issues, like threats from illness, do not command our immediate attention. Our minds have not evolved for such long-term planning, as we tend to look for short-term reward and security. In essence, executives understand the importance of risks and issues but seem to have a cognitive bias against them, primed as we are for "fight or flight," the classic crisis scenario. Even when risks and their management are advanced, such as enterprise risk management (ERM) systems within the financial sector, elements such as reputational risk are not adequately dealt with.

In his book, *Managing*, Mintzberg pointed out that businesses are often over-led and under-managed. Organizations place too much emphasis on preparing and training for crisis response, and far too little on establishing formal structures and training for complex issues and their management. Yet this seems somewhat strange given the rise of social networks and relational media, which have leveled the playing field, with bloggers and activists having the same access to the network as corporate giants. In the post-industrial world, dominance is being replaced by influence, central to which is an appreciation of what makes reputation.

Impact of Social Networks: Online Issues and Reputation Management

Social networks have transformed corporate communications and the ways in which risks and issues are handled. The speed and nature of online response are now critical as organizations struggle to stay on top of news-flow and circulating rumors, amplified through social media networks. User-generated content (UGC) has altered the power balance between brand owners and their consumers but often errors that lead to reputational issues are found deep within the organizational structures and operations.

Important Social Technologies in Managing Reputation

- ▸ Blogs, e.g. Technorati
- ▸ Microblogging, e.g. Twitter
- ▸ Social networks, e.g. Facebook, Bebo, LinkedIn, Google Plus
- ▸ Video/photo sharing, e.g. YouTube, Flickr
- ▸ Social bookmarking, e.g. Delicious, StumbleUpon
- ▸ Product reviews, e.g. Amazon
- ▸ Discussion groups, e.g. Google Groups
- ▸ Social news, e.g. Digg

Although the protection of online reputation is very important given the ubiquitous nature of social media, in the author's opinion too much emphasis is placed on search engine optimization (SEO) and the removal of online negative comment. Of course bad press and damaging comments must be swiftly and strategically dealt with and of course SEO and visibility are vital to any business and its reputation but it is equally important to address the reasons for such comment rather than simply to remove the symptoms. One cannot simply admire the "fruits" of the corporate tree while ignoring the roots of the business and, more importantly, the soil that it grows in. This reinforces the case for issue management being at the heart of a proper reputation management system as an effective means of providing analysis and valuable insights.

Issues are important to organizations not just because they are unsettled or contestable, thereby uncomfortable, but because they may have serious consequences and will impact on the organization's resources and brand equity in the long term.

Failure within organizations is usually attributable to someone or some group failing to notice or act—attention slips and responsibilities blur. Errors may not immediately cause a discernable problem, but problems may appear say six months later when another variable comes into play. This is why issue management is such a vital element of pre-crisis planning.

As tools for engagement, social media and networks are both friend and foe and must be carefully assimilated into any issue management strategy and tactics. Activists and NGOs such as Greenpeace have become skilled at exploiting issues against corporations, using new media as the forum for debate. For example, Nestlé has been subject to attacks from Greenpeace and other activists over the inclusion of palm oil in some products.

In March 2010, Greenpeace released an advertisement on YouTube that showed an office worker opening a Kit Kat biscuit. One of the chocolate fingers turns out to be a "finger" of an orangutan, which, when bitten, draws blood. Nestlé argued that this shocking pastiche infringed its intellectual property rights, which only resulted in more negative publicity for Nestlé. Like Kraft and Unilever, Nestlé was forced to reconsider its purchase of palm oil from the Indonesian company Sinar Mas, who Greenpeace accuse of significant deforestation that threatens the very existence of orangutans. Nestlé have now developed more robust sustainability strategies, which appear to recognize their global impact, especially from an environmental perspective.

What Is Reputation?

In a word, trust. However, given its amorphous nature, it is hardly surprising that no universally accepted definition exists. Charles Fombrun, CEO of the Reputation Institute, defines reputation as a "collective assessment of an organization's past actions and results that describes the organization's ability to deliver valued outcomes to multiple stakeholders."[1]

In its various perspectives and interpretations, reputation centers on the following common elements:

- ▸ A collective representation based on stakeholders' opinions.
- ▸ An aggregate evaluation that stakeholders make about how well an organization meets its customers' needs based on current and past actions.
- ▸ A holistic impression of a person or company based over time; it can be negative, neutral, or positive.
- ▸ A form of assessment, whereby an organization's performance is judged in the context of its past and current behavior.

As a critical intangible, reputation is rather like modern medicine—it is increasingly evidence-based, with a focus on prevention and understanding of root causes, and changing vital behaviors. In this regard, the importance of issue management can be highlighted. Issue identification and management are the equivalent of preventative medicine, the analysis of the patient's lifestyle to evaluate risks and issues (such as raised blood pressure and poor diet), and the prescribing of drugs that will help mitigate the risk of the medical condition (an ongoing risk or issue) becoming a crisis (such as a heart attack). Just as with modern medicine, people recognize the importance of analysis of symptoms and that early intervention can be critical in the successful management of a condition, but all too often people ignore warning signs and think only of today.

What Are Risks and Issues?

There are a myriad of perspectives and definitions of risk, but from a technical viewpoint, risk can be defined as:

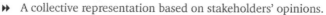

Risk = Probability of occurrence × Impact

The Institute of Risk Management defines risk as "the combination of the probability of an event and its consequences."[2] Consequences can range from positive to negative.

At its simplest, a risk is a future event that may have an impact on an organization. Generally, risk refers to a downside or negative state. An issue is a present problem or concern that has the potential to influence a brand or organization. As an issue can arise from a risk, it is critical that when involved with an issue management process, individuals should understand the risks faced by the organization, and the risks that current issues pose to the organization. Issues are not immediate problems, and therefore are often overlooked. As a concept, issue management is ancient, but in a business context it emerges properly in the late 1970s, along with stakeholder management.

Howard Chase is usually considered the father of issue management, and is credited with coining the term issue management; together with Barrie Jones, he defined an issue as "an unsettled matter which is ready for a decision." Most people, when referring to issue management, do so in the context of downside risk and negative outcomes. Issues can on occasion also have unintended upsides or positive consequences, for example as a result of changes in government policy or regulation that drives more business to one particular manufacturing or service firm while derailing linked businesses.

However, it is important to remember that the essence of issue management is to anticipate problems and opportunities and, by managing them correctly, create positive outcomes such as enhanced reputation and market share. The American clothing giant, Gap, suffered years of global protests based on charges from activists of labor rights abuses, environmental damage, and supply chain issues. Gap engaged in a complex but largely successful stakeholder engagement campaign that resulted in an improved image in the eyes of many activists. Many organizations try to gain "ownership" of an issue, which can often be achieved by working in collaboration with an NGO in an attempt to reduce an issue's impact. By owning and highlighting an issue, companies can tackle problems head-on and ask for the support and cooperation of detractors in an attempt to resolve the issue.

An issue can be categorized in many ways. Some issues are single or narrow-based, such as the impact a factory may be having on the health of local people, while others are broad-based, such as the impact of nanotechnology in the consumer goods sector. Some issues are local, some global. The type of issues faced by a business, and their complexity, is normally a function of the type of business, its impact, and visibility. A business as global and massive as BP will usually adopt a portfolio approach to issue handling, i.e., the ways in which a previous issue was approached and the lessons learned from it are very likely to influence how a new, yet related issue is handled.

Examples of issues faced by organizations:

- ▶▶ Child labor in the supply chain.
- ▶▶ The use of meat from cloned animals.
- ▶▶ Privacy and the use of data from social networking sites.
- ▶▶ Responsible marketing to children.
- ▶▶ The need to reduce an organization's carbon footprint.
- ▶▶ The benefits of environmental and social reporting by companies.
- ▶▶ Biodiversity and threats to key habitats, such as marine or rainforest ecosystems.
- ▶▶ Ethical sourcing of products and labor.
- ▶▶ IT security and data loss.
- ▶▶ Immigration and loss of jobs.
- ▶▶ Traceability of food and consumer goods.
- ▶▶ Promotion of responsible drinking.

What Is Issue Management?

Issue management is a strategic business-planning tool that helps organizations and NGOs gain legitimacy and credibility in their arguments on contentious, unsettled matters. It is a formal process that seeks to harmonize organizations' and stakeholders' interests, thereby reducing the gap between performance and expectation, and which aims to reduce negative outcomes for organizations.

Issue management also helps to shape public debate and public policy formation, the most common approach being advocacy, which involves campaigning and lobbying stakeholders in order to change attitudes and beliefs toward an issue.

Based broadly on the Howard Chase model, modern issue management as a process involves a number of sequential steps that attempt to anticipate, identify, analyze, and provide strategic options to tackle the issue in the best interests of the organization.

The key steps involved are:

>> environmental scanning;
>> issue identification;
>> issue monitoring;
>> issue analysis;
>> strategic options and responses;
>> implementation;
>> evaluation.

The various stages above are highly interrelated and not mutually exclusive (Figure 1). Issue management is not without its critics but in the author's opinion it is a skill and capability that is vastly underused in corporations. It requires resources and dedicated teams, in the same way that most corporations have a crisis management team.

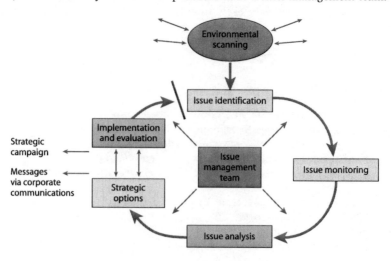

Figure 1. Issue management process

Environmental Scanning

This stage involves scouting the terrain and looking out for any emerging issues, based on opinions, discourses, and debates taking place in the environment. It is a form of intelligence gathering that requires the organization to acquire data and information, and from this produce some knowledge that will inform and guide them. Information can be gathered from a wide range of sources including formal and informal searching of:

- ▸▸ newspapers and general periodicals;
- ▸▸ academic journals;
- ▸▸ open-source intelligence;
- ▸▸ business-to-business publications;
- ▸▸ trade journals;
- ▸▸ NGO-based publications;
- ▸▸ social media and networks, especially specific bloggers/activists;
- ▸▸ online communities;
- ▸▸ government releases and speeches;
- ▸▸ expert opinion;
- ▸▸ market research;
- ▸▸ professional bodies' publications;
- ▸▸ dissertations and research publications;
- ▸▸ independent commissions;
- ▸▸ business news and intelligence organizations.

Researchers should attempt to detect political, economic, social, technological, environmental, and legal (PESTEL) events that may be relevant to the organization. In addition to the PESTEL scanning, one should also look at industry and the task environment. As well as outside threats, scanning also looks at potential internal issues, such as capabilities, resources, and asset availability. Once both external and internal analyses are completed, the results can be fed into a SWOT analysis.

Corporations normally set selection criteria for an emerging issue such as relevance, frequency of mention, the source, and reason for its being highlighted. The primary aim of the scanning stage is to provide intelligence about emerging issues and trends for the next stage: issue identification.

Issue Identification

This stage of issue management involves taking the intelligence gathered and working out whether the issue is going to become a problem for the organization, how the issue is being framed, and, indeed, if it has been given a name or slogan. It is important to realize that those who name the issue or debate often have a significant advantage over its outcome.

During this stage it is important to:

- ▸▸ Define and explain the issue, and how it is being framed and presented.
- ▸▸ Outline its angles and positions, and identify those with a vested interest, e.g. stakeholders' reactions.

➤ Identify potential sources of future information.
➤ Determine how complex and interdependent the issue is and whether it can be broken down.

Monitoring

Monitoring involves forecasting how an issue will develop, its intensity, and potential to cause fear or outcry among key publics. The skill at this point is to evaluate how trends are developing, particularly through online monitoring. Various online resources are available to monitor comments and the lifecycle of issues. It is also important during this stage to realize which stakeholders are influencers, and which are detractors.

Examples of organizations and software that can assist with online and social media monitoring include:

➤ Alexa (www.alexa.com);
➤ BlogPulse (www.blogpulse.com);
➤ Google Alerts (www.google.com/alerts);
➤ Google Analytics (www.google.com/analytics);
➤ Google Trends (www.google.com/trends);
➤ Icerocket (www.icerocket.com);
➤ Radian6 (www.radian6.com);
➤ Technorati (www.technorati.com);
➤ TweetMeme (www.tweetmeme.com);
➤ Twitter Search (search.twitter.com);
➤ Twitterfall (www.twitterfall.com).

Following and tracking online debates, discussions, and forums is integral to the monitoring process. Combined with the specific online monitoring techniques available, other techniques that can be employed to monitor the issue include:

➤ the Delphi forecasting technique;
➤ trend impact analysis;
➤ focus groups, on and offline;
➤ archival research;
➤ surveys;
➤ technology forecasting;
➤ scenario planning.

Some companies, e.g. PepsiCo, have developed social media command centers where they constantly monitor the opinions of consumers on Twitter and other social media about specific products.

Information can also be obtained from news and information sites such as Factiva, Taylor Nelson Sofres, and Brandwatch. Issues generally have a lifecycle development that can be represented graphically (Figure 2).

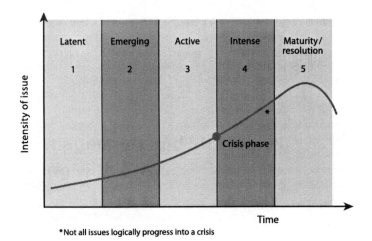

Time

*Not all issues logically progress into a crisis

Figure 2. Issue lifecycle

Issue Analysis

Analysis focuses on trying to establish the facts, position, premise, and possible outcome of the issue in question. This stage is the most critical as it requires the issue management team to dissect the arguments and link these with relevant stakeholders, taking into account their interests and power. Through the analysis, issues can be placed into clusters and priorities set. The questions to be addressed during issue analysis include:

▸▸ What are the various arguments being put forward and by whom?
▸▸ How will the public view and consider the issue?
▸▸ Which activists are involved and why?
▸▸ How can the issue influence public policy?
▸▸ Are arguments shifting and how has the issue been framed?
▸▸ Which stakeholders are implacably against, and which are not yet decided on their position?
▸▸ Is there misrepresentation of the issue?
▸▸ What are the facts and data to support the arguments?
▸▸ Is there conflicting information?
▸▸ Is there a broad spectrum of opinion?
▸▸ What are the concerns of the stakeholders and how are they likely to react?
▸▸ Which clusters of issues should be given priority?
▸▸ What issues are mission critical to the organization both in terms of timing and impact?
▸▸ How can the issue influence the current business model, its operations, and strategy?
▸▸ How mature or advanced is the narrative, and what is the type of language being used?
▸▸ At what stage is the issue within its own lifecycle—still emerging, active or intense, or is it reaching maturity and consolidation?
▸▸ What are the risks/benefits of responding to the issue?

▸▸ Are their false dichotomies within the arguments or fallacious aspects inherent in the debate?

In addition to analysis of current stakeholder interests, it is crucial to try to predict which stakeholders will show an interest in the future and those who have yet to declare their interests. The threat posed by a risk must be considered (Figure 3) and a cost–benefit analysis of acting upon the issue conducted.

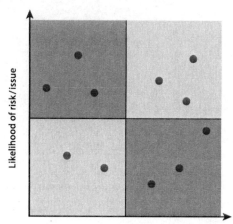

Figure 3. Risk threat assessment matrix

Strategic Options and Responses

Having analyzed the issues, an organization has to consider how it will respond and the strategic options available to it based on the constraints and resources available. Is the organization going to adopt an advocacy response by campaigning and lobbying specific stakeholders to influence the debate in its favor? Is it going to adopt a buffering strategy by keeping silent and avoid ownership of an issue? Exxon Mobil was accused of such a strategy by NGOs over the issue of climate change. In 2008, Exxon was accused of providing cash to skeptic groups allegedly to provide misleading information.

Cigarettes have long been the subject of debates and complex issue management and public affairs campaigns. The tobacco industry has lived with warnings (and sometimes accompanying graphic images of diseased organs) on tobacco packaging for over a decade.

In Australia, the government is planning to introduce some of the toughest laws against tobacco advertising ever seen; in 2011, the UK government is considering a similar approach. Tobacco giants such as Philip Morris in Asia have argued that their intellectual property rights and their brands will be massively damaged by measures such as the plain-packaging of cigarettes. Globally, tobacco manufacturers are under threat from governments seeking to restrict retail displays and branding in an attempt to make smoking less attractive to young people.

Despite the powerful health warning and potential benefits of this regulatory activity, the tobacco companies argue that as well as the destruction of their brands and potential infringements of their intellectual property rights, the standardizing of cigarette packaging would encourage further growth in counterfeit cigarettes. Strategic options left open to cigarette manufacturers are shrinking and will need to become ever more subtle and sophisticated to circumvent existing and potential bans.

During this stage, corporations must also prepare a detailed question and answer responses and have recommended positions on an issue. These then permit the development of consistent messages that convey the position of the organization to the stakeholders.

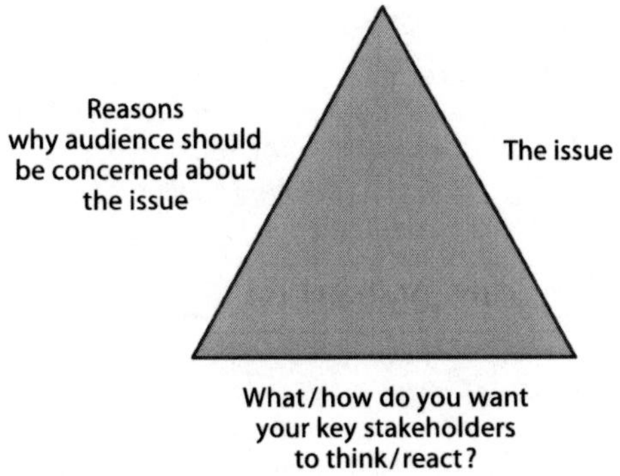

Message development is a vital part of any issue management process and feeds directly into corporate communications activities, such as website content, press and media releases, speeches from the CEO, interviews, spokespeople's comments, and engagement with social media (Figure 4).

Figure 4. Message development/framing triangle. (Adapted from Patterson and Radtke, 2009[3])

Typically message development requires:

- ▸▸ Identification of three or four key messages.
- ▸▸ Frame for the messages: how do you wish the issue to be presented and can the message be reduced to an attractive sound bite?
- ▸▸ The message triangle: outlining the message, why it matters, and what you want your key target groups to do.

The media are fundamental to the message-framing process, especially the portrayal of villain, victim, and hero within any given narrative. Corporations can ill-afford to be portrayed as the villain and are rarely the victims, so it is often best for them to position themselves as heroes.

Stakeholders, especially activists and campaigning NGOs, will often frame an issue in a manner that infuses it with emotive language, worrying statistics, or fear or about the future if nothing is done. To understand how an issue has been framed, one must collect samples of media articles relating to the issue and review them as follows:

1 Analyze the different articles and identify the common arguments and opinions used. Are there common phrases, sources, or people quoted? Who is deemed responsible for the problem and/or who could provide a solution?
2 From the above, clarify the core position, apparent solution, if any is being advanced, and predicted outcomes or impacts.
3 Gauge the public response and determine if the issue could be affected by public policy?
4 Establish what frames are being used.

Once a frame for an issue is understood, the corporation may be in a position to reframe the issue by changing the narrative and repositioning the problem, or by offering different, as yet unconsidered solutions.

Reframing requires complex messages to be simplified and misrepresentations or misleading data to be corrected, with alternative viewpoints advanced. It is always important for corporations to remember that arguments are complex and that there are no absolute truths, only relative positions and perspectives. NGOs often take the moral high ground in arguing concepts and present them in a simplified manner, which should always be challenged by engagement through dialectical methods.

Implementation and Evaluation

The implementation of a campaign will require issue communications via corporate communications tools, including:

- corporate or advocacy advertising;
- CSR activities;
- social media platforms: Twitter, YouTube, Facebook, etc.;
- use or endorsement of a position by a celebrity;
- speeches or interviews by CEO;
- forums and online communities;
- educational initiatives;
- published environmental or social reports;
- targeted media, press briefing, reviews;
- sponsored events;
- cause-related/social marketing campaigns;
- features, articles, or blogging;
- corporate website content.

Irrespective of the medium being used and analyzed during an issue advocacy campaign, it is important to be clear about objectives and what is being considered, including the scope and critical outcomes. Central to this whole strategic process is the importance of brand engagement, which can be measured using a wide range of metrics including:

- number of RSS feed subscribers;
- number of responses to surveys;
- number of comments and followers;
- number of sign-ups;
- number of "retweets";
- number of "likes";
- number of reblogs.

Whatever the form and mode of engagement, feedback must be evaluated, not just in terms of media noise and output, but also in terms of outcomes—have consumers or key stakeholders altered their beliefs or shifted in their opinions? Issues managed successfully, like most advocacy campaigns, are about changing peoples' attitudes, beliefs, and behavior.

Conclusion

The primary objective of any reputation management process is to build and protect the brand and secure its future equity. Issue management is one of the most effective tools available to any organization to gather intelligence, understand how the market and stakeholder networks are positioning themselves, and be in a position to defend and respond in a manner that maintain the organization's credibility and legitimacy. Issue management also provides a framework enabling corporations to make better judgments and decisions. Business is ultimately about making and implementing decisions, but so many of the decisions that are made in business are based on poor judgment and lack of reflective reasoning, the cost of which can be severe reputational damage.

Case Study

Too Much Too Young: The Issue of the Premature Sexualization of Children

The issue of the premature sexualization of children is broad and complex, filled with numerous sub-issues, moral outrage, and sensitivity. In February 2010, the UK Prime Minister, David Cameron, became directly involved, when he revealed he and his wife had to stop their daughter from listening to the pop music artist Lily Allen, because they believed the lyrics were inappropriate. Although not a new issue, the sexualization of children gained prominence in the United Kingdom during the previous Labour government as teen magazines pushed the envelope too far and brands such as Playboy became accused of grooming children to more readily accept the brand as adults. Playboy pencils and T-shirts for children became the subject of much news and general discussion as the issue was widened into how adults were negatively influencing the sensitive and important issue of what constitutes childhood and the ever-amorphous "well-being" of children.

As an industry-based problem, the issue had links with wider, complex, and emotive topics such as the United Kingdom's terrible record on teenage pregnancy and high levels of sexually transmitted diseases. Self-regulation also raised its head as individual companies had to consider their own responsibilities and response to growing public disquiet.

For too long, teenage magazines had pushed their luck in exposing children to sexual imagery, and behaved irresponsibly by seeming to tacitly encourage risky behavior and what many believed to be lapsed moral attitudes. Equally, pop videos had age-inappropriate imagery within the lyrics that shocked or offended, even sometimes on national TV.

In June 2011, the issue became intense after a six-month independent review into the commercialization and sexualization of childhood (the Bailey Report) was published. This produced a series of recommendations based on parents' concerns, such as restricting outdoor advertisements containing sexual imagery, putting age restrictions on music videos, and retailers offering age-appropriate clothing. Bodies such as the British Retail Consortium (BRC) also published family-friendly guidelines on how industry could respond positively and voluntarily to public feeling.

The Advertising Standards Authority (ASA) and regulator Ofcom became embroiled, welcoming the report and its recommendations. The regulator and other key stakeholders recognized that, if or when the report's recommendations become legislation, it could have a significant impact on specific companies and their brands. The retail groups were given 18 months to improve their act voluntarily or become subject to tough legislation. As the public discourse matured, so the issue seemed to come to an inevitable conclusion—either the retailers make sensible and credible changes or they would be forced to.

Some critics of the issue of commercialization and sexualization point to what they describe as creeping authoritarianism. What exactly was the responsibility of parents in the issue and is further censorship the answer? Others argued that parents cannot simply abdicate responsibility for their children's actions to the government.

Another aspect of the issue that went right to the heart of marketing practices aimed at children was the practice of paying children to promote products on social networking websites and at school. Toy and food brands were forced to rethink the practice of promoting to children using peer-to-peer recommendation.

The issue of premature sexualization of children is an interesting one as it evokes so many other interdependent issues and risks for brands. It challenges brand values and questions many of the techniques used by retailers to engage children. It is a classic example of an industry that simply went too far, and became subject to campaigning and a serious risk of being heavily regulated. Despite making much noise about CSR, many brands will have to seriously reconsider their approach as they become subject to the stigma of regulation and restriction.

More Info

Books:

Carroll, Archie B., and Ann K. Buchholtz. *Business and Society: Ethics, Sustainability, and Stakeholder Management*. 8th ed. Mason, OH: South-Western Cengage Learning, 2011.

Chase, W. Howard. *Issue Management: Origins of the Future*. Stamford, CT: Issue Action Publications, 1984.

Cornelissen, Joep. *Corporate Communications: A Guide to Theory and Practice*. 3rd ed. London: Sage, 2011.

Friedman, Andrew L., and Samantha Miles. *Stakeholders: Theory and Practice*. Oxford: Oxford University Press, 2006.

Heath, Robert L., and Michael J. Palenchar. *Strategic Issues Management: Organizations and Public Policy Challenges*. 2nd ed. Thousand Oaks, CA: Sage, 2009.

Rayner, Jenny. *Managing Reputational Risk*. Chichester, UK: Wiley, 2003.

Ringland. Gill. *Scenario Planning*. 2nd ed. Chichester, UK: Wiley, 2006.

van Riel, Cees B. M., and Charles J. Fombrun. *Essential of Corporate Communication*. Abingdon, UK: Routledge, 2007.

Articles:

Business Action to Stop Counterfeiting and Piracy. Submission to the UK Department of Health consultation on the future of tobacco control. September 8, 2008: Online at: tinyurl.com/44umasl [PDF].

Jones, Barrie L., and W. Howard Chase. "Managing public policy issues." *Public Relations Review* 5:2 (Summer 1979): 3–23. Online at: dx.doi.org/10.1016/S0363-8111(80)80020-8

Reber, Bryan H., and Jun Kyo Kim. "How activist groups use websites in media relations: Evaluating online press rooms." *Journal of Public Relations Research* 18:4 (2006): 313–333. Online at: dx.doi.org/10.1207/s1532754xjprr1804_2

Notes

1. Fombrun, Charles, and Cees van Riel. "The reputational landscape." *Corporate Reputation Review* 1:1 (Summer 1997): 5–13. Online at: dx.doi.org/10.1057/palgrave.crr.1540008
2. IRM, AIRMIC, and ALARM. "A risk management standard." 2002. Online at: www.theirm.org/publications/PUstandard.html
3. Patterson, Sally J., and Janel M. Radtke. *Strategic Communications for Nonprofit Organizations.* 2nd ed. Hoboken, NJ: Wiley, 2009.

Crisis Management and Strategies for Dealing with Crisis

by Jon White

Consultant, London, UK

This Chapter Covers

▸▸ Crises and their characteristics—what distinguishes crises from disasters, emergencies, and other exceptional situations.

▸▸ Crisis management—phases in crisis management, and the requirements in each phase for effective management.

▸▸ Techniques for anticipating crises, and preparations for dealing with them.

▸▸ The benefits to be gained by routine management from paying attention to crisis management.

▸▸ The demands made on management at times of crisis and the importance of psychological preparation.

▸▸ Practical conclusions.

Introduction: Crises and Their Characteristics

The term "crisis" is much used in the media coverage of events, in public discussion, and by organization leaders describing the situations that they face and try to manage. The consequences of failure to manage these situations may prove more or less damaging to their organizations. However, not all situations that are described as crises should be labeled as such, and it is important to distinguish real crises from other situations as a first step toward managing them as effectively as possible.

Before looking at the characteristics of crisis situations, we will examine a situation—the Deepwater Horizon oil spill in the Gulf of Mexico—that was recognized at the time as a crisis for the organization involved to draw out the features that define it as a crisis.

Case Study

BP in the Gulf of Mexico, 2010

On April 20, 2010, an oil rig—the Deepwater Horizon, which was operated for BP in the Gulf of Mexico by Transocean—was rocked by an explosion which killed 11 workers and allowed oil to escape from the wellhead, 40 miles off the coast of Louisiana and 5,000 feet below the surface of the sea. Oil flowed into the water for 87 days before the well was finally capped.

After the event, BP recognized that it was being subjected to unprecedented media and political scrutiny. For President Barack Obama the stakes were high—his predecessor, President George W. Bush, had been heavily criticized for his perceived slowness of response to the impact of Hurricane Katrina on the same US state in 2005.

In addition to the deaths of employees, the accident caused damage to the environment and economic damage to the affected states. For BP, the accident was a corporate crisis that threatened the existence of the company, wiping 50% off its market value and forcing it to set aside funds to meet potential claims against the company.

The management response to the accident and its aftermath was a reaction to a complex interplay of issues:

» the technical problems associated with attempts to cap a well in a deepwater operation;

» the organizational requirements of dealing with several partner and supplier organizations that were not part of BP, but were providing services, such as the operation of the rig, to BP;

» the number of involved stakeholders, from the US federal government, to local governments and the communities affected.

BP's CEO, Tony Hayward, became personally involved in the company's response to the accident, suggesting that he would not leave the site until the problem had been solved. He was, however, to be heavily criticized in his role and for a number of statements that he made to the media during the course of managing the company's response to the accident and its aftermath. His credibility was damaged, and he was replaced as CEO of the company as it sought to retrieve its reputation after the well was finally capped.

Media scrutiny of the company was intense, with attempts to deal with the problem of the oil leaking into the sea and to explain the company's actions under constant surveillance by the press and broadcast media, and in discussions that took place on the social media.

BP's experience in dealing with the Gulf of Mexico incident and its aftermath is already a classic case study, taking its place alongside other oil industry case studies dealing with Shell's experience with the Brent Spar in the mid-1990s and Exxon's disastrous Alaskan oil spill from the company's vessel, the Exxon Valdez, in 1989.

But what made the accident a crisis for the company? We will consider this question in the next part of the chapter.

Distinguishing Crises

In the academic literature on crisis management, crises are distinguished from other serious situations faced by organizations by a number of defining features.

Level of Threat

First, a crisis has to be serious in its consequences, involving loss of life, or threat to life, and serious injury or the possibility of serious injury, to numbers of people. It will also involve actual or possible damage to property. The first defining feature of crisis is the *level of threat* involved. The threat may also extend to the organization's existence, vital interests, or "raison d'être."

How an organization responds to a crisis will have an impact on its reputation, which is an aggregation of perceptions of its performance. Failure to perform to expectations at a time of crisis will result in damage to a company's reputation, which in some cases will be terminal.

There are also well-documented examples of corporate performance at times of crisis that enhance an organization's reputation. An example is the performance of Swissair (the airline went bankrupt in 2002) at the time of the crash of one of its aircraft off Nova Scotia, Canada, in 1998, a crash in which all 229 people on board the aircraft died. The airline's competent and sensitive handling of its obligations to those affected by the crash protected, maintained, and enhanced the airline's reputation.

Time Pressure
A second defining feature of crisis is *time pressure*. Threat or damage must be dealt with as soon as possible to minimize their consequences—whether these are further loss of life, threat to life, or damage to property. A good example here is the Japanese response to continuing threats of radiation leakage from the Fukushima nuclear plant damaged in the tsunami which followed an earthquake off Japan in March 2011.

Stress
A third defining feature of crisis is *stress*, as experienced by the decision-makers who have to deal with the situation. In crisis, their response will be marked by surprise, uncertainty, and flawed decision-making. In many crisis situations, the observation will be made that decision-makers are "out of position"—not where they need to be to deal with the situation as it develops.

Crises are unexpected, unforeseen events, which distinguishes them from disasters. Disasters, although serious in their consequences and sharing characteristics with crises, can be anticipated and plans made for dealing with them. For example, countries that experience earthquakes can prepare to respond to them when they occur, and take steps to minimize their consequences, by setting up early warning systems and buildings that can withstand earthquake damage.

Crisis management depends on classifying events or situations that will constitute crises for any organization. They will pose threats to life and property, and to the existence and reputation of the organization. They will need to be dealt with quickly to minimize their consequences, and they will make difficult demands on decision-makers and others who have to deal with them.

The Deepwater Horizon Incident as an Example of a Crisis
The BP case shows all these characteristics—the accident killed numbers of employees, damaged equipment, and created a huge oil spill that impacted the environment, the communities around the Gulf, and the livelihoods of their inhabitants. The company's vital interests—its reputation and ability to operate in deepwater environments in the United States and worldwide—were called into question, as were the abilities of the managers who tried to deal with the accident and the oil discharge and their consequences.

In addition, the crisis was played out in public, against sustained questioning and criticism from government, the media, the public, and investors in the company.

Categories of Corporate Crisis
The Deepwater Horizon incident was a "perfect storm" of a crisis. At end of the film *The Perfect Storm*, the fishing boat that is trying to ride through the storm is overwhelmed by the sea. How can organizations save themselves from being overwhelmed by such

"storms"? They need first of all to understand what they may be up against, by trying to understand what, for them, will constitute crises so that they can prepare for them.

Lerbinger (1997) has outlined a number of broad categories of corporate crises.

▸▸ *Crises involving technology:* In a world that is increasingly dependent on technology, when technology fails the consequences may be catastrophic. Examples of these crises are provided by the difficulties at the Fukushima nuclear plant in 2011 following the earthquake and tsunami in Japan, and the Bhopal industrial accident in 1984 when gas released from a Union Carbide plant in Bhopal, India, caused many fatalities.

▸▸ *Crises arising from confrontation:* These are caused when groups confront corporations or other authorities and criticize their actions, or go to more extreme lengths to express their opposition or discontent. An example of this is provided by the action of animal rights pressure groups in mounting strong, or even violent, opposition to companies that make use of animals in product testing or research.

▸▸ *Crises caused by malevolence:* These are crises caused by the malevolent actions of individuals or groups, such as terrorist groups placing bombs in unlikely locations to bring about maximum disruption of business and everyday life. The 7/7 attacks on London's transportation systems—the subway and buses on 7 July, 2005—are an example of a crisis created by malevolence.

▸▸ *Crises of management failure:* These are crises caused by management groups within the organization failing to carry out their responsibilities. Arguments have been made that the so-called financial crisis of recent years could be attributed to failure on the part of managers of financial institutions to manage the risks that their organizations were taking.

▸▸ *Crises involving other threats to the organization:* Examples include unexpected takeover bids.

"You never want a serious crisis to go to waste. And what I mean by that is [don't pass up] an opportunity to do things you think you could not do before." Rahm Emanuel, until late 2010 chief of staff to US President Barack Obama and now mayor of Chicago.

Crisis Management

How can the unexpected be prepared for and managed? How can the manager plan for that which cannot be planned for? How much attention should be given to planning for events or situations which may never happen? These are practical and difficult questions for managers thinking about crisis management to address.

Crisis management can be approached in terms of three phases of crisis management, and the requirements for managing each phase can be explored. Crisis management involves:

▸▸ crisis planning;
▸▸ crisis management—management of the crisis when it occurs;
▸▸ managing the aftermath of a crisis.

Crisis Planning

With hindsight, it is easy to ask whether or not an organization in crisis did enough to plan for the situation that arose. Questions along these lines were asked about BP's preparations for the oil spill which occurred in the Gulf of Mexico.

Crisis planning is an exercise in thinking the unthinkable—what, given the organization's interests, operations, plans, and links to groups such as suppliers, the community, and interest groups, could possibly go wrong for the organization? This exercise is one that should involve the most senior managers of the organization, and it may be difficult to get their attention and time for this—some will feel that they need not concern themselves with events that are unlikely to happen.

The exercise will typically generate a list of between 20 or 30 events and situations, which can be categorized and judged in terms of their likelihood of occurrence and impact. They may be placed on a scale of severity, ranging from crises (events or situations that affect the central interests or existence of the organization, involve threats to life and property, and require prompt action), disasters (similar, but more predictable), emergencies (less threatening situations, predictable, but still requiring prompt action), and exceptions to routine operations (predictable, requiring prompt remedial action). When events and situations have been categorized, plans can be made to deal with each category.

Crises require specific plans, which set out the situations that the organization has identified as crises. The plans set out arrangements for mobilizing the organization—identifying its senior managers and others who will be involved in managing the crisis situation. Crisis management requires two management teams—one to make decisions regarding the organization's response to the crisis, the other to implement the decisions made by this group and ensure that the organization deals with the demands of the situation. Arrangements have to be made for these two teams to work alongside each other, from facilities suitable for their work and with sufficient communication links between the teams, to the rest of the organization and to the outside world.

Crisis plans will identify roles in crisis management and the individuals who are to carry them out, and will set out arrangements for filling these roles over periods of time.

Communication at a time of crisis needs special attention. Will the communication links required be in place and sufficient? Who are the groups of people with whom the organization will need to communicate? What can and should be said at the outset in any crisis situation to groups such as the affected stakeholder groups (for example, the relatives of any employees injured in a crisis situation), or the media?

Some of this material can and should be prepared before any crisis situation develops. This can be incorporated into website content, into specific websites prepared for opening to the public at time of crisis, or into sections of already accessible websites.

A recent development in crisis communication has been to take into account the part played by the social media, allowing for stakeholder and public comment on the crisis situation as it develops. Planning for crisis communication now requires planning for possible developments in the discussion of crisis situations on such media, where the organization needs to decide what its approach to these channels will be before the crisis situation develops.

Once developed, crisis plans have to be tested, rehearsed through simulations, and kept up to date. It is particularly important to keep up to date the information about individuals who are nominated to play specific roles. All details of the plan can be tested against experience from simulations, where situations similar to those foreseen in the planning phase are presented to the organization to test the response of crisis management teams and the organization itself.

Managing the Crisis Itself

Despite the importance of planning, during a time of crisis the plans that have been developed may not fit the actual crisis situation. The situation may differ from any that was considered in the planning phase, or the crisis may overturn key features of existing plans. For example, the plans may call for the use of specific facilities from which the crisis is to be managed, but the actual crisis may involve the destruction of facilities intended for this use. Back-up plans should be in place, but there may be a need for improvisation at a time when the quality of decision-making is degraded by time pressure and stress.

Crisis management under these conditions is improved by preparation—although managers do not have specific preparation, they are prepared for stress and the difficulties of decision-making under stressful conditions. A characteristic of decision-making under these conditions is "group think." This is a term developed by the psychologist Irving Janis in the early 1970s to explain faulty group decision-making. In this, groups rely on their own resources and focus on group interests rather than on information from outside that might contradict prevailing views within the group. Group think can be avoided by ensuring an adequate flow of information to decision-making groups, which in turn requires sufficient communication links for these groups.

Organizations that face the possibility of demanding crisis situations need, where resources allow, to have in place advisors who at a time of crisis can monitor, comment on, and raise questions about the quality of decision-making and the need for additional information to inform decisions.

Managing the Aftermath of Crisis

After the immediate crisis situation has been brought under control—for example, after BP finally capped the well in the Gulf of Mexico—organizations have to manage the aftermath. This may involve correcting practices that led to the crisis, compensating those who have been affected, and reestablishing external confidence in the organization. Managing the aftermath requires longer-term effort, and will also involve communicating with important groups that changes have been made and that management will avoid similar situations in future. A primary interest here may be in repairing damage to reputation, as in BP's case. Exxon's experience with the Alaskan oil spill from the Exxon Valdez shows how the task of restoring reputation continues long after the crisis.

Techniques for Anticipating Crises, and Preparations for Dealing With Them

Senior managers can call on the advice of specialist groups to help them to anticipate crisis situations. These will include management consultants skilled in futures research, scenario planning, and risk assessment; internal and external groups that take a strategic perspective on the organization's interests; and specialists such as public relations and public affairs practitioners. These practitioners have expertise in dealing with issues and crisis management, communication during a crisis, and reputation management.

The techniques such advisors will draw on include the following.

▸▸ *Futures research,* which makes use of techniques such as scenario planning—a planning approach that looks into the future in a disciplined way, creating and examining plausible scenarios—or Delphi studies. The latter work through a series of rounds of questions to experts on likely developments and possible risks. Questioning is pursued with, and summarized to, the group of experts until consensus, or consensus on differences of opinion, is reached. The results of Delphi studies can be used to inform decision-making.

▸▸ *Risk assessments,* which weigh the likelihood of events or situations developing and their possible impacts, and making judgments on threats and vulnerability. A specialization in risk assessment relates to reputation risk assessment—what could happen to seriously damage the organization's reputation, and what steps should be taken to avoid damage to reputation.

▸▸ *Issues management,* where topics of concern to particular groups are identified and tracked through environmental scanning and monitoring. Involved here may be social research, analysis of traditional and social media content, and close attention to the concerns of special interest groups.

Benefits for Routine Management of Attention to Crisis Management

Advisors on crisis management, whether internal or external to the organization, will encounter scepticism from management regarding the time, effort, and resources to be committed to crisis management. Too often, organizations have to experience a crisis situation before they will take the task of crisis management seriously—and for some this will be too late.

A benefit of attention to crisis management that may be overlooked is that it improves routine management. By asking at the planning stage what could go wrong, current practices and processes can be reexamined from this perspective. Improvements can be made that will avoid problems, as well as improve management perspectives, skills, and decision-making.

The Importance of Psychological Preparation

Attention to crisis management, to crisis planning, and to rehearsal of the response to potential crisis situations also improves management capability. Management is essentially an attempt to bring order to the work of groups of people and to the use of resources to achieve objectives. Crisis situations disrupt the existing order—sometimes catastrophically (think for example of the 9/11 terrorist attacks in New York in 2001, or the Japanese earthquake and tsunami in 2011)—and make exceptional demands on decision-makers. Managers and decision-makers, prepared through training for these situations, will still find them very difficult to deal with, but they will feel psychologically prepared for them. After BP's experience in the Gulf of Mexico, the company's CEO Tony Hayward told a BBC documentary program that he had felt ill-prepared for the demands of the situation.

Training for crisis management involves the following.

▸▸ Working through simulations. Simulations set up situations as realistically as possible, through the use of real-time but simulated developments, actors, and creation of pressure on decision-makers. They allow decision-makers, working through developed plans, to see how the plans—and they themselves—perform against the demands of the simulated situation.

▸▸ Preparation for the communication requirements of crisis situations. Who will speak for the organization, what will they be able to say, and how will they cope with media interest in crisis situations? The training here will be very specific—how can individual managers be prepared for the encounter with the media? How should they present themselves, what should they be prepared to say and where, and how should they be prepared for the approaches to questioning that will be taken by the media?

"Humankind cannot bear very much reality." T. S. Eliot, "Burnt Norton"

Summary and Further Steps

▸▸ The reality of the modern world is that there are endless possibilities for things to go badly wrong for organizations, large and small. They confront scarcity of resources, political uncertainty, heavy social expectations, competition, and potential for conflict.

▸▸ It is essential that management groups prepare for difficult situations. These will be defined organization by organization, depending on their interests, their relationships, and their prospects.

▸▸ Preparation must be thorough and undertaken by the most senior and responsible managers in the organization, since they have the authority to see that the preparations made will be followed through.

▸▸ Crisis management depends on management accepting the necessity of preparation for potential crisis. This means lifting attention from the immediate, the short term, and day-to-day practical concerns to look to the future, and to anticipate disruption.

▸▸ The phase of crisis planning lays the basis for all the work that will be done in managing a crisis, and this depends on a commitment of effort by senior management.

▸▸ The other essential of crisis management is the psychological preparation of managers for the demands it will make of them. This adds to management capability and is a grounding for management in the modern world.

More Info

Books:

Griffin, A. *New Strategies for Reputation Management: Gaining Control of Issues, Crises & Corporate Social Responsibility*. London: Kogan Page, 2007.

Griffin, A., M. Regester, T. Johnson, and J. Larkin. *Risk Issues and Crisis Management in Public Relations: A Casebook of Best Practice*. 4th ed. London: Kogan Page, 2008.

Janis, I. *Group Think*. 2nd ed. Boston, MA: Houghton Mifflin, 1982.

Larkin, J. *Strategic Reputation Risk Management*. Basingstoke, UK: Palgrave Macmillan, 2002.

Lerbinger, Otto. *The Crisis Manager: Facing Risk and Responsibility*. Oxford, UK: Routledge Communication Series, 1997. (To be republished 2012.)

Movie:

Petersen, Wolfgang (dir). *The Perfect Storm*. Warner Bros, 2000.

Managing Your Reputation through Crisis: Opportunity or Threat?

by Magnus Carter

Mentor Communications, Bristol, UK

> **This Chapter Covers**
>
> ▸▸ Definitions of risk issues and crisis.
> ▸▸ How risk issues can escalate into crisis.
> ▸▸ How to prevent escalation.
> ▸▸ Why some crises threaten your reputation more than others.
> ▸▸ How to safeguard your reputation in a crisis.
> ▸▸ What to say and what to do.
> ▸▸ The important role of the media, including social media.

Introduction

We know that no organization is immune from crisis. The one thing that is predictable about crises is that they *will* happen, and a good crisis management plan is essential best practice. Yet my experience as a crisis communications consultant tells me that many organizations, including some substantial ones, do not have such a plan. And of those that do have a plan, surprisingly many consider only the direct threat of disaster, catastrophe, and physical emergency, and how to prevent such events from interrupting business.

My argument in this chapter has the following three fundamentals.

▸▸ That the greatest threat to organizations in crisis is often the damage caused to their reputation. You may be able to recover your ability to deliver product, for example, but if no one trusts your product any longer, the exercise is pointless.

▸▸ That reputation is most adversely affected where crises arise from risk issues that might have been foreseen and better managed. However, even disasters in which you may initially be seen as the "victim" have a nasty habit of throwing up challenges to your reputation, depending on how you manage the event.

▸▸ Managing your organization's reputation needs to be at the center of crisis management and recovery. It is not something you can "bolt on." Being seen and heard to manage risk issues and crises well can enhance your reputation and limit or mitigate damage from the event. So dealing with the media, including online sources, is not optional—it is essential.

Crisis and Reputation

The key to understanding how much of a threat to your reputation a crisis is likely to create and where that threat is likely to arise is to consider the following question: What is within your control, and what is beyond it?

Figure 1 illustrates the point. It was devised by Samuel Passow, a Harvard-educated journalist, author, and accredited mediator who is the head of consultancy services and executive training at the Conflict Analysis Research Centre at the University of Kent. The types of crisis that appear toward the left-hand end of the spectrum are the most likely to dent your reputation. In those toward the right, the early assumption is likely to be that you are the "victim." It is vital that crisis management plans do not focus entirely on the right-hand end of the spectrum. Always allow for mismanagement. And do not listen to the argument that such and such will never happen.

The spectrum of crises

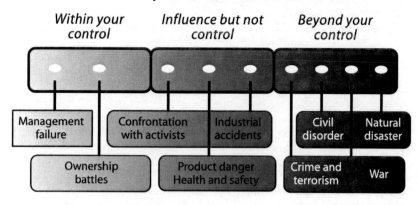

Figure 1. The spectrum of crises. (Devised by Samuel Passow)

Of course, how you manage a crisis is always under your control, so a crisis that begins at the right-hand end of the spectrum can move to the left if you are perceived to be mismanaging the situation, or if it is suspected that better management might have prevented or mitigated the crisis.

For example, in the Japanese earthquake and tsunami of 2011, sympathy for the plight of the nation and those affected was universal, as was admiration for the stoicism and robustness of individual and official responses. However, that did not prevent important questions being raised about Japan's nuclear safety policy in the light of what happened at Fukushima—questions that had serious repercussions for the reputation of the nuclear industry worldwide, as shown by Germany's almost instant decision to announce the ending of its nuclear energy program.

The Fukushima Daiichi plant was badly damaged by the 9.0 earthquake that struck on March 11, 2011. The Tokyo Electric Power Company, which owns the plant, had previously carried out geologic and sonic surveys to assess the power station's resistance to such events. They had put in place a number of additional precautions as a result of learning from a fire at another plant in the northwest of the country when it was hit by a magnitude 6.6 earthquake in 2007.

But Japan's Nuclear and Industrial Safety Agency said that, despite the surveys, it appeared that officials at Fukushima had not considered the scenario that a tsunami might hit the power plant at a time when they would need to use the diesel backup generators intended to provide emergency power to the reactor cooling systems. Fuel tanks for the generators, positioned at ground level just yards from the seafront, were among the first parts of the facility to be destroyed by the huge tsunami wave that swept inland following the earthquake.

Dr John H. Large, a United Kingdom-based independent nuclear engineer and nuclear safety expert, told the *Daily Telegraph*: "These plants should be designed to be resistant to tsunamis, but it appears they did not consider that a tsunami would hit the plant when they were using the back-up generators. The buildings will have been built to withstand a tsunami, but it appears the back-up generators were not." (Gray and Fitzpatrick, 2011).

This highlights an important aspect of crisis planning: the law of unfortunate coincidence, which says that whenever one thing goes wrong, so will another.

Risk Issues and Crisis

Mike Seymour and Simon Moore, in their work *Effective Crisis Management*, classify crises as either cobras or pythons. Cobras strike suddenly and take you by surprise, and are more likely to appear at the right-hand end of our spectrum. Pythons creep up over time and slowly crush you, and are more likely to appear at the left-hand end of the spectrum. Crucially, pythons do not start out as crises, and there is time to spot them and deal with them before strangulation occurs: at this stage, they can be classified as *risk issues*. But how to spot them before they become *crises*?

Let's start by defining what are in fact two stages of the same continuum. The *Journal of Management Studies* offers the following definitions:

> ▸▸ *Risk issue*—A point of conflict between an organization and one or more of its audiences, or a gap between corporate practice and stakeholder expectations. (In other words, a risk issue arises when you don't do what you say you do, or what others have a right to expect you to do).
> ▸▸ *Crisis*—An organizationally-based disaster which causes extensive damage or disruption and involves multiple stakeholders.

Every time we fail to meet customer expectations, we have raised a risk issue. Managed well, there is no lasting damage. Managed badly, the risk issue begins to escalate: other customers begin to join in, perhaps the media take an interest, and the risk issue tips over into crisis.

A notable and historic instance of this process is provided by the experience of Shell UK in the Brent oilfield in the North Sea. Brent Spar was a crude oil-storage and tanker-loading buoy for 15 years until it was decommissioned in 1991, having reached the end of its useful life.

An environmental outcry ensued when it emerged that Shell UK Exploration and Production (Shell Expro) was planning to dispose of the structure by sinking it in the Atlantic Ocean. As well as Greenpeace's occupation of the rig off the Scottish coast, many people boycotted

Shell products in a campaign which the company said lost it millions of dollars.

The publicity led the oil company to drop its plans in 1995, and no oil structures have been dumped at sea since then. In July 1999 European nations agreed to ban the dumping of offshore steel oil rigs.

Although Shell had carried out an environmental impact assessment in full accordance with existing legislation and firmly believed that its actions were in the best interests of the environment, it had severely underestimated the strength of public opinion. As a result, the oil industry now faces an expensive and environmentally questionable requirement to return all North Sea oil installations to shore when redundant, in contradiction of most scientific evidence.

Shell was particularly criticized for having thought of this as a "UK" (or even "Scottish") problem and for neglecting to think of the impact it would have on the company's image in the wider world. To quote the *Financial Times*: "In hindsight, Shell failed to detect the extent of public concern in continental Europe or to win adequate support for its argument that the best place for the Brent Spar was in a deep trench in the Atlantic. As a result, years of careful cultivation by Shell of an environmentally friendly image have been thrown away." And here's the *Wall Street Journal*: "Shell made a strategic error. In a world of sound bites, one image was left with viewers: a huge multinational oil company was mustering all its might to bully what was portrayed as a brave but determined band."

So, the issue of how best to dispose of a redundant piece of equipment in the most environmentally sound and safe way escalated into a crisis of public confidence—a threat to the company's reputation. The question is, how does this happen?

Crisis Escalation

In many cases, issues develop as a result of external processes or legislation, management directives, or working practices. Often, legislation or guidelines are simply viewed as "something that has to be done"—and although the operational implications are considered, the cultural and social impact is missed or ignored. This is a key element in the process known as "crisis incubation." The incubation of issues until they become crises results from a number of cultural factors.

▸ *Management values and perceptions:* The primary beliefs and values of an organization or its management may restrict decision-making or planning. In particular, autocratic management styles at the top tend to permeate through organizations and lead to contrary opinions and information being withheld. Processes and controls will only be created and implemented for perceived issues that fit the organization's demonstrated values (which are often not in tune with those which are publicly declared).

▸ *Denial of possibilities:* Organizations and managers will often not look beyond the identified issues and will deny that the organization requires processes to handle issues that may actually occur. This leads to…

▸ *Internalization:* Managers ignore or refuse to accept the opinions of people outside their own organization. This may be because they do not believe that

> outsiders have the expertise, or because outsiders' opinions or values do not match their own, or because they do not want their own expertise questioned.

▸▸ *Disempowered employees:* The combination of autocratic management and a failure to acknowledge external perspectives will usually result in a workforce that is reluctant to pass on knowledge gained on the shop floor or in encounters with customers. In this way, important information fails to reach decision-making levels, important decisions are missed, and a downward spiral of employee disenfranchisement begins.

▸▸ *Compliance:* Regulations or processes are, or are perceived to be, outdated or inappropriate for the particular organization, individual, or situation. As a result, the rules are not followed.

▸▸ *Monitoring:* Issues and processes are implemented but not monitored or evaluated to judge success, measure against original objectives, or assess impact or the need to change. Without constant monitoring, it cannot be established whether issues have been resolved or, at least, kept under control, or are actually heading toward crisis.

▸▸ *Blame culture:* Blame and finger-pointing hinders learning and can cause further unnecessary damage to the organization.

In the case of Shell and the Brent Spar, it is likely that the first three of these factors were at work. Shell knew it was right, but failed to recognize public perception and to engage in debate to put across its argument until it was too late and the company was forced into an embarrassing climbdown.

Avoiding a Crisis Culture

Arguably, a crisis culture stems from an organization's inability to address, identify, or resolve issues. An organization with a culture which is open to internal and external debate and advice about issues as they arise, which is prepared to initiate change as a result of that advice or debate, and which is prepared to communicate clearly how issues have been resolved is an organization that is far more likely to avoid crises in the first place, or to be able to defuse them quickly when they occur.

One of the most significant factors in both crisis incubation and postcrisis learning is blame. Identification and resolution of issues is far more difficult in a culture that fosters blame. Whistleblowers only exist—and are seen in an entirely negative light—because organizations lack transparency and fail to listen to, or address, issues raised in the day-to-day working environment by people at all levels within them. "Blowing the whistle" is an act of last resort by people who can no longer watch bad or dangerous practices being conducted by their colleagues. Whistleblowing marks the point at which an issue has incubated into a crisis, and a no-blame culture will help to avoid this.

The identification of issues—which may often be associated with someone's weakness or failure—is hindered by the fear of finger-pointing, blame, and accusation. In a no-blame culture, however, your ability to make rapid, clear decisions will be enhanced by a reduced fear of "getting it wrong."

In a crisis, the media and other external parties will be looking for someone to blame. *Don't give them the opportunity.*

How to Avoid a Blame Culture

▸ Focus on the culture or processes that have led to the issues, rather than looking at one individual. Remember, 70% of crises are thought to arise from organizational rather than individual issues.

▸ Accept and encourage constructive suggestion and criticism from all levels of the organization, and even from external stakeholders. Staff or stakeholders at the "sharp end" can often identify issues far more swiftly and clearly than middle or senior managers.

▸ Listen—don't dismiss advice, comments, suggestions, or criticism. Listen to what is being said. In particular, if the comment is aimed at an individual, look beyond the person and seek out the underlying issue.

▸ Focus on the bigger picture—many issues continue to incubate because organizations deal with the small, easily resolved technical issues and ignore the larger, more complex and difficult cultural issues.

▸ Ensure the involvement of representatives of all levels of the workforce when developing, enhancing, and reviewing processes or key operational activities.

▸ Provide opportunities for formal discussion in a nonthreatening environment—hold team meetings away from the office, or in a relaxed area. Set ground rules that encourage people to talk freely about issues rather than personalities.

▸ Provide opportunities for informal, ad hoc contact—in a kitchen or relaxation area, for example. Don't dismiss issues that are raised in informal discussions, as these are often the most revealing conversations. But understand the difference between informed comment and gossip.

Managing Issues to Avoid Crisis

The discipline of identifying and managing external risk issues has grown in importance. It received a kick-start in the 1960s from two US sources. The first was Rachel Carson's groundbreaking book *Silent Spring*, which argued that uncontrolled use of pesticides such as DDT was harming and killing not only animals and birds, but also humans. The second was Ralph Nader's *Unsafe at Any Speed*, a book which claimed that many American automobiles were a danger to drivers and pedestrians alike. The first marked the start of environmentalism, and the second, of consumerism—both of them forces that organizations would ignore at their peril.

Since then, we have witnessed the rise of consumer litigation and a growing recognition on the part of private business that reputation is its most important asset. As discussed elsewhere in the present volume, this becomes ever more important and urgent in the digital age, when news travels so fast and where consumers and activists can have influence and access on a par with companies and governmental agencies. I would also argue that social media have brought about a loss of deference toward organizations and an increasing emphasis on the "me" culture.

More and more organizations are rising to these challenges by putting reputation management at the center of management processes. This is sometimes given focus by establishing a reputation management group, drawn from all disciplines and all areas of the business, whose job it is to identify the issues that create risk for the organization. This should not be seen simply as a defensive operation: it enables your organization to support and adapt strategies, plans, and operations and can enhance your abilities to capitalize on opportunities, reduce risk, and secure competitive advantage.

Importantly, a reputation management group must not be allowed to degenerate into a talking shop. Neither can its task be delegated to the corporate communications function. To succeed, it must be locked into the decision-making process, and it must have the support and input of all management disciplines, recognizing that managing reputation is a fundamental task for all managers. Key features of a reputation management group are set out in the next section.

The multidisciplinary approach to risk management represented by a properly constituted reputation management group is essential. Without that, definitions of risk tend to become too narrow, often focusing on health and safety issues, for instance.

This narrowness of definition was surely one factor behind the problems that beset UK banks in 2008–09. Few organizations take risk management more seriously, and certainly none has more employees with the words "risk manager" somewhere in their title—and yet, if then Financial Services Secretary to the UK Treasury Paul Myners is right, on Friday October 10, 2008, the country was "very close" to a complete banking collapse after major depositors attempted to withdraw their money *en masse*. The focus of banks' risk management has developed and evolved over the past few years. That focus is now increasingly on reputational, regulatory, operational, and strategic risk, as well as the more traditional credit and market dimensions of risk. In 2008 that focus was still too narrow, and a blind eye was being turned to some of the banks' more aggressive lending.

On the other hand, perhaps the banking crisis simply illustrates a more general point. While identifying and managing risk issues can bring real reputational benefit and stave off many potential crises, there remains the problem that was identified by British Prime Minister Harold Macmillan toward the end of his premiership in 1963. Asked what he thought most likely to blow a government off course, he replied: "Events, dear boy, events." There will always be crises that come out of the blue. Indeed, we are all fallible, and therefore there will always be risk issues that no one spots until it is too late.

The Reputation Management Group

Members of the group should:

- be drawn from all disciplines/areas of the business;
- be able to draw on external expertise/advice if required;
- have decision-making powers, or board access.

The functions of the group are:

- to monitor public policy/legislation;
- to monitor key external issues;
- to monitor trends in public opinion.

The goals of the group are:

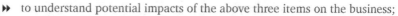

>> to understand potential impacts of the above three items on the business;
>> to adjust strategy, plans, and processes accordingly;
>> to develop and communicate organizational positions/responses, internally and externally.

What Issues?

The issues that are relevant or threatening will vary not only from organization to organization, but also with time and place. Here are just a few you may need to consider.

>> Climate change: flood risks, carbon footprint, carbon offset, etc.
>> Credit and interest rates
>> Health and safety (compliance)
>> Corporate governance
>> Ethical standards
>> Terrorism
>> Crime and security
>> Disaffected youth
>> Flu or other epidemics
>> Transport costs, overcrowded roads, etc.
>> Energy prices
>> House prices (impact on key workers)
>> Education standards
>> Board pay
>> Loss of key staff
>> Outsourcing
>> Call centers and customer service

How to Recognize Your Crisis

When crises are cataclysmic events ("cobras") they are comparatively easy to identify. If your factory burns down, that is clearly a crisis. Most crises, including all those that arise from risk issues, are less easy to define as such: there is more usually a continuum from controlled issues to out-of-control crises ("pythons").

The section below "How serious?" offers a checklist for evaluating your crisis and deciding a proportionate response. There is perhaps a simpler way of spotting the tipping point between issue and crisis: this is when you receive more than one media call, or when online discussions start to attract widespread responses. By this time, you need to be acting and communicating.

How Serious?

Here are 10 diagnostic indicators to help you to judge the seriousness of a crisis.

1 *Risk:* How much is at risk? Where are the risks?
2 *Control:* To what extent is the organization responsible for the crisis? Who else is responsible?

3 *Affected parties:* Who is affected by the crisis? More than one stakeholder group? How?
4 *Trajectory:* Is the crisis likely to escalate?
5 *Time:* How much time is there to maneuver?
6 *Interest:* Is the crisis likely to foster outside attention beyond the parties directly affected? Are the media likely to take an interest?
7 *Spillover:* Is normal business operation interrupted or affected? Are suppliers/customers likely to lose confidence? Will there be a bottom-line effect?
8 *Scope:* How many choices do we have? What is the quality of those choices?
9 Options: What is the organization's ability to influence the situation? Which parties in the situation need to be influenced?
10 *Communication:* What channels of communication will best help you to reach the audiences identified in indicators 3 and 9 above?

Communicating Your Crisis to Safeguard Reputation

Communication is not an optional extra in a crisis. It needs to be part of the management task, and it should be consistent with the actions you are taking. What you say must reflect what you do—and you won't be doing nothing, so you should never be saying nothing.

The temptation is to keep quiet in the early stages of a crisis, because you are likely to know very little: "We don't know enough about what's happening, we don't have solid information, so we can't really say anything." However, there are things you can say when you know very little, things that will help to manage your reputation from the start. And it is vital to say these things at the earliest possible opportunity. As long ago as 1970 the historian and satirist C. Northcote Parkinson wrote, "The vacuum created by a failure to communicate will quickly be filled with rumor, misrepresentation, drivel and poison." In an age of 24-hour news and globally accessible social media, that is truer than ever.

When it comes to giving information, there should be a presumption of openness. The question should be "Is there any good reason why we shouldn't reveal this?" rather than the more usual "Do we really need to tell them this?" A general spirit of openness and honesty will always enhance your reputation. Any suspicion that facts are being hidden will do the opposite.

Until the advent of the blogosphere and Twitter, the traditional media represented the only universal way of communicating with all your stakeholders at once. For the time being, it is still the case that traditional media coverage (TV, radio, press) is more influential than social media coverage when it comes to effects on your reputation.

As discussed elsewhere in this book, this may not remain true for ever, and it may already be untrue in some sectors (e.g. online retailing, and perhaps consumer electronics). It is important to understand also the close relationship between social media and journalism: most newsrooms now regularly monitor Twitter feeds and all are involved in and interact with blogs and discussion forums.

Organizations need to use all available communication channels to engage with stakeholders. In the case of both traditional and social media, conversations are more effective where there is an existing relationship. Twitter followers will not trust you if you simply create an account to answer criticism that is already out there. Journalists will have no reason to trust you if they have never heard from you before.

What to Say?

Whatever channels of communication you are using, what you choose to say is crucial. The good news is that there is a magic formula to help you to decide what to say. It can be applied to any type or scale of crisis, and indeed the same formula works well when speaking about risk issues, for example customer complaints. Applied wisely, and supported by real action, this formula can be a powerful aid in preventing issues from escalating into crisis.

The formula is encapsulated in the acronym CARE. Whatever the crisis, your media statements, interviews, blog postings, etc.—especially early in the crisis management process—should always be based on the following.

▸ *Concern:* For example, understanding the point of view of protesters, or showing sympathy for families of the bereaved. Do not be afraid of the word "sorry" if it is appropriate. However, note that "We are sorry this has happened" is not the same message as "We are sorry we got it wrong," but in either case the word has the power to defuse volatile reactions. The UK National Health Service Litigation Authority recognizes this in its guidance to hospital trusts, advising that, where it is clear that there has been a medical mistake, hospitals should apologize to those affected and their families at the earliest opportunity.

▸ *Action:* Your audience needs to know that you will be doing something, and as much as possible about what that might be. At the very least it should be told that there is to be some sort of investigation. Good crisis planning, to some extent at least, enables you to know what happens next.

▸ *REassurance:* This means, for example, saying that lessons will be learned, or that you have a good safety/security record, or that you have contingency plans in place. This message must be accompanied by the preceding two messages if it is not to come across as defensive and suspicious.

Who Should Say It?

Once one has accepted that there is positive advantage to be gained from communicating in a crisis, this question answers itself. Clearly, the best person to represent an organization when it wants to be taken seriously, or when it wants to indicate how seriously it is taking a situation, is the person at the top—probably the chief executive or chairman.

There are some exceptions to this rule, when you may decide to engage at a lower level. You may want to deliberately signal that the perceived crisis is not as serious as others may think. You may want to speak from specific expertise: for example, the technical director may be more appropriate in certain situations. Or there may be practical difficulties: the chief executive is on the other side of the world. Finally, you may believe that your chief executive does not possess the skills or aptitude needed to represent you well on camera. This is a matter of judgment, but the presumption should be that the most senior person available should be your public face, and that you should avoid the anonymity of "a spokesperson." This applies equally to issuing statements to the media or to content on your website or blog.

It is worth saying that no one is a "natural" at this. Getting the right combination of content, tone, and style of delivery is essential, and that takes practice. Media training is therefore a prerequisite, as is regular exercise testing of your crisis communications plan.

There were many factors that made life difficult for BP in the aftermath of the 2010 incident in the Gulf of Mexico, when the Deepwater Horizon rig blew up, killing 11 men and causing an oil spill that created massive pollution for more than three months. BP seemed to do the right thing in putting forward its then chief executive, Tony Hayward. The problem was that he was also in direct overall charge of BP's recovery operation. The lesson here is to keep the role of head of crisis recovery completely separate from that of spokesman.

In short, your public face should be the most senior person who is capable of presenting the best possible "face" of the organization and who is not operationally locked into the process of crisis management.

Classic Case Study

The Kegworth Air Crash

Serious air crashes tend to lead to a dip in ticket sales, sometimes related to a specific type of aircraft, sometimes to the airline involved, and sometimes both. For instance, the loss of an Indonesian budget airline Adam Air Boeing 737 on New Year's Day, 2007, in which 102 people died, led to a loss of more than 30% of the airline's sales, which took several months to recover.

However, in the case of the January 1989 crash of a British Midland Boeing 737 on to a superhighway embankment near East Midlands Airport, ticket sales actually increased in the following weeks—even though the crash killed 47 people. The communication around this incident by British Midland provided a model for all future crisis handling.

The airline chief executive, Michael Bishop, began giving interviews within an hour of the incident, when little was known about the circumstances. In the absence of facts, Bishop focused on expressing how he felt about what had happened and what he was going to do about the situation—in other words, he began to manage the flow and content of news to the media. His content was in line with the CARE formula. As a result, the airline was perceived to be caring and responsible—it was seen as part of the solution, rather than part of the problem.

There was little information in what Michael Bishop said, but he followed the golden rules:

- ▸ begin communicating at once—take the initiative;
- ▸ communicate from the top of the organization;
- ▸ treat all media seriously and don't neglect any outlet—especially those in your sphere of operation, including the regional press where you are located.

Summary and Further Steps

▸▸ When it comes to risk issues and crisis, *perception is reality*. Know and act on what people *think*.

▸▸ Risk issues need to be actively identified and managed to protect and enhance your reputation.

▸▸ A multidisciplinary reputation management group, with decision-making powers, can provide a focus for this.

▸▸ Well-managed risk issues reduce the likelihood and impact of crises.

▸▸ Foster a no-blame culture to ensure that risk issues are flagged up and the resulting policy is respected internally.

▸▸ Despite all your best efforts, crises will happen.

▸▸ Communicate quickly and openly in a crisis, using the CARE formula, and through all available channels. Aim to be seen as part of the solution, rather than the problem.

▸▸ Exercise regularly to test and revise crisis communication plans and to identify and support your spokespeople.

More Info

Books:

Anthonissen, Peter F. (ed). *Crisis Communication: Practical PR Strategies for Reputation Management and Company Survival*. London, UK: Kogan Page, 2008.

Carson, Rachel. *Silent Spring*. Boston MA: Houghton Mifflin, 1962.

Coombs, W. Timothy. *Ongoing Crisis Communication: Planning, Managing, and Responding*. 3rd ed. Thousand Oaks, CA: Sage Publications, 2011.

Fearn-Banks, Kathleen. *Crisis Communications: A Casebook Approach*. 4th ed. New York: Routledge, 2010.

Griffin, Andrew. *New Strategies for Reputation Management: Gaining Control of Issues, Crises & Corporate Social Responsibility*. London, UK: Kogan Page, 2009.

Holmes, Anthony. *Managing Through Turbulent Times: The 7 Rules of Crisis Management*. Petersfield, UK: Harriman House, 2009.

Nader, Ralph. *Unsafe at Any Speed: The Designed-In Dangers of the American Automobile*. New York: Grossman, 1965.

Parkinson, C. Northcote. *The Law of Delay: Interviews and Outerviews*. Boston, MA: Houghton Mifflin, 1971.

Regester, Michael, and Judy Larkin. *Risk Issues and Crisis Management in Public Relations: A Casebook of Best Practice*. 4th ed. London, UK: Kogan Page, 2008.

Seymour, Mike, and Simon Moore. *Effective Crisis Management: Worldwide Principles and Practice*. London, UK: Cassell, 2000.

Smith, Denis, and Dominic Elliott (eds). *Key Readings in Crisis Management: Systems and Structures for Prevention and Recovery*. New York: Routledge, 2006.

Ulmer, Robert R., Timothy L. Sellnow, and Matthew W. Seeger. *Effective Crisis Communication: Moving from Crisis to Opportunity.* 2nd ed. Thousand Oaks, CA: Sage Publications, 2011.

Article:

Gray, Richard, and Michael Fitzpatrick. "Japan nuclear crisis: Tsunami study showed Fukushima plant was at risk." *Daily Telegraph* (March 19, 2011).
Online at: tinyurl.com/43f27ue

Report:

Shell. "Brent Spar dossier." 1999. Online at: tinyurl.com/3mvaka7

Websites:

Greenpeace on Brent Spar: tinyurl.com/3hm9wz2

Institute of Risk Management: www.theirm.org

PR Media Blog on crisis communication: tinyurl.com/3zmruq9

Index